MANCHESTER
UNIVERSITY PRESS

A working-class crowd queues outside a cinema, c.1946

The British working class in postwar film

PHILIP GILLETT

MANCHESTER UNIVERSITY PRESS   Manchester and New York

distributed exclusively in the USA by Palgrave

Published by Manchester University Press
Oxford Road, Manchester M13 9NR, UK
and Room 400, 175 Fifth Avenue, New York, NY 10010, USA
www.manchesteruniversitypress.co.uk

Distributed exclusively in the USA by
Palgrave, 175 Fifth Avenue, New York, NY 10010, USA

Distributed exclusively in Canada by
UBC Press, University of British Columbia, 2029 West Mall, Vancouver, BC, Canada V6T 1Z2

British Library Cataloguing-in-Publication Data
A catalogue record for this book is available from the British Library

Library of Congress Cataloging-in-Publication Data applied for

ISBN   0 7190 6257 8 hardback
       0 7190 6258 6 paperback

First published 2003

10 09 08 07 06 05 04 03   10 9 8 7 6 5 4 3 2 1

Typeset in Photina and Frutiger display
by Carnegie Publishing Ltd, Lancaster
Printed in Great Britain
by Biddles Ltd, Guildford and King's Lynn

Contents

List of figures

List of tables

Acknowledgements

My thanks to Bruce Carson, John Sedgwick and Elizabeth Wilson at the University of North London for guiding me through my thesis, which formed the starting point for this book. I am indebted to the librarians throughout the country who have given their untiring assistance, and to the interviewees and correspondents who have shared their memories with me and put up with my silly questions. The enthusiasm and help of the staff of Manchester University Press have made publication a fairly painless process. Among the colleagues and well-wishers who have given help beyond the call of duty are Allen Eyles, Eric Fenwick, Annette Kuhn, Clifford Shaw and Mark Stephens. Credit is due to Colin Shindler for encouraging me to embark on academic research into the cinema, and to Colin Ward for daring me to take a new look at the familiar. My greatest debt is to my parents for introducing me to the delights of Saturday afternoon at the pictures.

Abbreviations

ABPC Associated British Picture Corporation
BBC British Broadcasting Corporation
BBFC British Board of Film Censors
BFI British Film Institute
COI Central Office of Information
CTA Cinema Theatre Association
NCO Non-commissioned officer
PEP Political and Economic Planning
PRO Public Record Office
WEA Workers' Educational Association

Exploring a lost culture

This book examines how the working-class people are portrayed in the British cinema. Leaving aside problems of definition, it is indisputable that class permeates British feature films, from Claude Hubert's silly asses to Norman Wisdom's little man in a cap. Sometimes it comes to the fore as in the films of Lindsay Anderson, though frequently it remains pervasive but unacknowledged.

Nor does class know its place and keep to the screen. In British screen romances of the 1930s, class often keeps couples apart until love finds a way to overcome social barriers.[1] The heroines were played by stars such as Jessie Matthews and Gracie Fields who had themselves risen from humble beginnings. So fairy tales do come true. They came true for Grace Kelly.

Films from the late 1950s reveal more breaches in the class barriers. The truculent working-class lad has no difficulty in attracting a partner from among his social betters, even if the relationship ends in tears. Romance is hardly the word to describe *Room at the Top* (d. Jack Clayton, 1958) or *Alfie* (d. Lewis Gilbert, 1966). In *Blow-Up* (d. Michelangelo Antonioni, 1967), the lad has made good, but living happily ever after is still a chimera. Even in this more liberal climate, differences of attitude and behaviour can pose a problem when parents encounter uncouth, lower-class behaviour on the part of a suitor. These tensions surface in *Look Back in Anger* (d. Tony Richardson, 1959) and *A Kind of Loving* (d. John Schlesinger, 1962). Thora Hird as Ingrid Rothwell's disapproving mum in the latter film would sympathise with the middle-class parents in *Private Road* (d. Barney Platts-Mills, 1971), as their daughter is lured into working-class ways. The difference here is that the villain of the piece is a well-spoken dropout. With youth culture allied to working-class culture, class and generational differences become difficult to disentangle.

But what precisely are films showing us? Are they charting a cultural shift, or merely presenting old ideas in new guises? The problems depicted in British realist films produced from the late 1950s onwards were not unique to a generation growing up during the Cold War. Fifty years earlier, the plays of Stanley Houghton dramatised young people rebelling against the class-bound (and gender-bound) prejudices of their elders. In *Hindle Wakes* (1912), there is the added tension that the fathers of the ill-matched couple once worked together, but one has gained from social mobility while the other has remained on the shop floor as his employee.

No industry can afford to alienate its customers, so it is axiomatic that the cinema industry seeks to please audiences. If people pay to see a film, a reasonable assumption is that it promotes values and attitudes more or less consonant with their own, or to which they aspire, however vicariously. Put more simply, they can empathise with the leading characters. Popular films are those offering greater consonance and to this extent they stand as testimony to the attitudes of audiences. As a check against rampant commercialism, censorship ensures that no film deviates too far from the consensus view. By this model, what is presented on screen, including attitudes towards class, is an ever-shifting compromise between censorship, public taste and commercial pressures. Successful films are those which get the balance right.

Whether overt or insidious, the presence of class imagery in films prompts three questions: whose assumptions are dominant in the collaborative process of bringing an idea to the screen, are the participants aware of these assumptions and what is the response of audiences? Viewing the films is an obvious first step in seeking answers, though the exercise may do little more than confirm prejudices. This is a particular danger when films from a generation or more ago are filtered through present-day sensibilities. It is tempting to judge the class attitudes of characters as regressive because ours must be progressive. In this way the past is remade for a new generation. We cannot see the films with an innocent eye. The caution applies to other social issues, though arguably views on gender and ethnicity are more explicitly formulated. Class is in danger of becoming the social difference which dares not speak its name.

A related difficulty is the way in which film contributes to societal memory. It shapes our view of phenomena as diverse as the First World War (ineluctably black and white), the Depression (the hopelessness which infuses newsreels of Jarrow marchers is contagious) and swinging London of the 1960s (Carnaby Street lived off its legend long after the swinging ceased). Other evidence is judged against the celluloid images, so that seeking corroboration dwindles into self-fulfilling prophecy and another myth is perpetuated.

How might this Gordian knot be cut? Biographies go some way to clarifying the assumptions of film-makers, though Anthony Asquith remains an enigma in spite of the attention lavished on him.[2] But this is akin to history being written by the victors, with attitudes being inferred from the views of a select few. Lesser lights of the cinema industry might see things differently, but they seldom merit biographies. Trade journals hint at whose interests are dominant in the making and marketing of individual films, but they are less revealing about power relations across the industry: a David Lean can impose his views on a producer in a way denied to a prentice director, while distributors and exhibitors function as gatekeepers for what the public is allowed to see, whatever the hopes of film-makers.

Business records provide tangible evidence of which films were popular, but the British cinema industry has often seemed intent on destroying all traces of its past. Instead, popularity has to be inferred largely from snippets in the trade press. John Sedgwick's POPSTAT is an attempt to overcome this deficiency by examining what was screened in a sample of cinemas, but inevitably the accuracy of a surrogate measure is open to question.[3] A few Board of Trade returns have survived, along with a run of weekly returns for the Gaumont, Sheffield, and these are summarised in the appendix.[4] Also included are the results of my own research in which the fortunes of the films discussed are compared in ten independent cinemas in working-class Leeds and in socially more amorphous southeast Essex.[5] As to what cinemagoers thought of the offerings presented to them and how the cinema influenced their lives, oral testimony offers tantalising glimpses.[6] The views of newspaper critics have the virtues of being contemporaneous and committed to print, and these are noted for 'quality' films.[7] For the mass of films which were beneath the notice of critics, recourse has to be made to the brief reviews in the trade press, where these are useful.

It is evident that a range of skills are needed in examining class in films. To the historian's expertise in the use of source material must be added the psychologist's insights into the formation of attitudes – not to mention the sociologist's rigour in defining class. This diversity helps to explain the evolution of film studies as an eclectic discipline, able to accommodate a range of interests in its nooks and crannies. The corollary is that exploring the impact of the cinema on society requires collaborative effort. The absence of such collaboration is apparent in the proliferation of studies of individual films and film-makers. Valuable as these are, the economic and social structures within which films are made and seen can too easily be forgotten. One objective of this work is to take a modest step in redressing the balance by considering the popularity of the films discussed.

A second objective is to demonstrate how film might be used by disciplines whose practitioners often display scant interest in its possibilities. When Terry Lovell surveyed sociological writings on the cinema in 1971, she found a meagre body of work; not much has changed in the intervening years.[8] Yet cinema-going is a curious activity: hundreds of people conniving in the fantasy that images of the iconic star projecting on a screen have significance. Given the weight of symbolism involved, it is surprising that no Erving Goffman has come forward to explore the phenomenon from the inside.[9] Among historians, Jeffrey Richards and Sue Harper have examined the relationship between the cinema and societal change, but they are exceptions.[10] Arthur Marwick has promoted the use of newsreels and documentaries as historical source material, but he is uncharacteristically dismissive of B-features, which can offer a less consciously manipulated view of the world than prestige productions.[11] Film does have something to offer other disciplines if professional caution can be overcome.

The third objective is to consider what films can contribute to the debate on the consequences of war. Should the postwar years be seen as a New Jerusalem, a reversion to the 1930s or a continuation of war without the bombing? Controversy has simmered since the 1960s, when Anthony Howard proposed that 'Far from introducing a "social revolution" the overwhelming Labour victory of 1945 brought about the greatest restoration of traditional class values since 1660.'[12] Marwick has remained consistently more optimistic, though he has his detractors.[13] Film offers a contemporaneous view of events – a view which could sway public opinion. The work of socialists like the Boulting brothers or Ted Willis can be considered from this viewpoint.

A final objective is to test received opinion. Raymond Durgnat's attitude to class in film is summed up in his idiosyncratic but indispensable *A Mirror for England*: 'A middle-class cinema will tend to acknowledge the working-class only (1) insofar as they accept, or are subservient to, middle-class ideals (2) where they shade into the feckless and criminal stream, and (3) humorously. All these approaches can be concertina'd into one.'[14] Durgnat was a pioneer in broadening writing on film beyond aesthetic considerations. The paradox is that by largely ignoring crime films and proletarian comedies like the Old Mother Riley series, he offers an approach predicated on the dominance of middle-class cinema. Nor are his insights entirely original: the humorous portrayal of working-class characters was noted by earlier commentators.[15] His cautious wording is tacit admission that not all working-class characters fit neatly into his three categories. Something more wide ranging and less value laden is needed to encompass the richness of working-class experience.

Brief Encounter (d. David Lean, 1945) is probably the best-remembered British film from the early postwar years, with Noel Coward's clipped dialogue being the subject of endless parody. Whatever the film's virtues, Lean's handling of class is hardly subtle. At the preview in Rochester, Kent, a working-class audience laughed at the love scenes; twenty years on, a middle-class audience in London did the same.[16] Perceptions of class changed over the intervening years, but what cues were being recognised which made the scenes appear class-bound to both audiences? Some method of identifying and codifying the signifiers of class is needed.

In the next chapter, the contentious issue of defining class is confronted and a sociological model for examining class in film is put forward. The third chapter examines the treatment of class in films about the Second World War. As the defining event of the period, the war cannot be omitted, even though it does not fit neatly into the proposed model. Subsequent chapters focus on aspects of working-class which were exemplified in films. The concluding chapter broadens the subject to consider the significance of the cinema for working-class audiences.

Because representations of the working class from the late 1950s onwards have received attention elsewhere, the films considered here are drawn from earlier years.[17] They offer snapshots of an urban working class trying to adjust to life in peacetime, before wartime controls gave way to the consumer society. Inevitably there are limits to what can be covered. The self-conscious attempt to capture reality in documentaries and newsreels merits more attention than can be given here. The same applies to the working class in the countryside. Racial issues were accorded little attention in British films until the late 1950s and are not considered. Period dramas are also omitted to avoid the conundrum of what message is being conveyed by characters in Regency dress when the original novel was published half a century before the film.

Release dates and running times are as given by Denis Gifford.[18] A feature film was defined as having a minimum length of 3,000 feet, which gives a running time of 33 minutes.[19] By this criterion, 491 British feature films were released between 1945 and 1950. Of these, the National Film Archive held viewing copies of 247 in 1996, with a dozen or so additional titles being available on video. Television companies around the world may hold the rights to other titles, but for practical purposes almost half the films released are lost or unobtainable. Among these are such potential gems as *The Agitator* (d. John Harlow, 1945), with a plot involving a socialist agitator who inherits a factory, and *The Turners of Prospect Road* (d. Maurice J. Wilson, 1947), in which the pet greyhound belonging to a taxi-driver's daughter wins a Dog Derby. The frustration of history is what has been lost; the lure is what might turn up.

Notes

1   Stephen C. Shafer, *British Popular Films 1929–1939: The Cinema of Reassurance* (London: Routledge, 1997), ch. 6.

2   R. J. Minney, *'Puffin' Asquith: A Biography of the Hon. Anthony Asquith: Aesthete, Aristocrat, Prime Minister's Son and Film Maker* (London: Leslie Frewin, 1973); Charles Drazin, *The Finest Years: British Cinema of the 1940s* (London: Andre Deutsch, 1998), pp. 185–99.

3   John Sedgwick, *Popular Filmgoing in 1930s Britain: A Choice of Pleasures* (Exeter: Exeter University Press, 2000).

4   For other surviving records see Julian Poole, 'British cinema attendance in wartime: audience preference at the Majestic, Macclesfield 1939–1946', *Historical Journal of Film, Radio and Television*, 7:1 (1987), 15–34; Allen Eyles, 'Hits and misses at the Empire', *Picture House*, summer issue (1989), 35–47. The Macclesfield records cover an earlier period than the Sheffield returns, while the Empire, Leicester Square, is a prestigious West End venue and atypical. Fragmentary records survive from the Daffodil, Cheltenham. These are held by the present owner of the building, Mark Stephens.

5   For a full explanation of the methodology, see Philip J. Gillett. 'British feature films and working-class culture 1945–1950', Ph.D. thesis, University of North London, 2000, ch. 6.

6   One example is Margaret O'Brien and Allen Eyles, *Enter the Dream House: Memories of Cinemas in South London from the Twenties to the Sixties* (London: BFI and Museum of the Moving Image, 1993).

7   For a definition of the 'quality' film see John Ellis, 'Art, culture and quality – terms for a cinema in the forties and seventies', *Screen*, 19:3 (1978), 9–49.

8   Terry Lovell, 'Sociology and the cinema', *Screen*, 12:1 (1971), 15–26.

9   His distinctive brand of sociology is displayed in Erving Goffman, *The Presentation of Self in Everyday Life* (Harmondsworth: Penguin Books, 1990). For its applicability to films, see Dudley Andrew, 'The neglected tradition of phenomenology', in Bill Nichols (ed.), *Movies and Methods*,

vol. 2: *An Anthology* (Berkeley, CA: University of California Press, 1985), pp. 625–32.

10 Representative of their approaches are Jeffrey Richards, *The Age of the Dream Palace: Cinema and Society in Britain 1930–39* (Basingstoke and London: Routledge, 1989); Sue Harper, *Picturing the Past: The Rise and Fall of the British Costume Film* (London: BFI, 1994).

11 Arthur Marwick, *Culture in Britain since 1945* (Oxford: Basil Blackwell, 1991), p. 57.

12 Anthony Howard, 'We are the masters now', in Michael Sissons and Philip French (eds), *The Age of Austerity 1945–1951* (Harmondsworth: Penguin Books, 1964), p. 33.

13 Arthur Marwick, *Britain in the Century of Total War: War, Peace and Social Change 1900–1967* (London: Bodley Head, 1968); Harold L. Smith (ed.), *War and Social Change: British Society in the Second World War* (Manchester: Manchester University Press, 1986).

14 Raymond Durgnat, *A Mirror for England: British Movies from Austerity to Affluence* (London: Faber & Faber, 1970), p. 48.

15 Glyn Roberts, *Film Weekly* (23 April 1938), p. 11, cited in Shafer, *British Popular Films 1929–1939*, p. 38; Richard Winnington, *Drawn and Quartered* (London: Saturn Press, [1948]), p. 106.

16 Kevin Brownlow, *David Lean: A Biography* (London: Faber & Faber, 1997), p. 203; Durgnat, *A Mirror for England*, p. 180.

17 Stuart Laing, *Representations of Working-Class Life 1957–1964* (Basingstoke and London: Macmillan, 1986); John Hill, *Sex, Class and Realism: British Cinema 1956–1963* (London: BFI, 1986).

18 Denis Gifford, *The British Film Catalogue 1895–1985* (Newton Abbot: David & Charles, 1986).

19 Donald Alexander, *Facts about Film* (London: Bureau of Current Affairs, 1946), p. 9.

2   Who were the workers?

Class is one of those phenomena like love, depression and the feel-good factor which resists definition, though we know it when we see it. This hardly satisfies sociologists, whose quest is to bring precision to their concepts. For those concerned with social structures, the grail is a quantitative measure, the ideal being ratio data such as income, with a known interval between each category. This can be used alongside dichotomous variables such as occupation (manual or nonmanual), housing tenure (owner-occupier or rented), housing type (terraced or semidetached), type of education (secondary modern or grammar) and length of education (ending at the secondary or tertiary stage). In practice, such precision can be illusory. Where the line should be drawn between a working-class and a middle-class income, or whether the owner of a corner shop in a slum district should be categorised as upper working class or lower middle class are matters of judgement rather than fact. Nor does income distinguish between the lifestyles of the genteel poor and affluent workers. A census might be expected to yield definitive conclusions, but using the 1951 census, the proportion of working-class people in Britain has been estimated variously at 64, 72 and 86.9 per cent.[1] The grail of a definitive measure remains elusive, leaving class as a semantic battleground for generations of sociologists. Like a dog with a particularly juicy bone, John Goldthorpe has devoted his career to the subject, refusing to be sidetracked during the Thatcher years when class slipped down the agenda. His career sums up changing perceptions of social differentiation – and its complexity.[2]

If at least two-thirds of the population were working class in 1951, a reasonable assumption is that a similar proportion of cinema patrons were working class. In all probability this is an underestimate. Using Board of Trade data for 1950/51, H. E. Browning and A. A. Sorrell calculated that admissions per person were higher in the industrial heartlands than elsewhere: 36 in Scotland, 37 in the North East, 35 in Lancashire and 34 in the East and West Ridings of Yorkshire, against a national average of 28. Only the Midlands went against the trend at 26.[3] The implication is that the working class were disproportionately exposed to the values promoted in films, including the representation on screen of people like themselves.

As a character on screen can become a real person to the audience, so the risk of emphasising measurement in sociology is that class assumes material reality instead of being merely a convenient way of grouping social phenomena. This is the social scientist's cardinal sin of reifying a concept. One way of avoiding this pitfall is to adopt Ervin Goffman's strategy and focus on how people perceive their own class position. One consequence is that the numbers change. In Gallup polls from 1948 and 1949, 45 per cent of respondents called themselves working class – a figure well below those proposed by sociologists.[4] As Arthur Marwick puts it somewhat acidly, 'I prefer "class" to mean what people in everyday life mean by it, rather than what Runciman or Weber tell me I should mean by it. I have never yet heard anyone speak of "working-status" homes, nor "middle-status" education. Sociologists, I fear, often preach in preference to practising.'[5] At first sight this returns the concept of class to the will-o'-the-wisp state from which sociologists seek to escape, but examine what class means to people and something more complex emerges. Certain defining characteristics keep recurring in the neglected body of social science research from the 1940s and 1950s. Cultural continuity is implied if these were apparent earlier in the century as evidenced by autobiographies of working-class people, though the risk must be acknowledged that these may be coloured by hindsight.

Neighbourhood referred to the surrounding district which inhabitants knew intimately. Particularly for women, most journeys outside the home were made on foot, so that the neighbourhood would not extend beyond easy walking distance of the front door: 'The Cockney fellow's street was his kingdom, and not lightly trampled on by outsiders. Even we small girls felt the bristling pride in belonging.' (Doris Bailey, born 1916, Bethnal Green, London).[6] In a wartime survey conducted in urban Scotland, 48 per cent of respondents went to a cinema within 600 yards of home.[7] Blackouts and bombing hardly encouraged adventurousness, but there was certainty in the known. Going outside the boundaries meant a loss of security and could be perceived as intimidating.[8] The neighbourhood mentality was highlighted by officers of a Junior Employment Board in the 1930s, who found that youths in a London suburb were unwilling to venture out of the area for work; even in the 1980s, working-class youths in Brixham, Devon, were unwilling to look for work elsewhere in Torbay.[9] During the war, mass entertainment, displacement by bombing, evacuation and work in factories might be expected to reduce women's ties to the neighbourhood, while child rearing and a lack of transport served to reinforce them. If the neighbourhood was less prominent in postwar anthropological literature, it was still influential enough to be enshrined in the doctrines of town planning which shaped postwar redevelopment.[10]

The neighbourhood implied more than the built environment, but *community* more aptly described the social network within the neighbourhood.[11] It is also the concept most at risk of being distorted by nostalgia. By means of gossip and threats, the community could define and police standards of behaviour which were not necessarily the norms of the wider society in such matters as sexual mores and attitudes to violence and private property.[12] There was little sense of community in the inner-city St Ebbe's district of Oxford in 1950: though 36 per cent of the population had been resident for twenty years or more, 60 per cent of families reported having no friends, compared with 30 per cent making a similar claim on the more modern Barton council estate.[13] Conversely, a study conducted on a Sheffield estate revealed that between 1927 and 1952, two-thirds of tenants married another resident, which might be expected to strengthen links within the community.[14] Ties were likely to be stronger in isolated settlements, or where everybody was dependent on a single industry. As a former miner wrote: 'The "lump" [a collection of houses plus a pub and a shop] is a closely coherent social organism more important in the life of the residents than the individual families of which it is composed.'[15]

Neighbours were those members of the community in close physical proximity. The nature of facilities in older urban areas – corner shops, shared WC blocks and washing lines strung across streets – made frequent contact unavoidable, although there was no reason why this should make for friendship rather than friction. On a Liverpool estate in 1951–52, families with four or more children asked for help more frequently than others, while older residents felt that there was too much privacy. The researchers concluded that 'the degree of contact between neighbours is regulated by convention, and there is probably rather less permitted or desired nowadays than in the past.'[16] Similarly, in Houghton, a modern and planned working-class neighbourhood of Coventry, the tendency was to be reserved with neighbours, though the district was sometimes described as poor because of the low standard of privacy.[17] Geoffrey Gorer's 1951 national survey confirmed these findings: people who visited neighbours had an income of less than £5 or more than £15 a week, which excluded most of the working class except the poorest and those who could flaunt their affluence.[18] This may be compared with evidence from the late 1930s: of 500 children who wrote essays on 'My home and who lives there', 16 per cent mentioned neighbours, compared with 61 per cent of the subgroup who lived in tenements. The latter children mentioned their parents far less frequently.[19] In the 1950s, a teacher in Liverpool could still write: 'The people of the tenements have no privacy. Everything is community life. If a mother comes here to see me, she brings a friend with her. One feels sometimes people don't want to be individuals. They go through life with arms linked, holding one another up.'[20] These clues suggest that if neighbourliness had once been important, a change was taking place by 1950 where there were smaller families and improved living conditions.

Family was an amorphous term, embracing not only the nuclear family, but the wider kinship network. A consistent feature of the studies is that kinship remained important, particularly for the wife. Townsend's thesis is convincing: a mother could be fifty-nine before her last child reached the age of marriage. This prolongation of the time spent caring for children was a major reason for the maintenance of family ties, particularly when there was a short period between children depending on parents and parents depending on children. The corollary is that a reduction in family size reduced family contact.[21]

The family promised not only emotional support, but help with such practical matters as child-minding, finding a job and a house, and support in old age.[22] With more official involvement in social welfare, these aspects of family life were declining. Mum had no power in the town hall.[23] Whatever the psychological benefits of familial closeness, it acted as a constraint on geographical and social mobility. This is apparent from a 1954 study made in a secondary modern school, probably in Leeds. These working-class girls generally had two or three siblings. Their preference was to spend leisure time outside the home and in the company of friends, siblings and boyfriends. Though most girls did not wish to follow their parents' occupations, they were unwilling to take work which the parents believed would necessitate living away from home.[24]

Home occupied an ambiguous place in the working-class world. Marriage could mean escape from an overcrowded parental home where there was parental discord and little privacy. Wanting a home was the most common reason for marriage, according to a postwar study conducted in London by Eliot Slater and Moya Woodside.[25] Diana Dors' character in *A Kid for Two Farthings* (d. Carol Reed, 1955) exemplifies the desire for a home packed with consumer goods. The risk was that a new home on an outlying estate could become all-enveloping for the wife, restricting wider contacts.[26]

If family links militated against the desire to leave the parental home, a lack of savings and the postwar housing shortage reinforced this pattern. In a study of industrial Wales dating from 1959, 50 per cent more couples shared a home with parents than before the war.[27] Similar results came from Sheffield and the East End of London.[28] Home was the place for the family, to the exclusion of the community – what Townsend calls the privacy of the hearth – with neither workmates nor neighbours generally being invited inside.[29] Overcrowding and the practice of heating only the living room were constraints on extending the social life of the home beyond the immediate family.[30] This enhanced the value of the street, pubs, cinemas and dance halls as meeting places.

The lack of privacy within the home deserves emphasis. Closeness was not necessarily perceived as a problem – at least until there was a basis for comparison among people in the same social group, which occurred as housing improved.[31] For the girls interviewed by Pearl Jephcott in 1945–46, these improvements had yet to be enjoyed at first hand.[32] Living in a spacious home must have been experienced vicariously through films, though whether with envy or frustration is not recorded.

Gender roles were generally unambiguous, though contradictory accounts imply that there was considerable variation according to local circumstances. Women in the poorest families and in large towns had more authority.[33] Fathers played a shadowy role in Liverpool, Oxford and London, though the mining community of Ashton was more patriarchal.[34] The social researcher Ferdynand Zweig sketched a complex picture of change for the miner's wife. Facilities such as pithead baths and canteens made life easier, but they gave her a different order of importance from when she scrubbed her husband's back and cooked his meals.[35] Ambiguity also showed in the husband's degree of involvement in housework and child rearing, with a north-south divide becoming apparent.[36] The northern attitude is summed up by John Barron Mays, who recounts how a working mother in Liverpool with a bed-ridden husband wanted her daughter to have time off school to look after him. When it was pointed out that two unemployed teenage sons were at home, the mother responded: 'I pray that as long as I've my strength, no man will ever be asked to cook in my house.'[37] Geoff Mungham suggests that male intolerance of bad language by women was the product of a strongly matriarchal society, though he offers no evidence.[38] Drunkenness and violence by the husband were less prominent than before the war. They hardly figured in Slater and Woodside's London study, though Gorer referred to them as persisting in the Midlands and they received mention in studies of poor communities.[39]

Respectability was a key component of working-class life, with a distinction being made between rough and respectable families. The former were usually poor, while the latter avoided this state by the application of hard work and self-improvement.[40] Though the distinction is clear, where to draw the line between the two groups was a fine social judgement. Zweig caught the complexities:

Working-class women divide themselves not so much by the jobs their husbands do – and still less by the jobs they themselves do – but rather by ways of life ... The main line of division is respectability, and the sense of respectability, i.e. conformity to accepted standards, is much stronger among women than men. A labourer's wife, if she is respectable and leads a clean reasonable life, doing her bit and coping sensibly with adversities, is much more respected and classed higher in the social hierarchy than a craftsman's wife who leads the irresponsible life of a waster.[41]

Zweig's views were echoed a generation later:

Social historians studying the working class in the recent past are almost overwhelmed at times by the total devotion and dedication shown towards the concept of respectability. It can be seen in the lives of almost all members of the working class, even in those who in the eyes of others were 'rough'. 'To be respectable' was in its original sense, to be respected, and in closely-knit communities, it was difficult to live comfortably without the respect of one's family and neighbours.[42]

One of the girls interviewed in the 1940s by Josephine Macalister Brew put it more succinctly: 'The closer you live together, the more respectable you have to be.'[43]

Respectability limited social interactions: children's contact with their rougher counterparts was discouraged, while families with social aspirations might be treated with suspicion for 'getting above themselves'.[44] Poverty militated against respectability by making it difficult to keep up standards. The important point was not to let it show. In Nigel Gray's words, the working class 'instead of fighting poverty, try to hide it like underwear under the cushions'.[45]

Status was linked inexorably to respectability. Superiority could be asserted by such means as clothing, speech or occupation. As a shipyard joiner recalls, 'Engineers thought they were better than boilermakers, they were more highly skilled. Boilermakers used to think they were the salt of the earth, because they literally built the ship, and if they didn't build the ship, the engineers couldn't finish it. There was a sort of class warfare.'[46] Status could also be indicated by the display of ornaments in the parlour. Creating a shrine in this way meant that the room was seldom used: 'You lived in the kitchen and you went in the parlour for your best room ... It was dusted and kept nice and never sat on [*sic*]. It was just used on special occasions ... [for] visitors, weddings, funerals, birthdays, happen on a Sunday'.[47] In Dennis Chapman's Liverpool study from the early 1950s, interviewers were shown into the formal room on 44 per cent of occasions in bye-law houses (nineteenth century terraced housing conforming to basic legal standards), compared with 22 per cent in semidetached houses.[48]

Status might imply an element of change, of a need to keep up with the Joneses, but the desire for respectability and for doing the proper thing meant that the prevailing attitude of the working class was one of *fatalism* and acceptance of the status quo, summed up in the third verse of the hymn 'All things bright and beautiful' by Mrs C. F. Alexander (1848):

> The rich man in his castle,
> The poor man at his gate,
> God made them, high and lowly,
> And ordered their estate.[49]

Subservience was less overt by the late 1940s, but the passive acceptance of one's role in life and the fatalism which this engendered were not completely lost.[50] C. S. Wilson saw the relative freedom of working-class children and the inherent opportunities for developing chance relationships which this provided as determining their attitude towards fate.[51] Life was a matter of chance, with gambling as a logical extension of this principle.

Conservatism was allied to fatalism and showed itself in an unwillingness to change working practices. This was more apparent in older industries like mining and shipbuilding. Though significant economically, it was not a prerogative of the working class.[52]

The Welfare State brought a reduction of *insecurity*, though after studying inner-city Liverpool in the late 1950s, Mays could still write that 'Old customs and habits die hard. The years of scarcity are for some a living memory. The days of full employment are still young, still uncertain. Suspicion of social discrimination and fear of possible unemployment even now activate the minds of many people.' [53] This attitude had not entirely disappeared by the 1980s: as though the National Health Service had never been, some elderly people living in the legacy of the Poor Law still referred to seeing their panel doctor.

Insecurity might be expected to result in planning ahead, but when allied to fatalism, the consequence was living for the present, which limited goal-oriented activities like saving and education.[54] As Jephcott reported glumly in the late 1940s, 'Some of the girls from poorer homes ... seem to have a feeling that any skill which costs money to acquire is the prerogative of the boy.' [55] The only certainty – death – was traditionally the subject of elaborate planning by means of life assurance.[56] But a more optimistic attitude was on its way. In a London School of Economics study from 1950, 88 per cent of the manual workers questioned considered that their children had a better chance of advancement than they did themselves, citing improved educational standards as the reason. Unskilled workers were less likely to prefer grammar school education for their children, however.[57]

Bernice Martin offers a perceptive analysis, linking several of the concepts discussed to the insecurity of working-class life in which a culture of control was the only hope of creating human dignity and a modicum of self-determination against all odds. She introduces the notion of liminal moments, set off against the rules, roles and categories of everyday life. These occasions when high spending was expected included funerals, weddings, holidays and Christmas celebrations.[58] Unfortunately she does not explore the role of the cinema as an alternative means of release from the culture of control, or as a source of different values.

A constellation of terms can be demonstrated as having significance in postwar working-class culture, albeit with considerable regional and occupational variations. Their presence reveals the varied stratagems which people used to define and differentiate their place in the world. In exploring the past, there is often no other way to study class, given that evidence has to be gleaned from the sources which survive, however inadequate. Such pragmatism will not satisfy all sociologists, but it allows David Cannadine and Ross McKibbin to write about class in twentieth-century Britain without becoming bogged down in terminology.[59]

The strengths of this approach become apparent when using feature films as evidence about class. The cues are visual and aural – and almost entirely qualitative. Though there is little ambiguity about occupation and the size of a house, to these signifiers of class must be added the minutiae of social stratification expressed in decor, clothing, speech, eating habits, etc. Such details are easily reproducible on screen, but, echoing Goffman, social values exist in the mind as much as in their outward manifestations. The skill of the film-maker lies in externalising the subjective awareness of being different experienced by a working-class child on entering a grammar school for the first time, or a labourer venturing into a solicitor's office. For an audience, empathy only becomes possible if they can experience that subjective awareness.

In the remaining section of this chapter, a five-dimensional model for examining images of the working class in films is proposed. A model in this sense functions as a checklist and should be judged by its usefulness. Unlike a theory, it is intended to have neither predictive nor explanatory powers. When audiences and critics identified working-class characters, such a model was implicit in their response. For working-class characters to be taken seriously, these defining features need to be delineated without imposing a theoretical framework so rigid as to exclude other potentially useful material.

Place in the authority structure

As generations of comedians can testify, working-class people are defined by their attitude to authority – and by the attitude of those in authority towards the working class. The vestigial salute implied in touching the cap and the failure to acknowledge it can speak volumes. Power and status are intrinsic to the equation, though they need not be vested in the same person, the uneasy relationship between Captain Mainwaring and Sergeant Wilson in *Dad's Army* (BBC TV, 1968–77) being a case in point.

At least in films, the lowly man who suddenly achieves wealth and tries to pass himself off as belonging to a higher social class is apt to betray his origins by his social gaffes. This is the stuff of comedy. As Stephen Shafer notes, such a fate is more likely to be avoided by the rich man who samples ordinary life.[60] The distinction rests on the artistic conceit that upper-class codes of behaviour are more complex than those of the working class. Working-class codes can be just as impenetrable, as John McCallum discovered when he visited an East End pub to research his role in *It Always Rains on Sunday* (d. Robert Hamer, 1947). Despite wearing old clothes and a cloth cap, he was immediately identified as an outsider.[61]

Working-class characters in films constantly confront authority in the shape of civil servants, policemen and employers. This tension runs through George Formby's films, where those with power struggle to keep the irrepressible George in his place. His fruitless attempts to obtain a drink on the Isle of Man steamer in *No Limit* (d. Monty Banks, 1935) illustrate that though a barman may have low status, he can connive in maintaining the social order – with George at the bottom.

The equivocal position of the supervisor has particular interest. Here is a member of the working class exercising power over former colleagues. This is exemplified in *Millions Like Us* (d. Frank Launder and Sidney Gilliat, 1943), where a wartime factory setting allows both gender and class differences to increase the potential for conflict with Eric Portman's foreman.

There is satisfaction in outwitting authority, even if authority ultimately wins out. Not that it need be faceless: in crime stories, the humble PC49 can assume the role of hero as readily as the amateur sleuth or the Scotland Yard detective. Where a clash with authority provides drama on screen, rather than being expressed in class terms, it may be transmuted into a battle between good and evil in the crime film, or between spontaneity and bureaucracy, as in any Ealing comedy.

Cohesion/fragmentation within the working-class community

The emphasis on community and shared experience becomes obvious where there is a dominant industry. The mine overshadows *The Proud Valley* (d. Pen Tennyson, 1939) and *Blue Scar* (d. Jill Craigie, 1949) as surely as fishing is woven into the fabric of *Johnny Frenchman* (d. Charles Frend, 1945) and *The Silver Darlings* (d. Clarence Elder and Clifford Evans, 1947). During the war, class cohesion could be subsumed within the desire for national unity in the face of a common enemy, as in *The Bells Go Down* (d. Basil Dearden, 1943). A glimpse of the postwar situation comes in *I'm All Right Jack* (d. John Boulting, 1959), with polarised attitudes reminiscent of *The Stars Look Down* (d. Carol Reed, 1939).

To generate drama, either the community is pitted against another social group (the enemy in some guise), or there is fragmentation from within. The latter can occur as characters acquire values derived from outside – often from education or the media. Many British realist films from the late 1950s onwards were predicated on the alienation of a central character from traditional working-class culture, though the middle-class culture which was the obvious alternative hardly seemed more alluring. A defining event can split the community; the shooting in *Odd Man Out* (d. Carol Reed, 1947) being a notable example. It can also draw the community together. This is evident in *Passport to Pimlico* (d. Henry Cornelius, 1945), where residents are temporarily united by the government's threat to seize buried treasure discovered on a Pimlico bombsite.

Optimists and sentimentalists generally see cohesion where pessimists and realists discern fragmentation. The thought-provoking films such as *Holiday Camp* (d. Ken Annakin, 1947), to be discussed in Chapter Four, are those in which competing positions are juxtaposed.

Internalised values

This concept embraces such abstractions as attitudes, mores and habits which mark a character as working class. A sense of fatalism, living for the present and the delicate balance between striving for respectability and getting above oneself are all to be found in films. *Millions Like Us* teems with differences in attitudes to matters like sharing rooms which help to define characters in class terms. Where film-makers are out of touch with the working class, they are more likely to resort to stereotypes. Bernard Miles' petty officer in *In Which We Serve* (d. David Lean and Noel Coward, 1942) is representative. A crucial issue is whether changes in internalised values are apparent over time. A comparison of postwar films with those made in the 1930s should reveal differences. Evidence may also be sought in the different attitudes of older and younger characters, though as each succeeding generation is apt to be seen as beginning the spiral into moral decline, this method must be treated with caution.[62]

The built environment

What kind of home do the characters inhabit? Is there a sense of oppressive overcrowding and dilapidation? Is family life centred on the kitchen? Are bedrooms (or beds) shared? Does the housewife attempt to keep the home clean and tidy, or does she surrender to squalor? Is the neighbourhood a place of cramped terraces? Where do people congregate? How is the workplace presented and how does it contrast with the home? Audiences unused to the world being presented may need to be brought into it by a device such as the middle-class narrator in *Waterloo Road* (d. Sidney Gilliat, 1945), or the introduction of a character who, like them, is a newcomer and who can explore the environment with them and share their feelings. Terry Lovell detects this process in early episodes of *Coronation Street* (Granada TV, 1960–current).[63]

The set designer has a major role in evoking a working-class milieu, which can be enhanced by the judicious use of location shooting and documentary material. A tight budget need not pose a problem: a limited number of sets can reinforce the sense of the characters' material impoverishment.

The built environment can be seen as a measure of the power and economic circumstances of the participants. It determines the nature of social interactions (the street gang or the gossiping housewives in the corner shop), as well as colouring the expectations of the characters and limiting their opportunities (the slum boy and the mill girl are both stigmatised). The industrial landscape can shape and oppress working-class characters, fuelling their frustration if they know something better.

Personal signifiers of class, notably speech, hairstyles and clothing

These are the outward manifestations of an individual's class. When the street market, the factory, or the slum is not there to provide a context, the flat cap is enough to place a character socially. Is the shabbiness apparent in *Love on the Dole* (d. John Baxter, 1941) still evident in postwar films, or was austerity reducing class-based distinctions in women's dress as Zweig discerned?[64] How are clothes worn? (The working-class Sunday best in all its glorious discomfort is still on parade in Gordon Parry's *Sailor Beware!* dating from 1956.) How are spivs presented? The essence of spivery is ostentation expressed in dress and accessories. How distinctive is young people's clothing? A sign of the emerging youth culture was that young men no longer dressed like their fathers. Such visual details are crucial in creating verisimilitude in films about ordinary people.

Though authentic northern or Glaswegian accents might limit the appeal of a film, speech places people geographically and socially. In one survey it appears as the most frequently-used way of ranking people by class.[65] The most well-known interpretative framework for examining the class aspects of speech in Britain is that devised by Basil Bernstein.[66] The restricted speech code used by the working class orients the user towards description rather than abstract concepts, with an emphasis on 'we', 'you' and 'they' pronouns to denote group membership. A shared set of values means that non-verbal communication and verbal shorthand are possible. By contrast, the use of an elaborated speech code depends on access to specialised positions within the social structure such as the professions, and aims at the delivery of an explicit meaning. The restricted code is primarily a means of reinforcing group values rather than presenting inner states to others; the elaborated code with its greater use of the 'I' pronoun gives awareness of orders of relationships, intellectual, social and emotional, its high level of abstraction emphasising structure rather than content.[67] In short, the working-class mother orders where the middle-class mother appeals. Although Bernstein was at pains to emphasise that the restricted code was not exclusively working class and not inferior, these caveats have not always been accepted by his critics.[68]

A development from the 1990s is discourse analysis, which focuses on such aspects of speech as the frequency of extreme case formulations ('always' and 'never') and degrees of variability in how objects are evaluated.[69] A difficulty with this approach is why one interpretation should be privileged over another. Adrian Coyle's suggestion that significant amounts of raw data overcome the danger of relativism is unconvincing – they might just as easily compound the problem.[70] A second limitation is the absence of a substantial body of research on class aspects of speech using this method. Here, quantity is desirable. Without it, the usefulness of discourse analysis in this context remains unproven.

Colin MacCabe accuses sociolinguistics of using banal sociological and psychological categories.[71] One response is that results are more important than methods. Banal or not, speech patterns cannot be ignored in considering the portrayal of working-class people.

The model offers a way of codifying images of class. It is less useful as a means of grouping films for the purposes of discussion, given that they straddle the five dimensions. Examining the work of one director might be appropriate for Hitchcock, but it is restrictive in the range of films which can be considered, it ignores the cooperative aspect of film-making and it is less satisfactory as a means of exploring the career of a jobbing director working in several genres. Considering the output of individual studios is possible with Hollywood films, but with a few exceptions such as Ealing and Gainsborough, it is less easy to apply to the cottage-industry approach to film production prevailing in Britain. Grouping films by genre has more potential, but means corralling disparate material on the basis of some theoretical unity – Raymond Durgnat identifies seventeen sub-genres of the crime film, many of which have little in common.[72] Colin Shindler offers a more promising approach, linking changes in American society to changes in the concerns apparent in films.[73] A potential danger, noted in Chapter One, is that films are selected for discussion because they fit the theory, while others are ignored. A variant on Shindler's approach is utilised here, grouping films by the recurring preoccupations of working-class life, such as community, upward mobility, the family and delinquency. What the films have in common is their concern for working-class characters. Above all, what remains important is that the films are meant to be enjoyed. Analysing them to the point of boredom is to obscure rather than illuminate what audiences of the past gained from their weekly visits to the pictures.

Notes

1 Rosemary Crompton, 'Non-manual labour', in James Obelkevich and Peter Catterall (eds), *Understanding Post-War British Society* (London: Routledge, 1994), p. 99; Geoffrey Browne, *Patterns of British Life: A Study of Certain Aspects of the British People at Home, at Work and at Play, and a Compilation of Some Relevant Statistics* (London: Hulton Press, 1950), p. 87; J. Rex, 'National class structure', in Eric Butterworth and David Weir (eds), *The Sociology of Modern Britain: An Introductory Reader* (London: Fontana, rev. edn. 1975), Table 1, p. 308.

2 Jon Clark, Celia Modgil and Sohan Modgil (eds), *John H. Goldthorpe: Consensus and Controversy* (Basingstoke: Falmer Press, 1990).

3 H. E. Browning and A. A. Sorrell, 'Cinemas and cinema-going in Great Britain', *Journal of the Royal Statistical Society*, series A (general), 117:2 (1954), Table 6, pp. 138–40.

4 George H. Gallup (ed.), *The Gallup International Opinion Polls: Great Britain 1937–1975* (New York: Random House, 1976), pp. 172 and 213.

5 Arthur Marwick, *Class: Image and Reality in Britain, France and the USA since 1890* (London: Collins, 1980), p. 15.

6 Cited in Steve Humphries, Joanna Mack and Robert Perks, *A Century of Childhood* (London: Sidgwick & Jackson, in association with Channel Four Television, 1988), p. 12. For earlier in the century, see Robert Roberts, *The Classic Slum: Salford Life in the First Quarter of the Century* (Manchester: Manchester University Press, 1971), pp. 132–40; Richard Hoggart, *The Uses of Literacy: Aspects of Working-Class Life with Special Reference to Publications and Entertainments* (Harmondsworth: Penguin Books, 1958), pp. 58–68.

7 Dennis Chapman, *The Location of Dwellings in Scottish Towns: An Inquiry into Some of the Factors Relevant to the Planning of New Urban Communities Made for the Department of Health for Scotland* (Wartime Social Survey NS 34, 1943), p. 24. See also L. G. White, *Tenement Town* (London: Jason Press, 1946), p. 17.

8 Madeleine Kerr, *The People of Ship Street* (London: Routledge & Kegan Paul, 1958), pp. 23–4 and 29; Margaret Stacey, *Tradition and Change: A Study of Banbury* (London: Oxford University Press, 1960), p. 155.

9 David Fowler, *The First Teenagers: The Lifestyle of Young Wage-Earners in Interwar Britain* (London: Woburn Press, 1995), p. 26; David Norman, Youth Employment Officer for Brixham in the 1980s (personal communication).

10 One example is Coventry City Libraries, J. P. Hayes, 'Convenience and

selectivity, and the planning of neighbourhood units', part of 'Coventry Sociological Survey', 1953.

11 For the prototypical working-class community, see Hoggart, *The Uses of Literacy*, pp. 80–6.

12 Peter Townsend, *The Family Life of Old People* (London: Routledge & Kegan Paul, 1957), p. 127; Terence Morris, *The Criminal Area: A Study in Social Ecology* (London: Routledge & Kegan Paul, 1958), pp. 177–8.

13 J. M. Mogey, *Family and Neighbourhood: Two Studies in Oxford* (London: Oxford University Press, 1956), Tables 7 and 26, pp. 18 and 96.

14 Mark W. Hodges and Cyril S. Smith, 'The Sheffield estate', in University of Liverpool, Department of Social Science, *Neighbourhood and Community: An Enquiry into Social Relationships on Housing Estates in Liverpool and Sheffield* (Liverpool: University of Liverpool Press, 1954), p. 90.

15 E. R. Manley, *Meet the Miner* (Wakefield: E. R. Manley, 3 Leeds Road, Lofthouse, 1947), p. 63.

16 Hodges and Smith, 'The Sheffield estate', pp. 110 and 117. Similar restrictions on contact with neighbours are noted in Lulie A. Shaw, 'Impressions of family life in a London suburb', *Sociological Review*, new series, 2:1 (1954), 193; Ray Gosling, *Personal Copy: A Memory of the Sixties* (London: Faber & Faber, 1980), pp. 17 and 104.

17 Leo Kuper, 'Blueprint for living together', in Leo Kuper (ed.), *Living in Towns: Selected Research Papers in Urban Sociology of the Faculty of Commerce and Social Science, University of Birmingham* (London: Cresset Press, 1953), p. 79.

18 Geoffrey Gorer, *Exploring English Character* (London: Cresset Press, 1955), p. 53. A similar pattern emerges in Janet H. Madge, 'Some aspects of social mixing in Worcester', in Kuper (ed.), *Living in Towns*, p. 290.

19 Charles Madge and Tom Harrisson (for Mass-Observation), *Britain* (Harmondsworth: Penguin Books, 1939), p. 219.

20 John Barron Mays, *Education and the Urban Child* (Liverpool: Liverpool University Press, 1962), p. 91.

21 Townsend, *The Family Life of Old People*, pp. 77 and 79; Stacey, *Tradition and Change*, pp. 115–23.

22 Pearl Jephcott, *Rising Twenty: Notes on Some Ordinary Girls* (London: Faber & Faber, 1948), p. 47; Shaw, 'Impressions of family life in a London suburb', 183; Gorer, *Exploring English Character*, pp. 45–6.

23 Michael Young and Peter Willmott, *Family and Kinship in East London* (London: Routledge & Kegan Paul, 1957), pp. 23–6.

24 D. J. Phillips, 'A study of the concepts of family life held by a group of adolescent girls', *Researches and Studies*, no. 10 (1954), 14–18.

25 Eliot Slater and Moya Woodside, *Patterns of Marriage: A Study of Marriage Relationships in the Urban Working Classes* (London: Cassell, 1951), p. 117. See also Jerry White, *The Worst Street in North London: Campbell Bunk, Islington, between the Wars* (London: Routledge & Kegan Paul, 1986), pp. 139, 146 and 214.

26 Slater and Woodside, *Patterns of Marriage*, p. 87; Diana Gittins, *Fair Sex: Family Size and Structure 1900–39* (London: Hutchinson, 1982), p. 140.

27 Colin Rosser and Philip Harris, *The Family and Social Change: A Study of Family and Kinship in a South Wales Town* (London: Routledge & Kegan Paul, 1975), Table 7.5, p. 250. See also Elizabeth Roberts,

Women's Place: An Oral History of Working-Class Women 1890–1940 (Oxford: Basil Blackwell, 1984), p. 43.

28 Hodges and Smith, 'The Sheffield estate', p. 85; Townsend, *The Family Life of Old People*, p. 27.

29 *Ibid.*, p. 12. Surprisingly, Hoggart also notes this, in spite of his stress on community. Hoggart, *The Uses of Literacy*, p. 34.

30 Winifred L. Whitely, 'Littletown-in-overspill', in Kuper (ed.), *Living in Towns*, p. 211; Mogey, *Family and Neighbourhood*, p. 133; Norman Dennis, Fernando Henriques and Clifford Slaughter, *Coal Is Our Life: An Analysis of a Yorkshire Mining Community* (London: Eyre & Spottiswoode, 1956), p. 182.

31 William Woodruff, *Billy Boy: The Story of a Lancashire Weaver's Son* (Halifax: Ryburn, 1993), p. 12.

32 Jephcott, *Rising Twenty*, pp. 15 and 34–5.

33 Gorer, *Exploring English Character*, p. 171.

34 A. P. Jephcott, *Girls Growing Up* (London: Faber & Faber, 1942), p. 129; Mogey, *Family and Neighbourhood*, pp. 59–60; Dennis *et al. Coal Is Our Life*, pp. 181–2 and 201. It is not always clear from the studies made in the 1940s whether the fathers were home or in the services. Attitudes from the interwar years are noted in Hoggart, *The Uses of Literacy*, pp. 41–58; John Burnett (ed.), *Destiny Obscure: Autobiographies of Childhood, Education and the Family from the 1820s to the 1920s* (London: Routledge, 1994), pp. 235 and 243.

35 Ferdynand Zweig, *Men in the Pits* (London: Victor Gollancz, 1948), p. 102.

36 Mogey, *Family and Neighbourhood*, pp. 17 and 65. For the interwar years, see Hoggart, *The Uses of Literacy*, pp. 55–8; Don Haworth, *Bright Morning: Images from a Thirties Boyhood* (London: Mandarin, 1991), p. 10.

37 Mays, *Education and the Urban Child*, p. 98.

38 Geoff Mungham, 'Youth in pursuit of itself', in Geoff Mungham and Geoff Pearson (eds), *Working Class Youth Culture* (London: Routledge & Kegan Paul, 1976), p. 88.

39 Gorer, *Exploring English Character*, p. 147; Slater and Woodside, *Patterns of Marriage*, Table 10b, pp. 290–1; Marie Paneth, *Branch Street: A Sociological Study* (London, George Allen & Unwin, 1944), p. 26.

40 George Orwell, *The English People* (London: Collins, 1947), p. 29; Kuper, 'Blueprint for living together', p. 78. For the interwar years, see Hoggart, *The Uses of Literacy*, pp. 77–80; Haworth, *Bright Morning*, p. 9.

41 Ferdynand Zweig, *Women's Life and Labour* (London: Victor Gollancz, 1952), pp. 123–4.

42 Elizabeth Roberts, *Women's Place*, p. 14.

43 J. Macalister Brew, *Informal Education: Adventures and Reflections* (London: Faber & Faber, 1946), p. 101.

44 Hodges and Smith, 'The Sheffield estate', p. 116; Elizabeth Roberts, *Women's Place*, pp. 195–6; Leslie Halliwell, *Seats in All Parts: Half a Lifetime at the Movies* (London: Granada, 1985), p. 19.

45 Nigel Gray, *The Silent Majority: A Study of the Working Class in Post-War British Fiction* (London: Vision Press, 1973), p. 139.

46 Cited in Peter Pagnamenta and Richard Overy, *All Our Working Lives* (London: BBC, 1994), p. 269. For earlier examples see Paneth, *Branch*

Street, p. 55; Ted Willis, *Whatever Happened to Tom Mix? The Story of One of My Lives* (London: Cassell, 1970), p. 12; Robert Roberts, *The Classic Slum*, p. 7.

47 Cited in Elizabeth Roberts, *Women's Place*, p. 129. See also Kuper, 'Blueprint for living together', p. 72; Pearl Jephcott, *Some Young People* (London: George Allen & Unwin, 1954), p. 56. For earlier in the century see Robert Roberts, *The Classic Slum*, pp. 17–18; Walter Southgate, *That's the Way It Was: A Working-Class Autobiography 1890–1950* (Oxted, Surrey: New Clarendon Press, 1982), p. 67.

48 Dennis Chapman, *The Home and Social Status* (London: Routledge & Kegan Paul, 1955), p. 73.

49 This verse had the distinction of being banned from use by the Inner London Education Authority in 1982 because of its inegalitarian sentiments. *The Penguin Book of Hymns*, ed. Ian Bradley (London: Viking, 1989), p. 28.

50 Ferdynand Zweig, *Labour, Life, Poverty* (Wakefield: EP, 1975), p. 89; Hoggart, *The Uses of Literacy*, pp. 91–4.

51 C. S. Wilson, 'The family and neighbourhood in a British community', M.Sc. thesis, University of Cambridge, 1953, p. 183.

52 Zweig, *Men in the Pits*, pp. 63 and 81; Correlli Barnett, *The Audit of War: The Illusion of Britain as a Great Nation* (London: Pan, 1996). For the tenacious clinging to habits and customs in Walter Greenwood's novel, *Love on the Dole*, set in the thirties, see Alan Swingewood, *The Myth of Mass Culture* (Basingstoke and London: Macmillan, 1977), p. 60.

53 Mays, *Education and the Urban Child*, p. 92.

54 For fatalism, see Ross McKibbin, *The Ideologies of Class: Social Relations in Britain 1880–1950* (Oxford: Oxford University Press, Clarendon Press, 1994), pp. 115–16; S. M. Miller and Frank Riessman, 'The working class subculture: a new view', *Social Problems*, 9:1 (1961), 91–4.

For saving, see Charles Madge, *Wartime Patterns of Saving and Spending*, National Institute of Economic and Social Research occasional paper 4 (London: Cambridge University Press, 1943), p. 16; Paul Johnson, *Saving and Spending: The Working-Class Economy in Britain 1870–1939* (Oxford: Oxford University Press, Clarendon Press, 1985), p. 41.

For conservatism in education see Mogey, *Family and Neighbourhood*, p. 75; Townsend, *The Family Life of Old People*, p. 101; Hoggart, *The Uses of Literacy*, p. 84.

For the view that the working class took a realistic view of their life chances, see David Hargreaves, 'Two subcultures', in Maurice Craft (ed.), *Family, Class and Education: A Reader* (London: Longman, 1970), p. 133.

55 Jephcott, *Rising Twenty*, p. 104.

56 B. Seebohm Rowntree, *Poverty and Progress: A Second Social Survey of York* (London: Longmans, Green, 1941), pp. 212–13; M. Fitzgerald (for Manchester University Settlement) *Ancoats: A Study of a Clearance Area. Report of a Survey Made in 1937–1938* (Manchester: Manchester University Settlement, 1945), p. 41.

57 F. M. Martin, 'Some subjective aspects of social stratification' and 'An enquiry into parents' preferences in secondary education', both in David V. Glass (ed.), *Social Mobility in Britain* (London: Routledge & Kegan Paul, 1954), pp. 67–9 and 166.

58 Bernice Martin, *A Sociology of Contemporary Cultural Change* (Oxford: Basil Blackwell, 1981), pp. 61, 71–3.

59 David Cannadine, *Class in Britain* (New Haven, CT, and London: Yale University Press, 1998); Ross McKibbin, *Classes and Cultures: England 1918–1951* (Oxford: Oxford University Press, 1998).

60 Stephen C. Shafer, *British Popular Films 1929–1939: The Cinema of Reassurance* (London: Routledge, 1997), pp. 77, 110–11.

61 John McCallum, *Life with Googie* (London: William Heinemann, 1979), pp. 18–19.

62 The theme is explored in Christopher Shaw and Malcolm Chase (eds), *The Imagined Past: History and Nostalgia* (Manchester: Manchester University Press, 1989).

63 Terry Lovell, 'Landscapes and stories – 1960s British realism', *Screen*, 31:4 (1990), 363.

64 Zweig, *Women's Life and Labour*, p. 124.

65 I. Reid, *Social Class Differences in Britain: A Sourcebook* (London: Open Books, 1977), Table 2.5, p. 27.

66 Basil Bernstein, *Class, Codes and Control*, vol. 1: *Theoretical Studies Towards a Sociology of Language* (London, Routledge & Kegan Paul, 1971). 'Interpretative framework' is Bernstein's own description of his work in preference to the more exacting term 'theory'.

67 *Ibid.*, pp. 76–147.

68 Denis Lawton, *Social Class, Language and Education* (London: Routledge & Kegan Paul, 1968), pp. 77–102; A. D. Edwards, *Language in Culture and Class: The Sociology of Language and Education* (London: Heinemann, 1976); Harold Rosen, *Language and Class: A Critical Look at the Theories of Basil Bernstein* (Bristol: Falling Wall Press, 1972).

69 Adrian Coyle, 'Discourse analysis', in Glynis M. Breakwell, Sean Hammond and Chris Fife-Schaw (eds), *Research Methodology in Psychology* (London: Sage, 1995), pp. 243–58.

70 *Ibid.*, p. 256.

71 Colin MacCabe, *The Eloquence of the Vulgar* (London: BFI, 1999), p. 51.

72 Raymond Durgnat, 'Some lines of enquiry into post-war British crimes', in Robert Murphy (ed.), *The British Cinema Book* (London: BFI, 1997), pp. 90–103.

73 Colin Shindler, *Hollywood Goes to War: Film and American Society 1939–1952* (London: Routledge & Kegan Paul, 1979).

3 The guns fall silent: recollections of war

Though hostilities provided a backdrop to many feature films made in Britain during the war years, the topic was largely skirted by film-makers once peace came. This accorded with public opinion: in a *Daily Express* survey from 1946, only 1 per cent of respondents preferred war films, while 42 per cent wanted human interest films.[1] By Denis Gifford's classification, there were 20 war films among the 491 British features released between 1945 and 1950 (4 per cent).[2] Eight of the twelve released by the end of 1948 concerned spies and resistance fighters, as though there was a feeling that it was time for hidden stories to be revealed. Among the offerings was *Against the Wind* (d. Charles Crichton, 1948), a routine resistance story which failed at the box office (Appendix, Tables 2 and 5). It was scripted by T. E. B. Clarke, who wrote in 1974 that the film should have come out five to ten years later.[3] This hindsight view suggests that a shift in taste took place by the 1950s. Statistics do not support this: Gifford classifies 21 of the 621 British films issued between 1951 and 1956 as war films (3 per cent). Though the proportion of war films declined, the 1950s cycle included such prestige productions as *The Dam Busters* (d. Michael Anderson, 1954), *Cockleshell Heroes* (d. José Ferrer, 1955) and *Reach for the Sky* (d. Lewis Gilbert, 1956).[4] Myths were being reinforced or remade for a new generation. By the 1960s, the cycle had run its course and the Cold War became the preoccupation of film-makers, notably with the James Bond series.

The Way to the Stars (d. Anthony Asquith, 1945) was adapted from two Terence Rattigan plays. It was made before the war ended, so that an opening sequence had to be added to prevent the film from seeming dated on its release.[5] This was shot on an abandoned airfield, with a voice-over explaining that the action took place when the base was operational. Even without this, *The Way to the Stars* has an elegiac quality which would have been inappropriate at the height of hostilities. It is the last of the wartime films rather than the first of the peacetime treatments of war, though Robert Murphy detects similarities of subject matter with *I Live in Grosvenor Square* (d. Herbert Wilcox, 1945).[6]

Pilot David Archdale (Michael Redgrave) marries Toddy Todd (Rosamund John), who runs a hotel close to the airfield. They have a child whom Toddy brings up alone after David is killed in action. When the airfield is taken over by the United States Air Force, she becomes friendly with an American pilot, Johnny Hollis (Douglass Montgomery). He is killed while attempting to crash-land his bomber. In a parallel story, novice pilot Peter Penrose (John Mills) is attracted to Iris Winterton (Renee Asherson), who stays in the hotel with her ever-complaining aunt (Joyce Carey). The uncertainties of flying on combat missions make Peter wary of embarking on a relationship. When Iris rebels against her aunt, Toddy urges Peter not to hesitate any longer. He proposes to Iris as she is about to leave the hotel and she accepts.

The obvious social distinction in the film is between officers and other ranks. Pilots are assumed to be commissioned officers, and commissioned officers are middle or upper class. The schoolmaster, Peter Penrose, soon takes on the speech of his roommate, the languid, upper-class David Archdale. Other ranks are working class and are peripheral to the story, reflecting Rattigan's preference for middle-class drama. The ever-pessimistic fitter and the comfortably-off hotel resident, Mr Palmer (who would be securely middle class if he were not played by Stanley Holloway), are there to provide light relief. In this, the film resembles *Brief Encounter* (d. David Lean, 1945).

Peter Penrose's gunner, Nobby Clarke (Bill Rowbotham, later to become better known as Bill Owen), is the only working-class character to be treated seriously. He shares a cigarette with Penrose on the airfield. The two men drink together in the hotel – the upper-class David Archdale gave them a lift there. Social distinctions signified largely by accent are apparent, but they are never emphasised. Instead, other distinctions emerge: between experienced and inexperienced pilots, ground and operational crews, and American and British fliers.

An officer who served throughout the war considers that as the RAF was only recently established, it was more egalitarian than the other services. Because fliers were the ones in contact with the enemy, desk-bound senior officers necessarily assumed a supporting role. This created different relationships from those found in the army or navy. He also recalls laughing at the portrayals of service life in films like *The Way to the Stars*.[7]

Children are important to the film. Toddy's son gives her a common interest with the American, Johnny Hollis, allowing him to show her pictures of his own family. In a scene which takes place after the fatal crash, children at a party are calling for him. A member of his crew who parachuted from the stricken bomber has to explain that Johnny cannot be there. Implicit throughout is the sense that hope is invested in the next generation.

The Way to the Stars won enough critical praise to be listed in 1951 as one of the films which everybody should see.[8] The exceptions to this general approbation were the Robsons, who detected a pathological obsession with lavatories which eluded everybody else.[9] Subsequent critical opinion has been less enthusiastic. Raymond Durgnat dismisses the film as a 'poignant lightweight', while Charles Drazin considers that the joins between Rattigan's two stage plays are too obvious.[10] For Sue Harper,

This ethic [of impassivity], though it has been "argued up" into a national characteristic by male historians and critics, is based on weakness rather than strength: there is nothing inherently praiseworthy about emotional inexpressivity. But *The Way to the Stars* mounts a forcible argument in favour of such repression, and the performance of the actresses is probably a testament to their compliance in the face of forceful direction.[11]

Nor is there anything inherently praiseworthy about overt emotional expressivity. Deploring its absence seems ahistorical. Whatever the later connotations of emotional reticence, it has to be accepted as a convention of British films of the period. Nor is inexpressiveness necessarily the same as reticence. If critics accepted that the performances were neither lifeless nor stolid, then emotional responses, however muted, were being successfully conveyed. The Americans Antonia Lant and Marcia Landy appreciate this, with Landy also detecting antipathy towards America.[12]

Why emotional reticence should be deemed an English characteristic is a separate issue. There is a case for seeing it as distinguishing the upper middle and upper classes. The self control which it implies is a hallmark of that related habit of mind, deferred gratification. Public school stories such as *The Guinea Pig* (d. Roy Boulting, 1948) espouse it. From the viewpoint of society's upper echelons, the working class live for the present. The converse of this lack of forethought is that they can express emotions more easily and enjoy themselves uninhibitedly. Such proletarian amusements as the music hall and the fun fair are not noted for their reticence.

The lack of emphasis on class in *The Way to the Stars* means that a class perspective gives little clue as to why the film struck a chord with audiences across the social divide. Uniquely, it was reissued before initial bookings were completed, as well as winning the Daily Mail National Film Award for 1946.[13] The managing director of Raymond Stross Theatres (a circuit of nine cinemas based in Norfolk, but with outposts in Belfast and Wales) hailed the film as one of the top British successes.[14] This was borne out by the large number of screenings in southeast Essex (Appendix, Table 7). *The Way to the Stars* was the British feature film screened most often in working-class Leeds over the period 1945–50 (Appendix, Table 6) and it achieved the sixth highest admission figure out of fifty-one films screened at the Majestic, Macclesfield, in 1945.[15] It was also named as the most outstanding film by 73 per cent of respondents to the Bernstein Film Questionnaire, putting it ahead of the other thirty-five films listed, British and American.[16] Most of Bernstein's Granada cinemas were in working-class suburbs around London. Paradoxically, the revelation of emotions in the film provides a key to understanding its popularity, notwithstanding Harper's accusation of emotional inexpressivity. Although by 1945 there was little enthusiasm for fighting (which Asquith never shows), every member of the audience had been touched by war. There was too much time in which to contemplate the fate of a loved one who might be on the other side of the world. Responses could be rehearsed to the point where bad news no longer came as a surprise. This is exhausted emotion rather than repressed emotion. Audiences could respond to the film's psychological reality in a way which transcended class. *The Way to the Stars* functions as emotional catalyst, capturing the sense of getting on with things because there is no alternative and giving audiences the opportunity to empathise with characters' ways of coping. In C. A. Lejeune's words, 'Again and again the audience is left to resolve its own tensions: an operation that is painful, unusual and good for the soul.'[17]

Drazin sums up 'Puffin' Asquith's acceptance of his failure as a musician: 'To know the sublime, yet to live without it – Puffin had learnt this lesson from an early age.'[18] This serves as a key to Toddy's character: she knows the sublime, yet she lives with its absence as her husband and then Johnny join the litany of the missing and the dead which stalks the film. The contrast is with Peter Penrose, who survives his missions (because he is cautious as a flier?) and who takes no emotional risks. Toddy has the conviction to persuade him that his chosen course is wrong. The overt display of emotion when he proposes to Iris is all the more powerful for the careful buildup. Writer, director and actors judge the pace to perfection, giving the lie to David Thomson's bilious assessment of Asquith as 'a dull journeyman supervisor of the transfer of proven theatrical properties'.[19]

Any understatement in the acting is belied by the lush score, the resonance of John Pudney's poem, whose words are revealed only to the characters who know loss, and the moments of emotional release, often expressed in dancing or singing (including a song by the young Jean Simmons). As a study of how war shapes relationships, *The Way to the Stars* remains the most emotionally charged of British war films, in spite of eschewing conventional heroics. Perhaps Asquith was exorcising his own demons: his father was prime minister when war was declared in 1914. If so, he let the film speak for itself. What he did reveal about its making was his use of improvised dialogue and of real people in real settings. In spite of this, he felt that an actor can 'give something more real than the real thing. That is to say, he will express more of the man's inner personality, show up more facets of his character, present us, in fact, with a more living figure.' [20] Asquith conveyed heightened reality and judging by the film's commercial success, audiences had no trouble with this. Hard of heart is the viewer who does not blink away a tear as the music swells and Rosamund John raises her eyes towards the night sky in the film's final moments.

An aspect of service life which appeals to film-makers and which is exemplified in *The Way to the Stars* is the opportunity to bring together a disparate group of men. A variant of this is the prison camp story. The dilemma for film-makers is that given a camp full of male prisoners, the result is a man's film in the same way as the western. One way of overcoming this is attempted in *The Captive Heart* (d. Basil Dearden, 1946). The film begins with a series of flashbacks which establish the prisoners' civilian lives. By alternating the action between the families left behind and life in the camp, two worlds are shown to the audience. At first, letters provide the link between them; when the men return home, the two worlds come together.

This is in essence a portmanteau film – a form which was in vogue at the time. Dai Evans (Mervyn Johns) and Corporal Horsfall (Jack Warner) belong to the respectable working class. In civilian life they work together as builders. Dai's wife dies in childbirth during his captivity; when he returns home, his daughter is four years old and is being looked after by Mrs Horsfall. The second story is that of David Lennox (Gordon Jackson), who comes from a Scottish lower-middle-class background. He has lost his sight in action – a fact which he omits to mention in his letter to his fiancee, breaking off their engagement. When he is repatriated, she is waiting for him, having been told of his blindness by his mother. Representing the professional classes in the third story is pianist Stephen Hartley (Derek Bond), who receives a letter telling him that his wife is having an affair. When he gets back, he discovers that the letter was malicious. The final story and the one accorded most attention is that of the mysterious foreigner, Karel Hasek (Michael Redgrave), who escaped from a concentration camp by assuming the identity of the dead Captain Mitchell. To avoid arousing suspicion among the camp authorities, Hasek has to keep up a correspondence with Mitchell's wife. In doing so, he falls in love with her, creating problems when he is repatriated – problems which love overcomes.

As in *The Way to the Stars*, rank is not stressed and social distinctions are left unstated. Conditions in the camp are the same for officers and men, which contributes to the emphasis on pulling together, in spite of the military hierarchy being maintained. Both groups are seen sharing the remains of the soap (though there is no shortage of Brylcreem, judging by Jack Warner's hair). Dai leads the choral singing, that symbol of unity which finds its way into other films including Dearden's *The Blue Lamp* (1950). Dissident figures such as Hasek are assimilated into the community of the camp. Yet changes are coming. As the senior officer, Major Ossy Dalrymple (Basil Radford), admits, 'I'm a social parasite – the sort we're fighting to get rid of.'

Dearden seems happier among the social parasites and their emotional turmoils, leaving their working-class compatriots as undeveloped characters. Jack Warner reprises his stalwart cockney, his wife on this occasion being Gladys Henson. All that can be said of their relationship on his repatriation is that it takes up where it left off. Dai is given equally cursory treatment, except that he leaves a loving wife and comes home to a loving daughter. One missed opportunity is to explore how a parent and child who have been kept apart by the war negotiate their relationship.[21] Perhaps the topic touched a raw nerve, for it was accorded little attention in films until *The Divided Heart* (d. Charles Crichton, 1954) and then it was distanced by being presented as a problem affecting refugee children.

The most interesting lower-class character in *The Captive Heart* is another outsider, the self-confessed burglar, Matthews (Jimmy

Hanley), who risks his life so that Hasek can escape detection by the German authorities. This is the same Matthews who declared earlier that 'Only suckers work.' His life prior to becoming a prisoner is not explored, though after being reformed by his experience in the camp, he is offered work with Dai and Corporal Horsfall in their building partnership as a sign of his integration into society. Matthews drifts into the film and drifts out again in a perfunctory fashion. Whether his change of heart is permanent is not pursued.

In several scenes, camp inmates are seen peeling potatoes, knitting and washing clothes. On the basis of such evidence, Pat Kirkham and Janet Thumim detect a feminising effect of camp life on the men.[22] Yet these are everyday activities in service life: peeling potatoes is an indicator of the inmates' low status. If camp life does feminise them, some differential effects might be expected between classes, with working-class characters clinging determinedly to traditional roles. This is hard to detect given the sketchy characterisation.

Nationally the film was a commercial success, coming eighth in the *Daily Express* public opinion poll for the best films of 1946 and third in popularity among the thirty-six films included in the Bernstein questionnaire, with 56 per cent of respondents rating it as 'outstanding' and 35 per cent as 'good'.[23] Performance figures from southeast Essex mirror this pattern, though the film only achieved two three-day runs in working-class Leeds by the end of 1950 (Appendix, Tables 6 and 7). Managers might have been deterred by the high charges for a successful film, though regional differences in taste cannot be discounted. Alan Burton emphasises the film's reliance on Ealing's stock pattern of realism and stock character types.[24] These may have limited interest in the film among audiences who found little to relate to in Ealing's notion of working-class life. *The Captive Heart* is an unconventional story let down by a conventional treatment.

A variant on the prison camp theme is *The Hasty Heart* (d. Vincent Sherman, 1949), set in a military hospital in Burma. The enemy in this case is disease, with a prickly Scotsman, Lachlan McLachlan (Richard Todd), coming to accept the friendship of the other men in his hut when he realises that he is dying. His companions are assorted nationals, including Yank, Kiwi and Digger. The absence of names emphasises their symbolic status. Though the dialogue implies that Lachlan is working class – his impoverished background is emphasised – his class is unimportant compared to his Scottishness. Inevitably the Englishman of the group is called Tommy. The cockney role seems made for Jack Warner, but this was an ABPC film and Warner was a Rank man. His substitute was Howard Marion Crawford, who more often played blustering, upper-class establishment types. The sixth patient in the hut is the Negro, Blossom (Orlando Martins), though as he cannot speak English, his involvement in the story is minimal. The film is effectively a three-hander between Lachlan, Yank (Ronald Reagan) and Sister Margaret (Patricia Neal). There are personality clashes aplenty, but the dimensions of class and nationalism are never pursued.

The Hasty Heart could be passed over were it not for its popularity. For his performance, Todd was voted best actor in the 1950 *Picturegoer* and *Daily Mail* polls, with *The Hasty Heart* being voted best film in the latter.[25] These accolades are surprising given that the leading character is so unsympathetic, the film boasts no major stars (Todd's previous work was mainly in the theatre) and its origins as a stage play are all too obvious. The film achieved moderate exposure in the sample Leeds cinemas, though it fared better in southeast Essex (Appendix, Tables 6 and 7), presumably on the basis of Todd's charisma.

The emotional subtlety of *The Way to the Stars* becomes apparent when comparison is made with *They Were Not Divided* (d. Terence Young, 1950). This was an early entry in the 1950s war cycle, with its emphasis on fighting rather than feelings. The film follows soldiers from initial training to action in an armoured division of the Welsh Guards. Two who become officers and stay in the same unit are upper-middle-class Philip (Edward Underdown) and the American, David (Ralph Clanton). The film focuses on their stories. After D day, the division pushes through France, accompanied by American tanks. The two men are killed while on reconnaissance in the Ardennes.

Turning civilians into fighters had already been used as the scenario of *The Way Ahead* (d. Carol Reed, 1944). *They Were Not Divided* adds nothing new to the subject. Initial training takes up the first third of the film, the rest being devoted to the progress of the tanks through France. Once again rank is not stressed, particularly among the Americans, though the distinction between officers and other ranks is apparent on the British side in speech and behaviour, with upper-middle-class officers assuming an omniscience denied to lesser ranks. As in *The Way to the Stars*, other distinctions become apparent: between Americans and the British, and the Welsh and the Scots. As usual, the Welsh contingent emphasise their solidarity with choral singing.

The film achieves a documentary feel by the use of actuality footage and handheld camerawork during the advance of the tanks. The avoidance of stars obviates the problem of sustaining credibility when a familiar face appears. At the same time, verisimilitude creates an interesting dilemma. Whether intentionally or unintentionally, the dialogue among the officers takes on the stilted quality familiar from wartime documentaries using amateur actors. This is notable in the speech of the divisional commander, Major Bushy Noble (Michael Trubshawe). The sense of watching a documentary is enhanced, but realism is left behind.

Other changes are detectable from films about fighting produced during the war. Burying the dead did not figure in the earlier films, while the characters have licence to question the rationale for war. One occasion is a home visit by Philip shortly before his death. He explains to his wife:

You get such an odd, sort of superficial slant on the war, being in an armoured division. You're always moving over places and people. They're the ones who really see and feel the war – the people who are fought over. Perhaps in the infantry it's different. Maybe their feelings are more profound about it all. They have a worse time than we do. But then, you see, the things that you remember are all the wonderful, funny things that happened, not any of the horrors and unhappy things at all. I think that's how wars occur over and over again: because of what you don't remember.

The pity is that such introspective moments come so rarely. On the film's release, critics commented on its superficiality.[26] Any possibilities for exploring the motivations of working-class soldiers opened up by *Waterloo Road* (d. Sidney Gilliat, 1945) are forgotten. As in *The Way to the Stars*, the assumption is that only officers lead interesting emotional lives, but because the emphasis on fighting means that their private lives are little explored, their deaths are less moving than those of the fliers in the earlier film. Instead, Anglo-American unity is stressed, recalling a host of wartime films from *Mrs Miniver* (d. William Wyler, US, 1942) to *A Canterbury Tale* (d. Michael Powell and Emeric Pressburger, 1944) and *Journey Together* (d. John Boulting, 1945). In the final frames of *They Were Not Divided*, miniatures of the Stars and Stripes and the Union Jack on the heroes' snow-covered graves lean towards each other. With the Cold War and a conflict looming in Korea, the alliance needed reinforcing.

They Were Not Divided was released in February 1950. On 25 June 1950, North Korean forces crossed the 38th Parallel. Although the film achieved good exposure in southeast Essex (Appendix, Table 7), the first screening was in April and the last in early July. A moderately successful film would normally have been booked by second and third-run cinemas for the rest of the year. The film was never shown in the sample Leeds cinemas, suggesting that it was overtaken by events. This was not the moment for films about fighting which ended with the leading characters being killed. That comes when film-makers are confident of being on the winning side.

Also released in 1950 was *The Wooden Horse* (d. Jack Lee). With its emphasis on the mechanics of escape, this became a prototype for prison camp films, from *The Colditz Story* (d. Guy Hamilton, 1954) to *Escape to Victory* (d. John Huston, US, 1981). There is no place for women or working-class characters in *The Wooden Horse*. The story is set in a camp for RAF prisoners populated solely by the middle and upper classes. The result is that the film sometimes resembles a boarding school story, with the escape attempt dwindling into a series of jolly japes in the dorm. Landy rightly contrasts this with the populist orientation of war films made during the war.[27] Whatever cavils might be made, the film was a box-office success judging by anecdotal evidence.[28] Its progress cannot be charted in the sample cinemas given its late appearance in the period studied.

Class conventions in the films considered are generally implicit. One is that working-class commissioned officers are never portrayed, because this would disrupt the social hierarchy. As a consequence, war is presented as a middle-class affair, in which the working class play a supporting role. Yet the socially divided world of *In Which We Serve* (d. Noel Coward and David Lean, 1942) seems far away. Coward's failure to perceive social change is again apparent in his script for *This Happy Breed* (d. David Lean, 1944), which is set resolutely in the past. This failure of vision is chronicled by Andrew Higson, although he fails to indict Lean on the same charge.[29]

By the 1950s, attitudes were changing. National service was part of every young man's life and a decade of this enforced melding of the classes broke down the traditional equivalence of 'other ranks' with 'working class'. Film-makers were equivocal about national service. Although it could stiffen the moral fibre, as in *Carry on Sergeant* (d. Gerald Thomas, 1958), it was not without problems. In *Private's Progress* (d. John Boulting, 1956), corruption entered the system. More seriously, in *The Bofors Gun* (d. Jack Gold, 1968), a mindless emphasis on discipline destroyed men. The heroics of war were still on display in *The Dam Busters* (d. Michael Anderson, 1954), but social differences were not reactionary in the same way as those found in films scripted by Coward. The key distinction was gender. Women could star in films about the resistance, notably *Odette* (d. Herbert Wilcox, 1950) and *Carve Her Name with Pride* (d. Lewis Gilbert, 1958), but at heart war was men's business.

War films reveal society's attitude to war. More subtly, they expose the divergence between values and beliefs prevalent when the film is made and those thought to be held during the war. Assumptions about the latter are inevitably coloured by films made at the time. In this way, myths are not only sustained by films, but evolve incestuously from them; the stilted speech of the officers in *They Were Not Divided* being a case in point. A logical extension of this process is that national servicemen learned how soldiers should behave by watching war films.[30] With the passing years, the more difficult it becomes to disentangle myth from reality.

Notes

1 Ernest Betts, 'But No More War Films', *Daily Express* (15 February 1946). Contained in BFI Library, 'British films 1946' cuttings file.

2 Denis Gifford, *The British Film Catalogue 1896–1985* (Newton Abbot: David & Charles, 1986).

3 T. E. B. Clarke, *This Is Where I Came In* (London: Michael Joseph, 1974), pp. 157–8.

4 Christine Geraghty, *British Cinema in the Fifties: Gender, Genre and the 'New Look'* (London: Routledge, 2000), ch. 10.

5 Rosamund John, interviewed in Brian McFarlane, *Sixty Voices: Celebrities Recall the Golden Age of British Cinema* (London: BFI, 1992), p. 142.

6 Robert Murphy, *Realism and Tinsel: Cinema and Society in Britain 1939–49* (London: Routledge, 1992), p. 113.

7 Squadron Leader Ken Cater MBE (retd) (personal communication).

8 Andrew Buchanan, *Going to the Cinema* (London: Phoenix House, 2nd edn, 1951).

9 E. W. and M. M. Robson, *The World is My Cinema* (London: Sidneyan Society, 1947), pp. 115–16.

10 Raymond Durgnat, *A Mirror for England: British Movies from Austerity to Affluence* (London: Faber & Faber, 1970), p. 14; Charles Drazin, *The Finest Years: British Cinema of the 1940s* (London: Andre Deutsch, 1998), p. 194.

11 Sue Harper, 'The years of total war: propaganda and entertainment', in Christine Gledhill and Gillian Swanson (eds), *Nationalising Femininity: Culture, Sexuality and the British Cinema in the Second World War* (Manchester: Manchester University Press, 1996), p. 201.

12 Antonia Lant, *Blackout: Reinventing Women for Wartime British Cinema* (Princeton, NJ: Princeton University Press, 1991), pp. 53–7; Marcia Landy, *British Genres: Cinema and Society 1930–1960* (Princeton, NJ: Princeton University Press, 1991), p. 171.

13 *Showmen's Trade Review* (18 January 1947), p. 83; *Daily Mail* (12 April 1947). Latter item contained in BFI Library, *'Daily Mail'* cuttings file.

14 *The Cinema* (1 January 1947), p. 59.

15 Julian Poole, 'British cinema attendance in wartime: audience preference at the Majestic, Macclesfield 1939–1946', *Historical Journal of Film, Radio and Television*, 7:1 (1987), Table 7, 26.

16 Sidney Bernstein, *The Bernstein Film Questionnaire 1946–7* (London: [Granada Theatres], 1947), p. 17.

17 *Observer* (10 June 1945), cited in Murphy, *Realism and Tinsel*, p. 71.

18 Drazin, *The Finest Years*, p. 186.

19 David Thomson, *A Biographical Dictionary of Film* (London: Andre Deutsch, rev. edn, 1994), p. 27.

20 Anthony Asquith, 'Realler than the real thing', *Contemporary Cinema*, 2:1 (1948), 10.

21 A point which recurs in many accounts is how fathers were seen as intruders into an established mother–child relationship. Barry Turner and Tony Rennell, *When Daddy Came Home: How Family Life Changed Forever in 1945* (London: Hutchinson, 1995).

22 Pat Kirkham and Janet Thumim, 'Men at work: Dearden and gender', in Alan Burton, Tim O'Sullivan and Paul Wells (eds), *Liberal Directions: Basil Dearden and Postwar British Film Culture* (Trowbridge: Flicks Books, 1997), p. 97.

23 *The Cinema* (5 March 1947), p. 57; Bernstein, *The Bernstein Film Questionnaire 1946–7*, p. 17.

24 Alan Burton, 'Love in a cold climate: critics, film makers and the British cinema of quality – the case of *The Captive Heart*', in Burton *et al.* (eds), *Liberal Directions*, p. 119.

25 *Picturegoer* (1 July 1950), p. 7; *Daily Mail* (25 May 1950). Latter item contained in BFI Library, *'Daily Mail'* cuttings file.

26 Edgar Anstey, Ernest Lindgren, Roger Manvell and Paul Rotha, *Shots in the Dark: A Collection of Reviewers' Opinions of Some Leading Films* (London: Allan Wingate, 1951), pp. 166–70.

27 Landy, *British Genres*, p. 174.

28 Durgnat, *A Mirror for England*, p. 125; Jack Lee, interviewed in Brian McFarlane, *Sixty Voices*, p. 158.

29 Andrew Higson, *Waving the Flag* (Oxford: Oxford University Press, Clarendon Press, 1995), pp. 246–58.

30 Macdonald Hastings, *Night Waves*, BBC Radio 3 (14 April 2000). Hastings was himself called up for national service.

4   People don't lock their doors: the working-class community

Following the fortunes of a community necessitates keeping several storylines before an audience. A contrast of personalities has to be presented and plots have to be sustained without any loss of tension. In this respect, the subject presents film-makers with structural problems akin to those encountered by novelists, playwrights, or the writers of soap opera.

Class antagonism by the community can move the action forward as well as demonstrating unity or disunity within the group. With the approach of war in the late 1930s, changes in censorship allowed industrial disputes to be portrayed on British screens for the first time.[1] The consequence was a string of films containing a pivotal clash between employers and employees, *The Stars Look Down* (d. Carol Reed, 1939) being an early example. *Master of Bankdam* (d. Walter Forde, 1947) is typical of the vogue at its height, with the action set safely in the past as though to minimise its relevance to current events. *Adalen 31* (d. Bo Widerberg, Sweden, 1969) illustrates that the theme is not a purely British phenomenon and that confrontation can promote an ideological agenda as well as serving as a dramatic device. This was a latecomer to the genre. Films about industrial relations have fallen from favour, with even left-wing film-makers like Ken Loach skirting expensive set-piece confrontations.

A distinction should be made between community and communality. Though there may be communality in the sense of sharing a class position, this need not imply the common interests, attitudes or values which are the hallmarks of a community. Even within a community, straying from convention may lead to conflict. Family loyalties, gender, age, education, morality and economic circumstances all have the potential to create discord.

There has to be some means of delimiting the community for the audience. In the countryside, the village provides an obvious social unit, while in towns, the street or neighbourhood is comparable. Writ small, the shared house performs the same function. There are other possibilities, less topographically determined, such as the community centred on the workplace. Leisure interests provide another locus; both the club and the holiday camp offering contexts which were exploited in British films of the 1940s.

The community writ large

Do films provide any evidence that the working-class community evoked by Richard Hoggart or Don Haworth survived the Second World War? [2] One well-loved portrayal of the community on celluloid, *Passport to Pimlico* (d. Henry Cornelius, 1949), must be set aside. This Pimlico is an urban village largely inhabited by lower-middle-class shopkeepers who are on nodding terms with the bank manager. No working-class person would venture into a bank – that bastion of power, wealth and status. As Patrick Hamilton, that chronicler of forgotten people, wrote of one of his characters: 'Esther's mother was ... a victim of this eccentricity – an eccentricity to be found more amongst the very poor than any other class. Mrs Downs, sane as she was, did not fully trust even Post Offices or Banks.' [3] Better to keep your few shillings in the teapot on the dresser than entrust them to a grand institution meant for your betters.

The working-class neighbourhood is shown to better effect in *It Always Rains on Sunday* (d. Robert Hamer, 1947). The setting is the East End of London. Aside from the sparing use of flashbacks, events take place during one Sunday, which enhances the sense of real events unfolding on screen. There are three interrelated plot strands. In the first, Tommy Swann (John McCallum) has escaped from prison and seeks help from his former fiancee, Rose Sandigate (Googie Withers). Unknown to her husband, George, and her stepdaughters, Vi and Doris, she hides Tommy in their home. He flees when a journalist visits the house, but is recaptured by the police after a chase across a marshalling yard. In the second strand, three local thieves try to dispose of a gross of stolen roller skates. Their leader, Whitey Williams (Jimmy Hanley), attacks the fence, the ostensibly religious Caleb Neesley (John Salew), for offering less money than they anticipated. In turn, Whitey is robbed by Tommy Swann before being arrested himself. The third strand comprises the involvement of Rose's stepdaughters with the Hyams brothers, the philandering bandleader, Morry (Sydney Tafler), and the local fixer, Lou (John Slater).

The pervasive power of law and order is the film's leitmotiv. The first person to be seen is a policeman, donning his cape against the rain. The detective, Sergeant Fothergill (Jack Warner), continually prowls the streets. Wrongdoers never go free. If they escape the law, they receive retribution in other ways. Morry's wife leaves him and his car is stolen. The fence, Caleb Neesley, dies as a result of Whitey's attack. Rose tries to gas herself when she is discovered helping Tommy. The exception to the rule of inevitable retribution is the upwardly-aspiring Lou, who talks his way out of every situation.

The other recurring theme is betrayal. Again with the exception of Lou, everybody is betrayed: George Sandigate by his wife's deceit, his daughters by their encounters with the Hyams brothers, Morry Hyams' wife by Morry and the three petty crooks by their fence. Rose suffers most: Tommy Swann does not recognise the engagement ring which he gave her and he has no compunction about hitting her when she impedes his escape. Lovable cockneys are in short supply. This is a world where people live by their wits rather than the law, and where the strong prosper at the expense of the weak.[4] The children learn this quickly: Alfie, the youngest of the Sandigate children, has no qualms about indulging in blackmail when he discovers Vi's affair with Morry Hyams.

Lou Hyams has a hand in every lucrative activity in the community, His clothing marks him as having plenty of money, though the police show no interest in how he obtains it. This was a prominent role for John Slater, who graduated into films from his work with Unity Theatre.[5] The panache of his performance cannot conceal that the complexities of the character were lost in the compression of the novel for the screen.[6] The scene in which Lou decries the squalor of the East End and urges his father and sister to move away serves no dramatic purpose when shorn of its context: his sister's aspirations to be a pianist and Lou's conflict with her socialist friend, Bessie Weinbaum, who loves the vivacity of the area.[7] For other characters, escape is not so easy. The stereotyped routes presented for boys are boxing, betting or thieving, while a girl can dream of finding a man or being discovered (Vi hopes that singing will open doors for her). And just as Tommy Swann's hopes of escape are thwarted, so these routes lead to dead ends.

The amusement arcade is Lou's legitimate business, though legitimacy is relative: Doris suspects that the machines are rigged. The amusement arcade is a recurring image in films of the 1940s, notably in Sidney Gilliat's *Waterloo Road* of 1945, to be considered in the next chapter. In common with the fairground, the arcade has a brashness which taints anybody coming into contact with it. Its associations with gambling mean that if not overtly criminal, it is never entirely respectable. This nether world is a natural haunt of that epitome of brashness, the spiv, whose contacts extend into the underworld, but who exists to make good the shortages experienced by respectable society.

According to Googie Withers, Hamer said of the film, 'I want to do this out in the streets where it all happens.'[8] Despite being a studio set, the street market, noisy with the patter of the costermongers, does convey the feel of East End life. A Yiddish voice is a reminder of the area's large Jewish population – and why a street market is held on a Sunday. Location shots of empty, rain-swept streets capture the desolation of Sunday evening. This is a time for being home, putting family bonds to the test. The only public places open are the church and the pub; in this community, the pub is more enticing. It is the pivot of Mr Sandigate's social life: a darts match prevents him from staying home with Rose on that fateful Sunday evening. Rose often goes with him. It was while working as a barmaid that she first met Tommy. The pub is where the reporter learns of the relationship between Rose and Tommy. The three petty crooks meet there to hatch plots. It is the easiest place to find people, as Sergeant Fothergill well knows.

As a legacy of the war, lamp posts are still painted white and the Sandigates keep leftover blackout material in the Anderson shelter. One bombsite is glimpsed. Yet much is unchanged from the 1930s. The dosshouse which the sergeant visits in his search for Tommy Swann is no improvement over the one depicted in *Dosshouse* (d. John Baxter, 1933) – and less welcoming with the harridan Mrs Spry (Hermione Baddeley) in charge. It is a reminder that postwar housing provision was predicated on the needs of the family. Single people such as the men depicted here still slipped through the net.

The dialogue might be called anglicised cockney. While being intelligible to most British audiences, it never draws attention to itself as glaringly wrong, providing cockneys suspend disbelief. Neither the Australian John McCallum nor the children let the side down, even if visual signifiers establish the setting more securely. The location seen most often is Coronet Grove, where the Sandigates live. Like the set of *Coronation Street* (Granada TV, 1960–current), it is closed by a railway viaduct. The two-storeyed terrace dating from the nineteenth century is characteristic of working-class London, with a continuous parapet concealing the

1   The aftermath: the damage caused by Morry's stolen car. Street scene from *It Always Rains on Sunday* (1947). The terraced housing is characteristic of London. The street lamp is still painted white from the blackout

roof line. The Sandigates' house has two rooms up and down. The parlour doubles as a bedroom for Alfie and is little seen. Most of the action takes place in the kitchen-cum-living room. The clothes airing on a clotheshorse in front of the range are a reminder of the housewife's ever-present dilemma of what to do with washing which is not completely dry. The unheated bedrooms are hardly visited during the day, so Rose can safely let Tommy sleep in her bed. The two teenage girls share a double bed in the back bedroom. Privacy is a luxury for the whole family, There can be no escaping to the bathroom. As the film reveals, savouring a soak involves the laborious task of boiling enough kettles of water to fill the tin bath placed strategically in front of the kitchen range (to say nothing of emptying the dirty water afterwards). Additionally, there is the complicated logistical exercise of ensuring that other members of the family are kept out of the way.

The film received enthusiastic coverage from the trade press.[9] It also found favour among highbrow critics, with Roger Manvell praising its sense of 'real streets, real people, real shops with stuff to sell, and real railway yards in which the final chase takes place'.[10]

2 Nobody uses the bedroom during the day: Rose (Googie Withers) hides Tommy (John McCallum) in *It Always Rains on Sunday* (1947). The washstand was common in a house with no bathroom

Audiences concurred: among the Ealing features for which box-office data is available, *It Always Rains on Sunday* generated the greatest revenue (Appendix, Table 2). The film did well in southeast Essex, probably because of the large number of former East End residents who lived there (Appendix, Table 7). This was their world brought to the screen. Success was patchy, however. The film only managed three three-day bookings in working-class Leeds by 1950 (Appendix, Table 6). In protesting against the quota, the manager of the New Tivoli in Edinburgh claimed that along with *Fame is the Spur* (d. Roy Boulting, 1947), *It Always Rains on Sunday* only yielded a profit of 16s 10d.[11] To confound the notion of a north-south divide in responses, the film came in the first quartile of attendances at the Gaumont, Sheffield (Appendix, Table 5).

'If togetherness isn't a dream, it's a lie ... yet that we must accept ... The next stage is to try and show some sort of inter-dependence, of *virtual* togetherness, in the structures of civilian life [original ellipses and italics].'[12] By stressing the notion of virtual togetherness, Raymond Durgnat implies the weakness of the concept of community. The social structures preclude real togetherness. The Sandigates, Tommy Swann and the petty thieves all belong to the working class – the class without power. The Hyams brothers and the fence Caleb Neesley have achieved some power – and assert it. There can be no bridging the gap between the two groups. The final reconciliation of George and Rose is the film's only hint of forgiveness or redemption.

Charles Drazin is less opaque than Durgnat, preferring to see the array of characters who lie, cheat, exploit, manipulate and murder to achieve their aims as a measure of Hamer's disillusionment, with Michael Balcon's influence tempering the film's darker elements.[13] The difference between the two explanations is one of levels. Drazin favours individual psychology, stressing Hamer's tortured vision of the world; Durgnat opts for a sociological approach, albeit equally coloured by despair.

The significance of the reconciliation between George and Rose is stressed in a 1949 article by Gavin Lambert. He concedes that Rose finds her emotional senses starved as she becomes acutely aware of the pleasures which she had missed. But the crucial point for Lambert is that Rose's poverty and loneliness are respectable, making her better able to bear the tragedy of that fateful Sunday. 'She at least has a husband to support her, unlike the pathetic waifs in French films.'[14] This contrasts with Janet Thumim's view from the 1990s that the film demonstrates 'women cannot be permitted to act autonomously but must be secured within the heterosexual couple, the prelude to the nuclear family, for their own protection [original underlining].'[15] While Lambert's gender bias is of its time, Thumim ignores the reality of women's opportunities in the late 1940s. Marriage gives the ex-barmaid respectability and a modicum of financial security. These factors are liberating rather than restricting. This comes across more strongly in the novel, where the superiority of the inhabitants of Coronet Grove is stressed.[16] If the alternatives are having a husband in jail or remaining as a barmaid and living in a rented room, would a working-class audience of the 1940s have considered that Rose made such a bad choice? The crucial question is why she tries to kill herself. It seems fanciful to assume that life has no meaning now her illusions about Tommy Swann have been shattered. A more convincing explanation is that she has transgressed the law, respectability and her marriage vows. She has nowhere to go and there is no one to whom she can turn.

For Charles Barr, 'The enduring strength of the film is the way it exploits its story to compress the conflict of Rose's life and soul into concrete dramatic images.'[17] The inner conflict is certainly externalised, but rather than being concrete, the result is as evanescent as the flickering images on the screen. Almost every scene involves somebody glimpsed through a window or in a mirror, which creates an unsettling effect some way from the canons of realism.[18] What cannot be doubted is that the film takes the audience far from the traditional East End evoked by Michael Young and Peter Willmott, where the bonds of family and neighbourhood are stressed.[19]

The community writ small

The shared house provides a dramatic device for bringing together disparate individuals, while emphasising that communality evolves by force of circumstance rather than voluntary association. The house is usually presided over by a landlady. Often a widow, she maintains her independence in a male-dominated world by relying on rent from her tenants. She often assumes the role of upholder of morality, stressing the respectability of her establishment. Two such figures appear fleetingly in It Always Rains on Sunday. Mrs Spry, who runs the dosshouse, has already been encountered. The other (played by Grace Arnold) rents a room to Doris's suitor, Ted Edwards (Nigel Stock). She turns the couple out into the rain rather than letting Doris visit Ted's room. She is seen dimming the gas light in the hall after they have gone. After all, gas costs money.

The landlady assumes a prominent role in London Belongs to Me (d. Sidney Gilliat, 1948), which was coproduced by Gilliat and Frank Launder. The film, like the novel on which it is based, opens just before the Second World War.[20] Behind the credits, aerial shots along the Thames establish the location. A street nameplate indicates that Dulcimer Street is in southeast London (the location is later revealed as Kennington). As the tall town houses are first seen, the voice-over makes clear that 'they've come down in the world a bit.' This is emphasised by the gasometers which dominate the skyline. The lodgers who inhabit this nether world between lower middle class and respectable working class are introduced. The elderly and impoverished Connie (Ivy St Helier) likes to think of herself as a resting actress. The widowed Mrs Boon (Gladys Henson) dotes on her rather simple son, Percy (Richard Attenborough). The respectable Josser family are coming to terms with the retirement of Mr Josser (Wylie Watson). Later, the phony spiritualist, Henry Squales (Alastair Sim), joins the household, ingratiating himself with the widowed landlady, Mrs Vizzard (Joyce Carey), who is ever hopeful of contacting her husband in the spirit world. As Andrew Davies notes, fortune-telling and spiritualism were integral to working-class women's networks.[21] They feature in *Love on the Dole* (d. John Baxter, 1941), though Sir Arthur Conan Doyle's interest in spiritualism serves as a reminder that this was not an exclusively working-class preoccupation.

Percy works as a garage hand, but he finds an extra source of income in respraying stolen cars. A former girlfriend, Myrna, is unaware that the car is stolen when she persuades him to drive her home. She panics when he fails to stop for the police. As she struggles to open the door of the moving car, Percy hits her. She falls into the road and is killed. Evidence found at the lodgings incriminates Percy, who is charged with murder and found guilty. The other residents campaign to save him from hanging. The news that his sentence has been commuted comes as they lead a march on Whitehall.

Several of the leading characters are trying – and failing – to cling to the remnants of their middle-class lives.[22] This is most obvious in the case of Henry Squales with his pedantic speech: 'I am never aware of what passes in a trance state. After all, it is not I who speak.' He knows what he has been reduced to. As he looks in the mirror before tricking Mrs Vizzard into letting him stay, he asks rhetorically, 'Henry Squales, have you sunk so low as to do this thing? There can only be one answer – yes, you have.'

The genteel Mrs Vizzard knows the poor condition of her house. When Mr Squales takes the basement room, she cannot conceal her surprise. As the shot of her poring over a ledger makes clear, she is reliant on the rent from her tenants, though she insists that her late husband left her comfortably provided for. She reveals to Mr Squales that she came to the house as a bride. It can hardly have changed since her husband died in 1922, except to become shabbier and more out of date.

Fred Josser works in an office, which puts him a cut above people like Percy Boon, who earn their living from manual employment. Yet when Fred retires after a lifetime with the same company, he still occupies a lowly position. His middle-class status is tenuous, despite the prompting of his ambitious wife (Fay Compton). His reward for years of saving is enough money to buy a country cottage. His wife is less keen. His daughter, Doris (Susan Shaw), wants to stay in London, though she does not contemplate leaving the parental home.

For all their aspirations, the characters are condemned to share the same rundown house. This gives a sense of eavesdropping on a working-class world, where fellow lodgers cadge a coin for the gas meter, or steal milk from the hall. Visual cues reinforce their lack of status. It is a world of garages in the arches of railway viaducts, and dowdy, gas-lit rooms with curtains pulled across the doors to keep out draughts. The leisure activities glimpsed in the film are working-class amusements: the cinema and the fun fair. Percy steals a car from a cinema car park lit by flashing neon signs as the muffled soundtrack of a film filters from the auditorium. It is in a small fun fair opposite the garage that he first encounters the car thief, Jack Rufus (Maurice Denham), and where Myrna works as a cashier. She is brasher than Doris Josser, though Eleanor Summerfield's portrayal contrives to give her vulnerability.

The characters' attempts to climb the social ladder always fail. Connie's white lie in calling herself a hostess is exposed when Percy and Doris visit the club where she works, to discover that she is a cloakroom attendant. Percy's attempt to impress Doris comes to nothing when the club proves to be crowded and uncongenial – and is raided by the police. His scheme to make money by stealing a car results in a murder charge. Mr Josser's dream of a country cottage evaporates when he uses his savings to hire a barrister for Percy's defence. Mr Squales' hopes of marrying Mrs Vizzard are dashed when his fraudulent activities as a medium are exposed. This is a house of losers.

Though Susan Shaw as Doris and Stephen Murray as her Uncle Henry might have strayed from a middle-class drama, working-class idioms such as Fred Josser addressing his wife as 'mother' give the dialogue an authentic ring. The social stratum which the characters inhabit is made clear by the women's emphasis on respectability. Mrs Josser does not like her daughter associating with a garage hand like Percy. When Doris goes out with the detective sergeant, Bill Todds (Andrew Crawford), first encountered when the police raid the club, Mrs Josser is still uneasy, remarking to her husband that 'It doesn't seem quite respectable.' Mrs Vizzard's response to Percy's arrest is, 'I'll never live it down. I've always done my best to keep this house respectable.' Respectability is worth clinging to when there are no other vestiges of status.

Deference is another characteristic apparent in both the dialogue and the acting. In Percy's case, this is in part the deference to age – an attitude which persisted into the 1980s, when career advancement no longer depended on length of service – but Fred Josser displays the deference of class. His bearing at his retirement presentation verges on the obsequious. The same attitude is apparent when he visits Percy's solicitor. Though Fred is paying for Percy's defence, he still addresses the solicitor as 'sir'. The anomalous position of the youthful Bill Todds presents Fred with a dilemma which shows in his forced conversation. How should he respond to a man who is young, but who represents authority and who might become one of the family?

3   Spit and polish: Percy Boon (Richard Attenborough) at work in *London Belongs to Me* (1948). A working-class townscape reconstructed in the studio by Roy Oxley from south London locations

What welds these disparate individuals into a community is the campaign to have Percy's death sentence commuted. This is spearheaded by Doris's Uncle Henry, who is forever seeking a cause to champion. To his chagrin, his place as leader is usurped by a priest with similar ambitions. The march on Whitehall begins in a mood of optimism, which is dissipated as the downpour begins and a wheel comes off the pram bearing the petition. When news of the reprieve reaches the supporters, they drift away. Even the priest loses interest. In the final scene, which foreshadows the ending of *Genevieve* (d. Henry Cornelius, 1953), Uncle Henry pushes the broken pram across Westminster Bridge, accompanied by Percy's fellow lodgers and Bill Todds. As in *Passport to Pimlico*, the community spirit engendered by one defining event cannot survive once that event loses its significance. Instead there is a resort to smaller, familial groupings symbolised by Doris's acceptance of Bill as a suitor.

The anonymous reviewer in *Picture Show* noted the omission of the ending of the novel, in which Fred Josser goes back to his office which is short-staffed because of the war.[23] Opting not to follow

4 Retrieving the evidence: Percy Boon (Richard Attenborough) at home in *London Belongs to Me* (1948). The fireplace with fender, rag rug and fire screen is unchanged from Victorian days

the stories of the characters through the war gives the film a tighter dramatic structure, the costs being the imposition of a sentimental ending and the loss is the Dickensian aspiration of a novel which teems with characters and subplots held together by the ironic tones of the narrator.

The world of Dulcimer Street, like that of Coronet Grove in *It Always Rains on Sunday*, was known to many working-class people in southeast Essex. This may account for the success of *London Belongs to Me* in the area (Appendix, Table 7). In Leeds, with its large stock of artisan dwellings, the grand houses of Dulcimer Street which had 'come down in the world a bit' were less familiar to cinemagoers and none too appealing. Here, the film was another poor performer (Appendix, Table 6). This cannot be attributed to high booking charges, given that there was ample time for rentals to fall as the film was relegated to second and third-run cinemas.

It is tempting to interpret *London Belongs to Me* as a condition-of-England film for the austerity years, with the community spirit engendered by the war being dissipated and the middle class sinking into genteel poverty. But the novel was first published in 1945 – too early for disillusionment to set in. Nor did critics of the time see the film from that perspective. The general critical response was muted, with Forsyth Hardy's verdict being typical: 'The vivid figures of the novel seem flat and lifeless ... The Dulcimer Street of this film is a long way from the Waterloo Road which directors Frank Launder and Sidney Gilliat once made so real and memorable.'[24] Subsequent commentators have scarcely been more enthusiastic – if they refer to the film at all. Durgnat gives it a passing mention, while Robert Murphy dismisses it as sentimental.[25] With hindsight, both Launder and Gilliat conceded that the book contains too much material for the film.[26] In spite of these negative responses, *London Belongs to Me* remains a compulsive study of tragedy striking the claustrophobic world of the shared house and drawing its inhabitants together. If Alistair Sim's portrayal of Mr Squales threatens to dominate the screen, at least it lightens the prevailing mood of despair.

The other lodging house saga is *The Gorbals Story* (d. David Mac-Kane, 1950). Based on a play by Robert McLeish, this was the only work of the left-wing Glasgow Unity Theatre to reach the West End stage or the commercial cinema.[27]

Artist Johnnie Martin (Russell Hunter) recalls the other residents of a Glasgow lodging house in his days as a newspaper boy. The house is presided over by another formidable landlady, the widowed Mrs Gilmour, though she is away for much of the film. Peggie and Hector (Betty Henderson and Roddy McMillan) provide the sensible, respectable core around which the life of the house revolves. In Mrs Gilmour's absence, Peggie takes the opportunity to disobey her by giving shelter to a destitute couple. Another young couple, the Potters, are expecting a baby. Willie Mutrie (Howard Connell) is forever avoiding work and dreaming of the pools win which will solve his problems. His long-suffering wife, Jean (Marjorie Thomson), has a sharp tongue, but indulges Willie by giving him money for his betting. Ahmed, the youthful peddler, attempts to maintain his cultural identity by his insistence on eating his own food, in spite of the good-natured gibes of the others.

The British working class in postwar film

He courts Magdalene, while Johnnie hopes to marry Nora Reilly (Isabel Campbell), who lives with her parents.

There are few happy endings. The Potters delay too long in calling a doctor, with the consequence that both mother and baby die. Willie's pools selection comes up, but he confesses that he spent the stake money on a fish supper for Jean instead of posting the coupon. In spite of vowing never to drink again, he goes to the pub with Hector. Both men get drunk, hardly aware that they cause the fight which erupts around them. When Johnnie proposes to Nora, her violent father objects, forcing the couple to renounce each other. Johnnie seeks oblivion, first in a dance hall and then in drink. He returns to the tenement for his cutthroat razor, determined to seek revenge. As a storm breaks, Peggie talks him out of his chosen course.

Tennessee Williams' *The Glass Menagerie* received its first London production two years earlier in 1948. The author described it as a memory play.[28] The film of *The Gorbals Story* is similar in structure and mood, with the artist providing a commentary on events, the heightened, poetic dialogue, the emotionally charged atmosphere as the storm gathers and the prevailing sense of people imprisoned within an enclosed world. Though Johnnie becomes successful in material terms, *The Gorbals Story* does not show how he achieves his ambition to become an artist. The mature Johnnie is little more than a device for introducing the stories of the other characters.

Although no date is specified, the clothes and the emphasis on unemployment place the action in the interwar years. The film portrays people coping with poverty, though they are not on the lowest rung of the social ladder, as Peggie acknowledges when she wraps food in newspaper and throws it to the children outside the window, with instructions to 'Blow your nose on the paper.' Vermin are a constant concern. Peggie is worried that the fish and chip wrappers left in the toilet will attract rats. Hector is philosophical at the prospect: 'If they sleep on your feet and don't nibble your toes, they keep you warm.' It is a communal world, where food is shared (apart from Ahmed's exotic dishes) and men wash and shave at the kitchen sink.

The yearning for something different is voiced by Nora, as she tells Jean what being with Johnnie means to her:

It's nice being with someone you understand and who understands you. It makes you feel quiet inside – quiet, as if you had a home of your own, really your own, where if you wanted to go away and shut the door, you could keep out the people, even those you love. Yet they would understand. It would be so peaceful.

In this impoverished place, even such a modest aspiration must remain a dream.

Though Hector and Willie go to the pub together, their reasons differ. For Willie, gambling and drinking are the only routes of escape. Hector's demeanour and his clothing – he visits the pub in a three-piece suit and a bowler – signal his respectability. For him, drinking is part of the pattern of daily life rather than an escape. For Johnnie, when the dance hall fails to offer consolation after his relationship with Nora has been thwarted by her father, the pub is a last resort: 'I thought to myself, this is what I am part of. This is what I was born to. Why should I struggle? Why struggle?'

The strength of family relationships is unquestioned. The landlady is only prevented from watching over her lodgers because she is called away to look after her ailing sister. Jean's indulgence towards Willie is underpinned by the couple's devotion to each other. This becomes explicit when he tells of his dream of taking her on holiday and buying her dresses. As she comforts him, she tells him, 'Remember, I took you for better or for worse and whatever you are or whatever you've done, you're my man and I love you. And you love me still, don't you?' And for all his feckless behaviour, Willie is faithful. Similarly, Peter Reilly's possessiveness towards his daughter, Nora, may be misplaced, but it reveals a fierce loyalty. Even Ahmed is accepted when he proposes to Magdalene. Only Johnnie, the creative artist, is destined to remain an outsider. He is the only character seen to travel far from his roots.

The Gorbals of the interwar years symbolised poverty. Major change only came with redevelopment in the 1960s. Many elements of traditional working-class life feature in the film, including drunkenness, gambling and poor housing. 'Escape' and 'struggle' occur frequently in Johnnie's narrative. The problem is universalised: 'How long will they endure environments like that? How long will they remain painted in drab and dirty colours, sullying the canvas of our social conscience?' Yet the closeness is portrayed affectionately. Escape from that world implies loss.

Because the film was not taken up by the circuits, its release in January 1950 went largely unnoticed. By the end of the year it had been little shown in southeast Essex; it managed a three-day booking in Leeds (Appendix, Table 6). This lack of commercial success is unsurprising. The film's stage origins show rather too obviously, while the Glaswegian speech rhythms probably deterred English audiences. Nor was there much enthusiasm for reexamining the 1930s world of poverty epitomised by *Love on the Dole*. *The Gorbals Story* must be deemed a commercial failure, but an honourable failure. It has sunk so far into obscurity that

Margaret Dickinson's work exploring the byways of postwar British film culture fails to mention it.[29] As a testament to the power of socialist theatre in Britain, *The Gorbals Story* deserves better.

The community of work

Though work can define a community, it can be difficult to portray dramatically: whatever the virtues of Robert Tressell's novel *The Ragged-Trousered Philanthropist* (1914), house-painting is not the stuff of a box-office hit. The consequence is that work rarely assumes a central place in feature films, leading to a split between work and personal life.[30] The obvious exceptions are occupations with visual or dramatic interest such as mining or nursing. One of the few attempts to find drama in more humdrum activities is *Chance of a Lifetime* (d. Bernard Miles, 1950).

Factory owner J. Courtney Dickinson (Basil Radford) faces a rebellious work force. When he challenges them to run the business, they take him at his word. George Stevens (Bernard Miles) and Ted Morris (Julien Mitchell) assume control of the administration, while Adam Watson (Kenneth More) manages the workshop. The team face hostility from suppliers and the bank manager, but they ensure that the business survives by mortgaging their homes. When an order for a new design of plough falls through, Dickinson surprises his business colleagues by helping to find alternative markets for the product. George and Ted are relieved to hand back the management to him, but Dickinson cedes control to Adam.

As a snapshot of British industrial practices, *Chance of a Lifetime* makes Correlli Barnett seem restrained in his criticisms.[31] This is the family firm at its lowest ebb. The factory is outdated and ill kept, while Dickinson is autocratic and out of touch with his workforce. Both design and selling appear to be his sole prerogative, so it comes as no surprise that he works long hours. As he tells the men, 'It's seven days a week, working twelve, fourteen hours a day.'

The film presents rather than challenges the Marxist distinction between capital and labour. Interest often resides in the characters who inhabit the divide. One is the works manager, Bland (John Harvey). In spite of dressing like the last of the spivs, he deserves sympathy. His position allies him with management, but both sides make him the butt of their anger. Bland is the only person to lose his job.

The second transitional character is Palmer (Russell Waters), the old bookkeeper. When George and Ted take over the office, their first task is to discover whether Palmer is on their side. He is equivocal. To confound their expectation that white-collar workers are well paid, they discover that he earns eight pounds a week – roughly the earnings of a semiskilled manual worker. Had they seen his home, where he lives alone except for his dog, they might have been less surprised. It is an impoverished place reached from an alley, the door opening directly into the living room. A kettle boils on the range. Nothing can have changed since before the war. The promise of an increase in salary prompts Palmer to side with his fellow workers.

The third transitional character and the most developed is Dickinson's secretary, Miss Cooper (Josephine Wilson). She is on social terms with her employer to the extent of visiting his home. While he is in charge, she acts as an intermediary, smoothing over problems with the workforce. A woman's touch achieves what men cannot do. At first, divided loyalties make her hesitant about working for men from the shop floor, but their consideration wins her over. While continuing in her post, she keeps Dickinson abreast of what is happening.

Although no women volunteer to run the business – how this might have transformed the film – at least some of women's wartime roles in industry have been retained. Women work on the shop floor; a woman drives the tractor for the demonstration of the new plough. During an argument in the canteen, it is Hattie Jacques who injects some much-needed vivacity into the film when a coin is tossed inside her dress.

For Durgnat, the film makes working-class spectators feel doubly incompetent by simplifying the mutual distrust between workers and management and ignoring workers' organising skills in trade union branches and friendly societies.[32] The scriptwriters never resolve the structural difficulty of sustaining dramatic tension once the workers take control and the opportunity for confrontation between management and workers is removed. There is one potential point of conflict when reorganisation of the workshop causes a temporary loss of earnings and talk of a strike. The union officials are uncertain where their loyalties lie. Audiences must have sympathised: the film-makers' approach gives little incentive to root for either side.

The story of the film's exhibition makes up for any drama lacking on screen: its rejection by the circuits, its championing by the backer, Filippe del Guidice, and its imposition on the Odeon circuit by the Board of Trade.[33] Critics gave the film a favourable response. *The Times* film correspondent praised its integrity and flawless acting, Milton Schulman found it amusing, exciting and moving, while Richard Winnington singled out the photography and the acting.[34] The Rank card was less enthusiastic, calling the film an 'Unspectacular production, but one of general interest'. A flavour of what one audience thought comes from a Mass-Observation survey made in London. Of a hundred respondents, half considered the film 'outstandingly good', while the other half saw it because they had nothing else to do or because they visited the same cinema regularly.[35] The response of audiences generally was less equivocal: they stayed away. The film reached second-run cinemas by the end of 1950, but only accrued a modest number of screenings in Leeds and southeast Essex (Appendix, Tables 6 and 7). As del Guidice admitted to Miles: 'It is a bitter pill to swallow but we must swallow it. The film has done badly, notwithstanding the genuine efforts of the Odeon people to boost it in every possible way.'[36] This differs from his earlier judgement on Rank's marketing of the film: 'There is no doubt they will kill it.'[37] Half a century later, the film comes across as worthy rather than engrossing – hardly the fare to entice people to the local Odeon on a wet Saturday night in 1950.

Also released in 1950 was *The Blue Lamp* (d. Basil Dearden), scripted by T. E. B. Clarke from an idea by Ted Willis and Jan Read. In Paddington Green, new recruit PC Andy Mitchell (Jimmy Hanley) is shown the ropes by old hand PC George Dixon (Jack Warner). A jeweller's shop is robbed by two working-class youths, Tom Riley (Dirk Bogarde) and Spud (Patric Doonan), who graduate to robbing a cinema. When Dixon intervenes, Riley shoots him. Riley's girlfriend, runaway Diana Lewis (Peggy Evans), becomes nervous. In an act of bravado, Riley goes to a police station to clear himself, but only succeeds in implicating himself in the robbery at the jeweller's shop. The police follow him home, intervening when he tries to strangle Diana. He escapes, but is captured in a crowded greyhound stadium.

Two communities are represented in the film. Both are comprised largely of working-class people. The first is the police force, whose inner workings had already been introduced to audiences in *Night Beat* (d. Harold Huth, 1948). The camaraderie of the canteen extends beyond the confines of work. Choir practice and darts occupy spare moments between patrols, while the Dixons' home is open house, with officers dropping in for meals. The second community is that of the neighbourhood, embracing villains as well as law-abiding citizens. When George is in hospital after the shooting, a costermonger asks after him, while making clear that such concern in no way reflects any liking for the police as an institution. In the stadium, a bookmaker who has an uneasy

5 At home with the Dixons: George and Emily Dixon (Jack Warner and Gladys Henson) welcome Andy Mitchell (Jimmy Hanley) in *The Blue Lamp* (1950)

relationship with the law mobilises his men to look for Riley. Tic-tac men signal the progress of the chase. Riley has no chance against the will of the community.

The stable nuclear family is notable by its absence. If Tom Riley and Spud have families, they are by definition ineffective, for parental control has not been exercised. Diana Lewis comes from a large family, but all it offers her are violence, poverty and overcrowding. The Dixons lost their son, presumably in the war. They take Andy Mitchell as a lodger, but he becomes a surrogate son to the extent of calling Mrs Dixon (Gladys Henson) 'ma'. This blurs the distinction between family and community. The communality of the police force becomes the film's substitute for the family. Whether it exemplifies a true community is an open question.

Dearden's sureness of touch in the scenes involving children deserves acknowledgment. Carol Reed has received more credit in this respect.[38] Women fare less well in *The Blue Lamp*, being marginalised and stereotyped. Only Diana and Mrs Dixon have significant roles in the story and they have little to do except respond to situations, Diana by crying and Mrs Dixon by being stoical. Like cinematic representations of waging war, policing is men's

6 PC Andy Mitchell (Jimmy Hanley) interviews Mrs Lewis (Betty Ann Davies) after she is beaten up by her husband in *The Blue Lamp* (1950). A lower-working-class tenement flat

business. Feelings can only be hinted at by a change of tone or a stiffening of the upper lip.

Authority is stamped on *The Blue Lamp* even more firmly than on the earlier Ealing film, *It Always Rains on Sunday*. Police provide both the opening and closing images. Just as quasi-military discipline is imposed on the police by senior officers who have themselves risen through the ranks, the police function as NCOs, imposing a benign discipline on the wider working-class community. The uniformed police are drawn from that community as the Dixons' respectable working-class home and the off-duty banter about gardening make clear, though the extent to which the officers have cut themselves off from their social origins by their choice of career is not explored. They address the middle class as 'sir' or 'ma'am'. Lower-class men are more likely to be called by their forenames, though the young Andy Mitchell addresses Mrs Lewis as 'madam' when asking about her errant daughter. Even those outside the force recognise rank and defer to it. Mrs Dixon calls the chief inspector 'sir' when he breaks the news that George is dead. Age can also signify authority. The costermonger ordered to move on by George is addressed as 'son', even though he is in his thirties.

Detectives play an ambiguous part in the authority structure. They are generally middle class, with gradations only partly based on rank. The social gap between Sergeant Roberts (Robert Flemyng) and Inspector Cherry (Bernard Lee) is difficult to discern, unlike the chasm which separates the sergeant from Constable Campbell (Bruce Seton). The latter is seen eating in the canteen, unlike his fellow detectives, and his clothes are conspicuously not made to measure. In spite of being a detective, Campbell belongs among the other ranks.

The film was shot on location in Paddington.[39] The feel of inner-city London in the late 1940s comes across strongly, with peeling house-fronts betraying a decade of neglect and bombsites an everyday feature. Bogarde claimed that *The Blue Lamp* was the first British example of *cinema vérité*, with the chase across electrified railway lines being made without permission, while nobody in the stadium was told of the filming.[40] Aside from the police station, few interiors are shown except for Tom Riley's lodgings and the Dixons' living room. Both are dated. In Riley's rented room, furnishings are minimal. The sleeping area is curtained off and across one corner is a washstand. The Dixons' home is more comfortable. The kitchen is an alcove off the living room, removing the clear distinction between food preparation and eating which marked middle-class homes. This enhances the sense of informality. On Andy Mitchell's first visit, a beer bottle and a sauce bottle are on the table as Mrs Dixon serves dinner. When other policemen drop in for a meal, socks are hanging over the range. The table and the Welsh dresser dominate the room, the latter being used for displaying china as much as storing it. When Mrs Dixon is told that her husband has died, she turns to the dresser. She arranges in a vase the flowers which were intended for him. Andy Mitchell let the chief inspector into the house. If Mrs Dixon had opened the front door to a senior officer, she would doubtless have invited him into the parlour.

By 1950, film-makers were finding an acceptable form of working-class speech. Tom Riley presents a textbook example of Basil Bernstein's restricted linguistic code with its emphasis on the imperative verb form and a preference for 'you' or 'they' among pronouns: he tells Diana to 'Keep your mouth shut, see? You don't know nothing. Understand?' Turning commands into questions and the use of the double negative are other obvious characteristics in this example. Working-class speech in British films was to be little changed until censorship was further relaxed a decade later and a new generation of actors including Albert Finney and Tom Courtenay brought regional accents to the screen.

The film caused dissension among the censors. For Lieutenant Colonel Arthur Fleetwood-Wilson, it was 'A sordid, vicious, unpleasant story'. His report continues, 'I deplore this type of film being produced in this country. I feel certain that it does a great deal of harm to those of the younger generation who are criminally minded.' Frank Crofts was more lenient: 'Without his revolver, Riley showed what a coward he really was.'[41] Critical responses were equally mixed, with Dilys Powell and James Monahan praising the film's authenticity and documentary feel, while Frank Enley in *Sight and Sound*, Denis Forman and the film correspondent of *The Times* all detected a theatricality in the characterisation.[42]

Later critical approaches to *The Blue Lamp* reveal the concerns of commentators and changing societal attitudes to gender, youth, crime and the police. Barr focuses on the disruption and restoration of order.[43] Stuart Laing sees in the film the lack of regulation associated with a competitive and acquisitive society.[44] Landy detects the masking of repressed and repressive sexuality, while both Hill and Murphy stress the juxtaposition of steady, dependable Andy Mitchell with the rootless Tom Riley.[45] The danger is that readings based on latter-day preoccupations divorce the film from its historical context. In spite of cautioning against such 'twisted teleology', Andy Medhurst cannot resist the temptation.[46]

This is another film which came too late in the sample period for its popularity to be fully assessed once it left first-run cinemas. With this handicap, it still did well in southeast Essex (Appendix, Table 7). On the evidence of the trade press, audiences generally were enthusiastic. On its northwest London circuit release, *The Blue Lamp* did better at the box office than the Danny Kaye vehicle, *The Secret Life of Walter Mitty* (d. Norman Z. McLeod, US, 1947), while a month later, the *Kinematograph Weekly* described *The Blue Lamp* as 'still raking in the shekels'.[47] It was one of the few films of the period to produce a profit for its producers.[48] A *Picturegoer* reader in south London described queuing for two hours with thousands of others to see the film in a suburban cinema.[49] This success was not emulated in the sample Leeds cinemas, where the film only managed a single three-day run by the end of 1950. It was new enough and popular enough to command a high rental which independents in the back streets of Leeds could not afford.

The presentation of delinquency in *The Blue Lamp* will be considered in Chapter Eight. Whether the film's plea for a sense of community in the face of this threat to order came from Dearden, Balcon, or Willis cannot be known. The denouement, with Riley's capture in the stadium, is exciting, but it rings hollow. This is the community of never-never land, which was more usually recreated in the Ealing comedies. The grit of *It Always Rains on Sunday* is missing. The risk is that reality takes a back seat as *The Blue Lamp* comes to be seen as a model of traditional policing.

The world of leisure

Mass leisure implies more than the provision of leisure facilities. The act of people coming together connotes shared interests and values which bind the group and distinguish members, however transiently, from others. Two examples of leisure activities performing this function in films of the 1940s are the holiday camp and the cycling club.

The holiday camp was predicated on a population with enough leisure time and money to enjoy a week at the seaside. Crucial to the camp's success was the widespread adoption of holidays with pay. By the end of the war, two-thirds of workers were entitled to a week's paid holiday, though as the grumbles of the men in *Chance of a Lifetime* make clear, this had yet to reach some firms by 1950.[50] Along with the wartime improvement in manual workers' earnings came limited opportunities for spending the extra money during the austerity years which followed. Allied to these factors were a desire to spend gratuities after leaving the services and a more general acceptance of mass catering brought about by the government-inspired National Restaurants and the wider provision of works canteens. For a while the holiday camp had everything in its favour. With the coming of cheap air travel and the package holiday, the decline of the camp paralleled that of the cinema under the onslaught of television.[51]

The atmosphere of the holiday camp at the peak of its popularity is captured in *Holiday Camp* (d. Ken Annakin, 1947). The idea for the film came from Godfrey Winn, newspaper columnist and friend of that king of holiday camps, Billy Butlin. The involvement of so many hands in the script – Muriel and Sydney Box, Peter Rogers, Mabel and Denis Constanduros and Ted Willis – does not augur well. In practice, such plot devices as the throwing together of strangers who share chalets can be exploited, so that the stories are woven together more successfully than in other examples of the portmanteau film. For a week, the campers are part of a community.

One family sampling holiday camp life are Joe and Ethel Huggett (Jack Warner and Kathleen Harrison) with their son, Harry (Peter Hammond), and daughter, Joan Martin (Hazel Court), who brings her own child. Harry loses at gambling, but Joe avenges the family honour by winning the money back and leaving the gamblers penniless. Joan meets Jimmy Gardner (Jimmy Hanley), a sailor who has been let down by his girlfriend. Misunderstandings abound, but by the end of the film, Joan and Jimmy are reconciled. Joan's chalet companion, Angela (Yvonne Owen), hopes to become engaged to Squadron Leader Binkie Hardwicke (Dennis Price), who is ostensibly on holiday. At the end of the week, she leaves without discovering that he has been arrested on suspicion of murder, and that Elsie Dawson (Esma Cannon), who also came to the camp looking for romance, went for a walk with him the previous evening and never returned.

Spinster Esther Harman (Flora Robson) finds something familiar about the voice on the camp's public address system. On visiting the control tower, she discovers that the announcer was blinded during the First World War and has no memory of his earlier life. Now he is happily married. She leaves without revealing that he was once her fiance. She befriends a young couple, Michael (Emrys Jones), who is working as a musician at the camp, and Valerie (Jeannette Tregarthen), who has been living with an aunt. When the aunt discovers her niece's pregnancy and disowns her, Esther offers the lovers a home.

Sydney Box encouraged Annakin to direct *Holiday Camp*.[52] Annakin's background as a documentary director shows in the location shooting. The film preserves such set pieces of holiday camp life as the arrival of guests at the railway station, where a fleet of coaches waits to ferry them to the camp, and the melee at the camp entrance as the bewildered newcomers unload their luggage. These episodes make the film as valuable a historical record as the Blackpool scenes in *Sing As We Go* (d. Basil Dean, 1934) and *Hindle Wakes* (d. Arthur Crabtree, 1952).

On the coach journey, the characters' clothes can be seen to advantage. Particularly among the women, clothes do not distinguish classes, reflecting the leavening effects of rationing and utility styles. Older women wear hats. Elsie Dawson betrays her age by wearing one. Jimmy is resplendent in his naval uniform. Joe wears a cap. His pocket watch is prominent, though as the week progresses, he relaxes enough to put on an open-neck shirt with the collar outside his sports jacket in the fashion of the time.

When the guests arrive at the camp, the men's clothes are noticeable. The sports jacket is the norm, though several men wear suits – one has a three-piece suit. The raincoat was a prerequisite for any journey away from home in an age before the car and is much in evidence. There is no distinction of dress by age, though in a later scene, Harry Huggett wears a school blazer, denoting that the Huggetts belong to the respectable working class who can

7   Time to go home: external scene from *Holiday Camp* (1947).
                          A pageant of men's clothing

afford such things. The adoption of formal clothing should not be
seen as indicative of shortages. The notion of leisure wear hardly
developed until the 1960s. In spite of the uniformity, social distinctions are detectable. The squadron leader's clothes are smarter
than Joe's, while the ostentation of the card-sharps' clothes betrays
their intentions.

These opening scenes show the range of people holidaying at
the camp. They include the middle class (Squadron Leader
Hardwicke, Esther Harman and Valerie), as well as the working
class (the Huggett family). This social mix is not entirely fanciful:
the roster of luminaries who sampled holiday camp life, albeit
with some prompting from Billy Butlin, included the Archbishop
of York, Lady Violet Bonham Carter, Anthony Eden and Hugh
Dalton.[53] If class differences are not abolished in the camp, the
communal atmosphere makes them more difficult to sustain. Behaviour which is frowned upon outside is legitimised, so that
campers are urged to kiss strangers on the dance floor and select
the most attractive girl in the bathing beauty competition. In these
surroundings, the villainous squadron leader has no difficulty in
finding working-class victims such as the naive chambermaid, Elsie
Dawson.

8   The spivs close in: Charlie (Denis Harkin), unnamed female
(Betty Nelson) and Steve (John Blythe) select their victim in
Holiday Camp (1947), but Joe (Jack Warner) knows their game

As Colin Ward and Dennis Hardy caution, 'The Camp is indeed
a universal symbol of the twentieth century, along with barbed
wire and the Unknown Political Prisoner.'[54] Two years after the
war ended, memories of other uses for camps were still vivid.
Holiday camps had been used to house internees and service personnel. This does not go unremarked:

ESTHER: Where does the announcer's voice come from?
ELSIE: The control tower.
ESTHER: The control tower. Sounds like a prisoner-of-war camp.
ELSIE: That's right – only we're the prisoners.

Like the prison camp, the holiday camp was an enclosed community, though without the barbed wire. Larger camps boasted
ballrooms, bars, theatres and sports facilities. It was not that campers were prevented from venturing beyond the gates; they had no
need to. Failing to take advantage of everything on offer was
tantamount to foolishness in an age of austerity. As Joe tells Ethel
while she struggles with her morning physical jerks among the
rows of campers on the beach: 'Stick it, mother. Good money we're
paying for this. You don't want to waste it.'

The working-class community

Authority might be expected to take a back seat on a holiday; instead it assumes more subtle forms. Uniformed staff – the redcoats – are the NCOs of the camp, their function being not to maintain discipline, but to facilitate pleasure. One steers a reluctant Ethel onto the ballroom floor. Others are seen urging girls to take part in the beauty contest. From the window of the control tower, Esther watches them jollying a crowd of campers. As one of Yvonne Roberts' interviewees who worked in the camps puts it, 'Everybody wants to be a Redcoat . . . because the blazer gives you the authority to be the kind of person you really are.' [55]

Two phenomena of the time captured in the film are of particular interest. The first is the one-parent family. The war had turned this into a social problem which could no longer be ignored. The film rehearses several responses. Valerie is pregnant and single. Her reaction is melodramatic: to jump off a cliff into the sea, preferably with her boyfriend, Michael. Her aunt's response – to have nothing more to do her – was more usual among older members of the middle class and the respectable working class. Thinking of her own lost love, Esther takes a pragmatic and sympathetic line more in keeping with the times.

For the Huggetts' daughter, Joan, the one-parent family is already a reality. Her status is made clear as she tells Jimmy, 'Of course I'm married. You don't imagine I'd have a child like that if I wasn't, do you?' A conversation with Angela in their chalet reveals that Joan is widowed. Practical support in such matters as baby-sitting comes from her parents, though Ethel sees the stay at the camp as an opportunity for Joan to find a husband. If the film does not show Joan's situation resolved by marriage, at least it allows the possibility.

The other phenomenon of the time is the situation of Esther Harman, whose life has been devoted to looking after her ageing mother. Ray Seaton and Roy Martin are alert for symbolism, seeing the old woman as representing Mother England of the previous generation. [56] The two women holidayed in Torquay, that quintessentially middle-class resort with no holiday camps. Now that Esther is alone, she is making an effort to embrace the new.

For many young women, the First World War took away the opportunity for marriage. As a consequence, the maiden aunt of late middle age was a feature of family life in the 1940s and 1950s. She has been neglected by social historians, though she regularly appears in Agatha Christie novels as the paid companion. A disproportionate number of such women came from the large working-class families characteristic of the early years of the century. Like the grandmother, they were on hand to help with child-rearing, dispense wisdom and defuse parent–child conflicts. In this case, the middle-class Esther acts as fairy godmother to the young lovers, Michael and Valerie. The choice she offers Michael is between his music and Valerie. True to his middle-class upbringing and the demands of the box office, he puts Valerie first.

The scenes of holiday camp life provide so much visual interest that the film's dialogue takes second place, though accent provides a convenient shorthand for assigning characters to their roles in the drama. Middle-class Esther is introspective. Joe and Ethel Huggett are the family-centred cockney couple. Elsie Dawson's speech marks her as working class: she is the naive one. If the speech of the younger people is less class-bound, this is indicative of the dictates of drama schools from which many young actors graduated, as much as any reduction of class differences in the real world.

A holiday is an occasion for presenting a facade to the world, safe in the knowledge that when the week is over, the other guests will not be seen again. The stories in *Holiday Camp* are those of people with something to hide. The card-sharps pose as ordinary guests to entice punters into their chalet; Joe Huggett assumes the facade of an incompetent gambler to outwit them. Elsie, the chambermaid, tries to hide her age from herself, only to expose it to everybody else by taking part in the bathing beauty contest. Valerie hides her pregnancy. Esther tries to conceal her dislike of life in the camp. The squadron leader has more to hide than anybody.

For Murphy, 'the holiday camp is treated very much as a microcosm of British society and Dennis Price's irrational, war-obsessed killer functions effectively as an embodiment of post-war anxiety, jolting the film out of cosy complacency and acting as a sinister antidote to Jack Warner and the Huggetts.'[57] The problem with this interpretation is that an institution like a holiday camp is not a microcosm of anything. It has its own rationale for existence, its own history, and generates its own dynamics. Society is messier. The holiday camp displays aspects of the wider society, but it is a commercial organisation aimed at purveying pleasure. It can be seen more usefully as society's mirror image, in which the traditional rules and proprieties of behaviour do not apply: work is replaced by fun, the woman can pursue the man, while the mother can abdicate to the staff responsibility for supervising her children.

There is a further problem with Murphy's approach. The risk in treating any institution as a microcosm of society is that the characters have to take on a mythic status almost too heavy for them to bear, so that they risk becoming portentous or stereotyped.

One example is the squadron leader. Annakin makes clear that it was Muriel Box who worked the character of sex murderer Neville Heath into the film.[58] A former borstal boy, Heath was arrested in Bournemouth in 1946 while posing as an RAF officer. His trial caught the public's imagination.[59] This is not the same as seeing him as 'an embodiment of post-war anxiety', though Murphy is surely right in seeing Binkie Hardwicke as 'jolting the film out of cosy complacency'. At the same time, Heath's proletarian origins cast doubt on the squadron leader's middle-class persona.

The fate of Elsie Dawson is left unresolved. As the film progresses, she becomes a tragic character rather than a figure of fun. With her story, the film takes on a darker hue rather than concluding on the anticlimax of the end of the holiday. In the process, the notion of the working-class character as a figure of fun is subverted. As with the squadron leader, the class role which seemed so uncomplicated is brought into question.

Martha Wolfenstein and Nathan Leites took the film seriously enough to write about it not long after its first release. Their general contention was that 'Ultimate fulfilment of … film's promise to reveal everything can be achieved if actors were to play themselves.' Citing *Holiday Camp* as a rare example of this among British films, the authors continued, 'The self portrayal occurs in a film expressing the breakdown of the traditional British value of privacy. The scene is a crowded vacation camp where inmates are organised into mass dancing and kissing games approximating Huxley's orgy-porgy forecasts.'[60]

Presumably something other than naturalistic acting is implied. Patricia Roc, Charlie Chester and Gerry Wilmot appear as themselves in the film, though what this signifies is debatable. It might be argued that the presence of stars only emphasises the film's artifice. The practice was not as unusual in British films as Wolfenstein and Leites imagined: they should have watched the Old Mother Riley comedies, which abound in stars making cameo appearances (see Chapter Ten). Nor does the holiday camp necessarily symbolise a breakdown of the traditional British value of privacy. As Ward and Hardy point out, 'a chalet at Butlin's was for many couples their first experience of domestic privacy.'[61]

Rather than accepting the sinister overtones detected by Wolfenstein and Leites, the function of the camp can be summed up by a speech made when Esther visits the control tower. Its socialist tone makes Ted Willis the probable author. The blind (middle-class) announcer takes Esther to the window and throws it open, letting the noise of the campers reach them. The announcer was played by Esmond Knight, who had been blinded during naval service.

ANNOUNCER: Do you see what I see?

ESTHER: What do you see?

ANNOUNCER: One of the strangest sights of the twentieth century: the great mass of people all fighting for the one thing you can't get by fighting for it – happiness. When I first came here, I thought I couldn't stand it – the noise, the crowds, the frantic search for pleasure. Then I saw it wasn't really a crowd at all – just separate individuals, each one of them with a different set of problems and worries, hopes and fears, each one of them tired and dispirited, eager for peace and yet frightened to be alone. And I thought, if I can help to make them happy, just for a while, if I can enable them to forget their everyday anxieties while they're here, then I've done a little to repay the great happiness the world has given me.

This credo applies equally well to the cinema.

Holiday Camp was popular with audiences nationally, being one of the few Rank films to make a profit (Appendix, Table 1). This popularity was apparent in southeast Essex (Appendix, Table 7). It was repeated in Yorkshire: as well as appearing in the first quartile of attendances at the Gaumont, Sheffield, *Holiday Camp* was the only film among those considered in this chapter to have more than a token showing in the sample Leeds cinemas (Appendix, Tables 5 and 6). One reason for this popularity may be that the film is not tied to a London location; another is its association with holidays – particularly as many Yorkshire people were likely to know the Filey camp used for location shooting.[62] More important than either of these factors is the film's rich texture, with plenty of variation in mood and pace as well as a host of storylines. The characters are recognisable enough for audiences to empathise. Elsie Dawson's fate and whether Joan gets her man do linger in the mind. The moment when Joe and Ethel lie in the sand dunes and talk of life together does have poignancy, as it must for couples who married in the aftermath of war and were bringing up families in the late 1940s. Underlying the film's obvious appeal is the sense of a masked ball being played out for the audience – of characters harbouring dreams and never quite showing their real selves. The exceptions are the innocent – Ethel Huggett – and the intellectual – the blind announcer, who is willing to conspire in the dreams of others if it brings them happiness. For a director making his first feature, *Holiday Camp* is a notable achievement.

Like the holiday camp, cycling has hardly captivated film-makers, though in 1948 came *Jour de Fête* (d. Jacques Tati, France) and *Bicycle Thieves* (d. Vittorio de Sica, Italy). Critically, they have fared better than the British entry in the canon, *A Boy, a Girl and a Bike* (d. Ralph Smart, 1949), scripted by Ted Willis.

In a Yorkshire mill town, wealthy young David Howarth (John McCallum) is attracted to Susie Bates (Honor Blackman), a mill girl who belongs to the local cycling club. He joins the club, buying a bike from crooked dealer Bill Martin (Maurice Denham). The bike was stolen by the delinquent Charlie Ritchie (Anthony Newley) to pay a gambling debt owing to Martin. Ada Foster (Diana Dors) overhears Martin and Charlie talking. Matters come to a head when the cyclists go camping. Charlie tries to destroy the bike so that the theft will not be discovered, but he is too late. Bill Martin's son has let Ada down by not taking her to a dance and in revenge she tells the others about the plot.

David Howarth proposes to Susie. Her boyfriend, Sam Walters (Patrick Holt), becomes jealous, picking a fight with David. Later, rivalries are forgotten as David takes part in the championship race and wins for the team. When the club organiser, Steve Hall (Leslie Dwyer), finds a home for Sam and Susie, he does not reveal that David has provided it.

Along with rambling, cycling was taken up by the working class and the lower middle class from the 1890s. H. G. Wells' *The Wheels of Chance: A Holiday Romance* (1896) evokes this early freedom – a theme used by Alan Bennett in *A Day Out* (BBC TV, 1972). Enthusiasts came together in clubs, which enhanced the ability of working-class people to organise themselves. A noticeable feature of the film is how much time the cyclists devote to running the club. This expertise spills into the wider community: Steve Hall is on the council's housing committee.

The hostility of David's family to his new hobby illustrates that cycling remained a low-status pastime. In addition to giving young women freedom from chaperones, rambling and cycling threatened the hegemony of the ruling classes by increasing mobility and hence the contacts between lower-class communities. The threat could be more specific, the most notorious example being the ramblers' challenge to private land ownership in the 1932 Kinder Scout mass trespass.[63]

Outsiders can disrupt the community. The obvious example is David Howarth, who precipitates a rift between Susie and Sam, even if he does step back so that it can be healed. In the championship, David stands in for another outsider crucial to the plot, the mysterious Londoner, Bert Gardener, who joins the club at the same time as David. Bert equivocates when his wife wants to go back to London. Only when he is arrested as an army deserter does the reason for his reluctance become clear.

Charlie and his widowed mother, Nan (Megs Jenkins), are the other outsiders. Nan is being wooed by Steve Hall. She has been assimilated into the community, though the same cannot be said of Charlie. Nan blames his unruly behaviour on evacuation. Steve diagnoses the absence of a father's firm hand as the cause and hints darkly that the boy needs disciplining. Presumably he has corporal punishment in mind, though the film allows him no opportunity to carry out his threat.

It is not only outsiders who are disruptive. As with many of Diana Dors' characters, Ada's power to upset the equilibrium of the community resides in her sexuality. After David and Sam fight over Susie, Ada turns her charms on Sam, though without success. The difference between Ada and the outsiders is that her disruptive potential can be contained by the community. Her activities are treated tolerantly and she remains not only a member of the club, but a friend of Susie. As Charlie is young and impressionable, his disciplining can also be kept within the club. The contrast is with Bill Martin, who is given over to external authority in the shape of the police.

Though women are active club members, they occupy subordinate roles. They are not involved in its organisation, the exception being Nan Ritchie, who acts as treasurer and in whose cafe the meetings are held. Running a business qualifies her as an honorary man. In the championship heats, women are relegated to being spectators. At the championship, even Nan takes on the traditionally feminine task of dispensing refreshments. (David's family is conspicuous among the spectators – his mother and sister are the only women wearing hats.)

Location shots take up much of the film, with the Yorkshire setting more effectively establishing a sense of place than the variable dialects.[64] Shots of a mill interior give a feeling for the world of work, where noise is more noticeable than any visual signifiers. The high incidence of deafness among mill workers is unsurprising.

The only home in the town shown in any detail is that of Susie Bates. Her father is a dustman. With three generations living in the house, including Susie's two younger siblings, the living room is overcrowded. This was an age when widowed parents were assimilated into the household, though not without tensions showing. A telling scene shows the difficulties of Susie and Sam in finding somewhere to talk about their future. In the living room, her father is bickering with grandma, while his wife temporises. Susie's sister is with her boyfriend in the parlour. Bedrooms are not a proper place to talk, so Susie and Sam retreat to the greenhouse, to dream of the home which one day they will make for themselves. The contrast with David's country house, set in its own grounds and where a grand piano fails to dominate the panelled morning room, is not laboured.

The characters are grouped into families or proto-families, the exception being Diana Dors' Ada. The family does not necessarily cure disruptiveness: in the case of the Martins or the Gardeners, it conspicuously fails to do so. More often, the cycling club is seen exerting control to maintain the values of the community. Not that wayward behaviour is necessarily bad. It can function as the grit in the oyster. Whatever problems Susie's flirtation with David causes, it reveals the limits of his own family's control over him and ultimately leads to a home for Susie and Sam. To see the family or the club merely as proscribing or curing certain forms of behaviour is to underestimate the forces for societal change and the capacity of social institutions to adapt to change.

A Boy, a Girl and a Bike was never screened by independents in southeast Essex. This cannot be attributable to high rental charges, for Rank never took the opportunity to rerun the film in their own cinemas there after its initial release (Appendix, Table 7). Independents in Leeds also judged that its commercial potential was minimal (Appendix, Table 6). On the evidence of the film's reception at the Gaumont, Sheffield, they were right: it came in the bottom quartile of attendances (Appendix, Table 5). As the manager commented, 'well balanced programme cannot understand why we have not taken more money.'[65]

Recent commentators have ignored the film. An exception is Landy, who takes a Darwinian view of cycling:

Cycling is a signifier for the working-class community in the film, testing the mettle and morality of the men and serving as a means of eliminating discordant elements ... The film adheres to a rigid notion of community. Susie does not get her rich man and abandon her social class. Though the film flirts with such an alliance, it ultimately frustrates hopes for a Cinderella ending and aligns itself with the working-class characters.[66]

Landy's rider holds out the possibility for change:

The film harbours a tension between realism and melodrama. The realism opens up a space to see the characters as struggling over issues of economy, family and gender, but the melodrama insists on the maintenance of the family as the cohesive force that binds the community, curing the disruptiveness generated by generational, sexual, and class differences.[67]

The scope for change seems small – and melodrama wins.

In McCallum's words, the film 'only aimed to entertain on a fairly simple level, and it did this reasonably well'.[68] Though lacking artistic pretension, it captures the place and the time as surely as its more illustrious rivals. Few film-makers ventured into Yorkshire, which makes this portrait of a mill town during its postwar Indian summer all the more valuable. In passing, the film dramatises the deserter's fear of discovery and what housing shortages meant to those involved – something which official records cannot convey.

Of the six films considered, three are set in London. This is not unexpected given that London was both the largest conurbation and the centre of the film industry. If the films are typical, one implication is that audiences nationally became familiar with the more unsavoury aspects of working-class London. The films in which ordinary people from other parts of the country did appear were little seen. The British cinema of the 1940s might have been a mass medium, but it was also a selective medium.

Mutual dependence as much as emotional ties bind the communities. Individuals may come together over particular issues (*London Belongs to Me*), but crime can be divisive (*It Always Rains on Sunday*). Older women like Peggy in *The Gorbals Story* are often crucial in maintaining communal bonds, while the sexuality of young women like Ada Foster in *A Boy, a Girl and a Bike* threatens them. One consequence is that men can appear weak and vacillating, though Jack Warner's characters deny this possibility.

Many of the communities presented would hardly make present-day audiences yearn for the world we have lost. Only *A Boy, a Girl and a Bike* comes near to satisfying the received notion of a traditional working-class community. The film happens to be set in a small northern town, which may be no coincidence given the appeal of such locations to television audiences, Holmfirth in *Last of the Summer Wine* (BBC TV, 1973–current) being an obvious example. Most of the mills have gone. The mill towns with their cobbled ginnels and precipitous flights of steps linking the streets still huddle in the valleys, but now they are dormitory towns or tourist attractions. Their power to evoke nostalgia is an acknowledgement of the changes which have taken place. A film can amuse and entertain, while at the same time prompting speculation about how we mould our imagined past. The world of *It Always Rains on Sunday* can be conveniently forgotten.

Notes

1 Tom Dewe Matthews, *Censored* (London: Chatto & Windus, 1994), pp. 105–6.

2 Richard Hoggart, *The Uses of Literacy: Aspects of Working-Class Life with Special Reference to Publications and Entertainments* (Harmondsworth: Penguin Books, 1958); Don Haworth, *Bright Morning: Images from a Thirties Boyhood* (London: Mandarin, 1991).

3 Patrick Hamilton, *The West Pier* (London: Constable, 1951), p. 170.

4 For this approach to life in the East End of London, see Dick Hobbs, *Doing the Business: Entrepreneurship, the Working Class and Detectives in the East End of London* (Oxford: Oxford University Press, 1989).

5 Colin Chambers, *The Story of the Unity Theatre* (London: Lawrence and Wishart, 1989), pp. 185 and 189. In 1961, Sydney Box paid credit to what the Unity Theatre had done for the film industry (*ibid.*, p. 369). Among the names mentioned by Chambers are Bill Owen, Alfie Bass, Ted Willis, Herbert Lom, Maxine Audley, David Kossoff, Warren Mitchell, Lionel Bart, John Bluthal, Walter Lassally and Stanley Baxter.

6 Arthur La Bern, *It Always Rains on Sunday* (London: Nicholson & Watson, 1947).

7 *Ibid.*, pp. 77–84 and 135–50.

8 Googie Withers, interviewed in Brian McFarlane, *Sixty Voices: Celebrities Recall the Golden Age of British Cinema* (London: BFI, 1992), p. 235.

9 For a range of reviews, see *Cinema and Theatre Construction*, 15:3 (1948), 4–7.

10 Roger Manvell, 'Recent films', *Contemporary Cinema*, 2:1 (1948), 18–21.

11 *Kinematograph Weekly* (8 July 1948), p. 13.

12 Raymond Durgnat, *A Mirror for England: British Movies from Austerity to Affluence* (London: Faber & Faber, 1970), p. 201.

13 Charles Drazin, *The Finest Years: British Cinema of the 1940s* (London: Andre Deutsch, 1998), pp. 76–8.

14 Gavin Lambert, 'Film and the idea of happiness', *Contact*, no. 11 (1949), 64.

15 Janet Thumim, 'The female audience: mobile women and married ladies', in Christine Gledhill and Gillian Swanson (eds), *Nationalising Femininity: Culture, Sexuality and the British Cinema in the Second World War* (Manchester: Manchester University Press, 1996), p. 253.

16 La Bern, *It Always Rains on Sunday*, p. 7.

17 Charles Barr, *Ealing Studios* (London: Studio Vista, 2nd edn, 1993), p. 70.

18 Tim Pulleine sees the mirror sequences as offering Rose an expressive alternative world. Tim Pulleine, 'Spin a dark web', in Steve Chibnall and Robert Murphy (eds), *British Crime Cinema* (London: Routledge, 1999), p. 32.

19 Michael Young and Peter Willmott, *Family and Kinship in East London* (London: Routledge & Kegan Paul, 1957).

20 Norman Collins, *London Belongs to Me* (London: Collins, 1945).

21 Andrew Davies, *Leisure, Gender and Poverty: Working-Class Culture in Salford and Manchester 1900–1939* (Buckingham: Open University Press, 1992), pp. 79–81.

22 For a similar point see Durgnat, *A Mirror for England*, p. 36.

23 *Picture Show* (18 September 1948), p. 8.

24 Forsyth Hardy, 'Safety first for British films?', *Film Forum*, 4:1 (1948), 1.

25 Durgnat, *A Mirror for England*, pp. 36 and 242–3; Robert Murphy,

Realism and Tinsel: Cinema and Society in Britain 1939–49 (London: Routledge, 1992), pp. 159–60.

26 Geoff Brown, *Launder and Gilliat* (London: BFI, 1977), pp. 122–3.

27 Chambers, *The Story of the Unity Theatre*, p. 282.

28 Tennessee Williams, *'Sweet Bird of Youth'*; *'A Streetcar Named Desire'*; *'The Glass Menagerie'*, ed. E. Martin Brown (Harmondsworth: Penguin Books, 1962), p. 229.

29 Margaret Dickinson (ed.), *Rogue Reels: Oppositional Film in Britain 1945–90* (London: BFI, 1999).

30 John Hill, *Sex, Class and Realism: British Cinema 1956–1963* (London: BFI, 1986), pp. 138–40.

31 Correlli Barnett, *The Lost Victory: British Dreams, British Realities 1945–1950* (London: Pan, 1996).

32 Durgnat, *A Mirror for England*, p. 70.

33 BFI Library, del Guidice papers; *Daily Film Renter* (27 February 1950), p. 3; Edgar Anstey, Roger Manvell, Ernest Lindgren and Paul Rotha (eds), *Shots in the Dark: A Collection of Reviewers' Opinions of Some Leading Films* (London: Allan Wingate, 1951), pp. 158–63.

34 *Ibid.*, pp. 159–63.

35 'Film and public: *Chance of a Lifetime*', *Sight and Sound*, new series, 19:9 (1951), 349–50.

36 BFI Library, Bernard Miles papers, letter dated 9 September 1950 from del Guidice to Bernard Miles.

37 BFI Library, Bernard Miles papers, letter dated 9 March 1950 from del Guidice to Bernard Miles.

38 One example is Drazin, *The Finest Years*, pp. 55–70.

39 Paddington in wartime is evoked in Marie Paneth, *Branch Street: A Sociological Study* (London: George Allen & Unwin, 1944).

40 Dirk Bogarde, interviewed in McFarlane, *Sixty Voices*, p. 26.

41 BFI Library, BBFC scenario notes, note 24, 12 April 1949.

42 Anstey *et al.*, *Shots in the Dark*, pp. 127–30; Frank Enley, 'The Blue Lamp', *Sight and Sound*, new series, 19:2 (1950), 76–7; Denis Forman, *Film 1945–1950* (London: Longmans, Green, for British Council, 1952), pp. 24–5.

43 Barr, *Ealing Studios*, p. 83.

44 Stuart Laing, *Representations of Working-Class Life 1957–1964* (Basingstoke and London: Macmillan, 1986), pp. 112–13.

45 Marcia Landy, *British Genres: Cinema and Society 1930–1960* (Princeton, NJ: Princeton University Press, 1991), p. 467; Hill, *Sex, Class and Realism*, p. 70; Murphy, *Realism and Tinsel*, p. 166.

46 Andy Medhurst, 'Dirk Bogarde', in Charles Barr (ed.), *All Our Yesterdays: 90 Years of British Cinema* (London: BFI, 1986), p. 347. The point has been made before. See Steve Chibnall, 'The teenage trilogy: *The Blue Lamp, I Believe in You* and *Violent Playground*', in Alan Burton, Tim O'Sullivan and Paul Wells (eds), *Liberal Directions: Basil Dearden and Postwar British Film Culture* (Trowbridge: Flicks Books, 1997), p. 143.

47 *Daily Film Renter* (8 March 1950), p. 9; *Kinematograph Weekly* (13 April 1950), p. 12.

48 *Daily Mirror* (28 April 1950). Contained in BFI Library, 'British films 1950' cuttings file.

49 *Picturegoer* (13 May 1950), p. 3.

50 PEP, *British Trade Unionism: Six Studies* (London: PEP, 1948), p. 94.

51 Colin Ward and Dennis Hardy, *Goodnight Campers! The History of the British Holiday Camp* (London: Mansell, 1986). For contemporary accounts of holiday camp life, see Kenneth Adam, 'Anatomy of Butlin', *Pilot Papers*, 1:2 (1946), 81–90; Hilde Marchant, 'Life in a holiday camp', *Picture Post* (13 July 1946), reprinted in Tom Hopkinson (ed.), *Picture Post 1938–50* (London: Allen Lane, The Penguin Press, 1970), pp. 192–6.

52 Ken Annakin, interviewed in McFarlane, *Sixty Voices*, pp. 5 and 6.

53 Peter Hennessy, *Never Again: Britain 1945–51* (London: Jonathan Cape, 1992), p. 315.

54 Ward and Hardy, *Goodnight Campers!*, p. 105.

55 Yvonne Roberts, 'Is everybody happy?' *New Statesman* (26 August 1977), cited in Ward and Hardy, *Goodnight Campers!*, p. 89.

56 Ray Seaton and Roy Martin, 'Gainsborough in the forties', *Film and Filming* (June 1982), p. 17.

57 Murphy, *Realism and Tinsel*, p. 215.

58 Ken Annakin, interviewed in McFarlane, *Sixty Voices*, p. 6.

59 Harry Hopkins, *The New Look: A Social History of the Forties and Fifties in Britain* (London: Readers Union and Secker & Warburg, 1963), pp. 50–1.

60 Martha Wolfenstein and Nathan Leites, *Movies: A Psychological Study* (Glencoe, IL: Free Press of Glencoe, 1950), pp. 289–90.

61 Ward and Hardy, *Goodnight Campers!*, p. 75.

62 Ken Annakin, *So You Wanna Be a Director* (Sheffield: Tomahawk Press, 2001), pp. 25 and 26.

63 Mike Harding, *Walking the Peak and Pennines* (London: Michael Joseph, 1992), p. 107.

64 Filming took place in Wharfedale, West Yorkshire. John McCallum, *Life with Googie* (London: William Heinemann, 1979), p. 44.

65 CTA, weekly returns for Gaumont, Sheffield, 13 August 1949.

66 Landy, *British Genres*, p. 449.

67 *Ibid.*, p. 449.

68 McCallum, *Life with Googie*, p. 44.

Family fortunes: portrayals of the working-class family

Most films concerned with working-class life offer some image of the family. In *Holiday Camp* (d. Ken Annakin, 1947), it is the stable, coherent social unit of the Huggetts. In *It Always Rains on Sunday* (d. Robert Hamer, 1947), the family generates conflict and divided loyalties, though the film holds out the hope of something better. In *Good Time Girl* (d. David Macdonald, 1948), the family is the wellspring of faulty socialisation. In *The White Unicorn* (d. Bernard Knowles, 1947) and *When the Bough Breaks* (d. Lawrence Huntington, 1947), children are as much a source of heartbreak as pleasure. The films considered in this chapter have the family as their centrepiece.

A family seen struggling through the war are the Colters in *Waterloo Road* (d. Sidney Gilliat, 1945). The story is told towards the end of the war by the local GP, Dr Montgomery (Alastair Sim), and is an extended flashback to a day in the blitz of 1941. Jim Colter (John Mills) is married to Tillie (Joy Shelton). While Jim is serving in the army, Tillie lives in Jim's parental home, along with his sister, Ruby (Alison Leggatt), and her husband. Ruby writes to Jim, telling him of Tillie's involvement with local amusement arcade owner, Ted Purvis (Stewart Granger). Jim goes absent without leave, intending to confront his adversary at the arcade, but Ted is not in there. Instead, one of Ted's cronies knocks Jim out during a scuffle. After being tended by Dr Montgomery, he continues his quest, eventually coming upon Ted and Tillie in Ted's flat. The two men fight as an air raid rages, with Jim emerging as the victor. As the flashback ends, Dr Montgomery is seen giving a toy railway engine to Jim and Tillie's son. The couple have stayed together.

Gilliat followed Hitchcock's habit of making an uncredited appearance in his own films, though he is harder to spot.[1] This is one of many devices in British films of the 1940s which remind audiences of the artificiality of what they are watching.[2] It is as though film-makers were reacting against the documentary tradition by not taking themselves too seriously. *Holiday Camp* (d. Ken Annakin, 1947) has stars appearing as themselves. In *Spring in Park Lane* (d. Herbert Wilcox, 1948), Michael Wilding's character is informed that he looks like Michael Wilding. *Waterloo Road* has its own self-regarding moment, aside from its director lurking among the extras. As an air raid warning sounds, the doctor encounters a husband and wife heading away from the shelters:

MRS WILSON: We're going to the pictures to see Mickey Rooney. You can't stay cooped up every night. You can have too much of a good thing.

DR MONTGOMERY: In my opinion you can have too much of Mickey Rooney, but perhaps that's a personal point of view.

Gilliat needed to retain a sense of humour. He recalled that filming was 'prolonged and troubled'. Arthur Crabtree, the cameraman, wanted to direct the film himself. Maurice Ostrer, head of production at Gainsborough Pictures, disliked the project and quarrelled with its producer, Edward Black. When Black resigned, Ostrer delayed the film's completion.[3] As if echoing events behind the camera, a continued friction with authority runs through *Waterloo Road*. The military police are the most obvious manifestation of power. They are the enemy, with the Germans relegated to being a background irritant who occasionally drop bombs. This is evident in the subplot involving a Canadian renegade whom Jim encounters in Waterloo Station – a man who joined the army to fight and who deserted when service life proved to be a matter of routine and discipline rather than getting to grips with the enemy. When his unit is posted overseas, the Canadian is happy to give himself up – until he discovers that he will be arrested instead of being allowed to fight.

Jim's battle with authority is woven through the film as he seeks to evade the military police until he has settled his score with Ted. His adversaries are not portrayed as being overly hostile. When Jim is arrested at Waterloo Station, the officer in charge gives him the opportunity to return to his regiment on his own. When Jim rejects this, he is escorted on the train as far as Clapham Junction. On the journey, the corporal accompanying him offers him a cigarette as they chat. This is the unforced conversation of two men who share the same class position. Yet the corporal is still the enemy. When he is distracted by another passenger, Jim has no compunction about seizing the chance to escape. He goes home, though he has to leave by the back door when the corporal and a policeman come looking for him. Jim's mother defends her son, voicing her own attitude towards authority: 'Why don't you leave our boys alone? They're doing their bit, aren't they? Always badgering 'em, badgering 'em.' Though the corporal sees her concealing Jim's belt, he contents himself with a friendly warning that her son should give himself up.

Jim battles with military authority; the audience is shown authority's human face. The tension between the two viewpoints means that the evasion of the military police by Jim and the Canadian seems like a game. This may be interpreted as directorial uncertainty or an attempt to counter war-weariness with humour. Marcia Landy accords it greater significance: 'French leave is justified in the context of the imperative to bolster morale on the home front, to diminish threats to domestic stability.'[4] By this reading, marital harmony takes precedence over duty.

Civilian authority is represented by the police and air-raid wardens. The power of the police is apparent as they check identity papers in the dance hall which Jim visits in his search for Ted. He uses his uniform to outwit authority by pretending to be on the side of the police as they round up miscreants. Yet civilian authority is weak, as the constable's hesitation at breaking up the fight in the amusement arcade illustrates. He takes the easy option, blaming Jim for the affray. Only Dr Montgomery's intervention saves Jim from being charged. Ultimately it is the all-knowing, middle-class doctor who wields power most effectively, if benignly, though his legal authority is limited.

While other characters are preoccupied with the problems of survival, Dr Montgomery can reflect on the past and speculate on the future. The film was made in 1944, when the future was uncertain. Not surprisingly, aspiration takes precedent over detail, though the sort of postwar world the doctor envisages is clear enough. He takes a dim view of Ted Purvis: 'Hope he's not still having his cake and eating it when the war's over.' As in *The Way to the Stars* (d. Anthony Asquith, 1945), made at the same time, the importance of children is stressed. On his way to the Colters' house, the doctor surveys the rubble of the blitzed street and muses, 'We'll need good citizens when this is all over. Millions of them.' He leans over the pram in the Colters' back yard to declare, 'Well Jimmy, my boy, you've got the future. It's all yours.' His medical views are less progressive. He admonishes Tillie for picking up her baby when it cries, warning that this encourages attention seeking. John Bowlby's theories on the dire effects of maternal deprivation were to become the psychological orthodoxy in postwar Britain.[5] Bowlby would certainly have disputed Dr Montgomery's advice.

As well as acting as narrator, the doctor is the film's conscience – and perhaps the mouthpiece of Gilliat, who wrote the script in addition to directing. He records that the flashback element was to lead audiences back into the blitz, which had been over for a year. It had resumed by the time the film was released, rendering the device unnecessary.[6] Raymond Durgnat seems to have strayed into a different film when he describes Sim as the crooked doctor helping the spiv to seduce Jim's wife (Rosamund John) [sic]. More usefully, he sees *Waterloo Road* as affirming the working man's right to little revolts rather than insisting on discipline as salvation – the route favoured in *The Bells Go Down* (d. Basil Dearden, 1943).[7]

The doctor is first seen wending his way through a street market, with no hint that this is wartime. The period is established by shots of the cellars at Waterloo Station being used as air raid shelters, the ubiquitous service personnel milling around the concourse and the mounds of rubble towering above the remaining houses in Jim's street. Roads are closed because of unexploded bombs. Missing is the tape crisscrossing windows to hold shards of glass in place in the event of a bomb blast. Even in the tattooist's shop where Jim hides from the military police, the plate glass window is unprotected.

The Colters' home is in a terrace with that distinctive London feature encountered in *It Always Rains on Sunday* of a parapet high enough to conceal the roof line. Here the houses are lower in the social scale, lacking even vestigial front gardens. Having a front door opening into a hall rather than directly into the living room gives a modicum of social tone, but this is belied by the railway viaduct at the rear. Trains are continually passing the Colters' kitchen window. The noise and the lack of privacy are reminders that this is working-class territory, though the nearness of the railway is not always perceived as a problem: in the final shot, Tillie waves to Jim who is leaning out of a train window. The corporal is standing behind him, smiling benignly, but keeping firm hold of Jim's belt.

During the war, 220,000 houses in Britain were destroyed or damaged beyond repair.[8] This represented around 2 per cent of the national housing stock, with working-class areas like the East End of London suffering disproportionately. By 1951, the number of households sharing houses in England and Wales was greater than in 1921, indicating the continued pressure on housing.[9] The problems of sharing a house come over clearly in *Waterloo Road* as Jim's sister, Ruby, squabbles with Tillie, while his mother tries to mediate. Fred is the man of the house. He avoids quarrels by finding a second home in the pub, or retreating to the back yard where he keeps pigeons. The image of the caged bird is a convenient metaphor for working-class lives – it occurs in *It Always Rains on Sunday* – but it also reflects the realities of the working-class home in which there was little room for pets. When the birds are released to fend for themselves, they come back. Home might not be ideal, but for the pigeons as much as for Jim, it is known and it is the place to which they return. The moral is not lost on Antonia Lant.[10]

The interior of the Colters' house is not shown in any detail, though the cramped conditions and dated decor of the living room are evident: the runner on the mantlepiece is a Victorian hangover, along with the overlarge clock and the elaborate ornaments, while every piece of wall space is used for displaying pictures. The house has electric light, though in common with the Sandigates' home in *It Always Rains on Sunday*, there is no bathroom or hot water supply: Fred is seen washing at the shallow sink in the scullery. Close by it is that essential washday accessory, the mangle. Food is cooked on the range.

Jim is marked as working class by his home. There is little attempt to delineate his position by speech. His training as a locomotive engineer suggests that he is upwardly mobile. As Tillie looks at a photograph of her wedding in a photographer's window, there is a flashback to the couple setting off on their honeymoon. From the train they see the home they intend to buy. It is an interwar terraced house – modest enough, but as Jim says, a change from the Waterloo Road. They intend to furnish it by hire purchase, though he has qualms about this. The respectable working class were wary of long-term debt.

The modernity of Ted Purvis's flat contrasts with the clutter of the Colters' home. Ted is a more flamboyant (and more interesting) character than Jim. Robert Murphy considers him to be the screen's first fully-fledged spiv.[11] He has evaded conscription by buying a medical certificate. He is first seen shaving in the communal shelter – his electric razor is a rarity for the period. One of his acolytes ministers to him, like a butler fussing over his master. The trappings are those of a wealthy man, yet Ted is placed firmly in the working class by the location of his flat above the amusement arcade and more importantly by his opportunistic lifestyle which teeters into petty criminality. The members of his gang are introduced in the amusement arcade scenes. Like the fun fair in Gilliat's *London Belongs to Me* (1948), the amusement arcade attracts those on the fringes of the law. Ted's charm is apparent as he cajoles Tillie into spending the afternoon with him, even though she only keeps their date in order to tell him that they cannot go out together. Gilliat is unwilling to let him off lightly for this. Not only does Ted lose his fight with Jim, but Dr Montgomery pronounces that the hapless spiv really does have a heart condition.

In general, morality is not underlined so obviously. As a glimpse of the problems of marriage in wartime, *Waterloo Road* remains affecting. Its structure follows that of the western, with the hero stalking the villain, to dispense justice and win his girl in the last reel. Visually, trains and train journeys punctuate the action as much as in that other railway film of 1945, David Lean's *Brief Encounter*. The difference is that *Waterloo Road* shows the working class at the bottom of the hierarchy of authority, but coming to their own accommodation with the system. The film was rooted in reality for working-class audiences, which may account for its appeal in working-class Leeds (Appendix, Table 6). As Richard Winnington declared, Gilliat 'has kept alive that instinct to portray the working classes of Britain as they really are', though other critics disapproved of the emphasis on crime.[12] Nor were audiences enthused at the Majestic, Macclesfield, where out of the fifty-one films screened during 1945, *Waterloo Road* ranked thirty-first in terms of attendances.[13] Middle-class audiences had Alastair Sim to guide them through this alien landscape. As the film was described as doing 'huge business' in the West End of London, they must have enjoyed the experience.[14] This success was repeated in socially mixed southeast Essex (Appendix, Table 7). Perhaps for audiences tired of the wartime regulations, the appeal was Mill's defiance of authority – or perhaps it was Stewart Granger being a cad.

By the time the Huggett family were introduced to audiences, the war was over. Ethel and Joe Huggett made their first appearance in Ken Annakin's *Holiday Camp* (1947). The subsequent Huggett films were not intended as sequels. While Annakin was making *Wedding Bells* in the following year, again with Kathleen Harrison and Jack Warner, Harrison suggested using the name Huggett because 'It brought us luck.'[15] *Wedding Bells* was retitled *Here Come the Huggetts* and was followed in 1949 by *Vote for Huggett* and *The Huggetts Abroad*, both directed by Annakin. The couple have three daughters: Jane (Jane Hylton in *Here Come the Huggetts*, Dinah Sheridan in *The Huggetts Abroad*, but missing from *Vote for Huggett*), Susan (Susan Shaw) and Pet (Petula Clark).[16] A script for *Christmas with the Huggetts* was submitted to the BBFC in 1949, but the film was never made.[17] Instead of fading into obscurity, the family reemerged on the BBC Home Service in *Meet the Huggetts*, which became staple Sunday radio listening from 1953 until 1961.[18]

Here Come the Huggetts introduces the family in their suburban home. Joe works in a local factory. Susan and Jane are working, though Pet is still at school. The plot contrasts the wedding of Princess Elizabeth and the Duke of Edinburgh with the ups and downs of Jane's wedding. A subplot involves the complications which ensue when Ethel's niece, Di (Diana Dors), comes to live with the family and Joe persuades his employer to give her a job in the office. In *Vote for Huggett*, Joe is persuaded to stand for the local council, with businessmen on both sides of the political divide hoping to gain from the contest. In *The Huggetts Abroad*, the family set out to emigrate overland to South Africa, but their tribulations in the Sahara cause them to return home.

The Huggett films exemplify the difficulty of attuning to the social hierarchy of another period. The family's social status is described as working class by Murphy and Sarah Street; Jeffrey Richards is more circumspect in defining the Huggetts as upper working/lower middle class, while Landy, less attuned to the nuances of the British class system, ignores their social position entirely.[19] A safe description of their status is transitional, with a working-class outlook confronting the trappings of middle-class life.

Ethel and her ever-complaining mother (Amy Veness) are located firmly within the respectable working class. The bond between mother and daughter is reinforced by Ethel's limited horizons. She is the one who shows most alarm when the prospect of emigrating is mooted. She is equally flustered at the prospect of being thrust into the limelight as a councillor's wife. Joe is more comfortable with upwardly mobility. In *Here Come the Huggetts* he has been promoted from the shop floor, though he is still deferential enough to address his employer, Mr Campbell, as 'sir'. The obvious signs of Joe's newly-acquired status are his car, the telephone and the suit which he wears at home as well as at work. Cars were a rarity for the working class at the time. Rising working-class incomes made the purchase of a car a possibility, but production was aimed at the export market and wartime credit controls were still in place. Using the Hulton Readership Survey definition of working class, 3 per cent of social classes D and E owned one or more cars in 1949, compared with 11.5 per cent of class C (the lower middle class) and 26.5 per cent of classes A and B (the upper middle class).[20] When Joe is called out at night to a fire at the factory, he discovers that one of the younger members of the family has borrowed his car. For a new generation, it represents leisure; for Joe, it is an extension of his work. He resorts to his bicycle. Resplendent in suit and bowler hat, he pedals to the fire. Draped over his shoulder is a stirrup pump, that relic of the war which adorned many garden sheds into the 1950s. Hanging from the handlebars is a bucket of water. This is British improvisation at its best – and at its least effective.

Cost, nonavailability and a lack of cultural acceptance also limited the spread of the telephone, though the number of domestic users increased from 1,196,577 in 1939 to 1,266,275 in 1945 and 1,837,247 in 1950.[21] Joe's promotion necessitates having a telephone at home. Its installation provides an excuse for an extended comedy sequence on the unhelpfulness of the British workman. Ethel's suspicion of the new technology betrays a working-class conservatism which is not shared by the younger generation. It is Pet who has to dial when Ethel wants to speak to Joe at work.[22]

The precariousness of Joe's status becomes apparent when he is demoted as a consequence of Di's incompetence. Later, when it is revealed that Joe has saved the company money, Mr Campbell reverses his decision. In *Vote for Huggett*, Joe is sure enough of his social position to accept an invitation to the golf club. He causes a few sniggers by wearing a check jacket and plus-fours for the occasion. As one of the businessmen remarks, Joe looks like the comedian Sid Field in his famous golfing sketch.

In *The Huggetts Abroad*, Joe is in charge of the packing department at the factory. An accusation of pilfering prompts him to walk out. His speech still retains such working-class idioms as turning a statement into a question: he cannot argue against his dismissal because 'I haven't got any proof, see?' Emigration is the next step. On the journey, Joe becomes unofficial leader by virtue of his age and service experience. He knows how to gain the compliance of foreign customs officials by giving them alcohol, though he addresses senior officers as 'sir'. Serving in the forces has made him a man of the world, as much as being confined to the home has made Ethel parochial, Yet Joe cannot shrug off his working-class origins.

Joe's daughters are difficult to identify in class terms by their voices or their clothes. The blurring of class distinctions in fashions which Ferdynand Zweig detected (see Chapter Two) was also noted by James Laver: 'Often it is quite impossible to tell what class a girl belongs to – until she opens her mouth, or is joined by her boyfriend. The social distinctions in male dress, subtle and obscure as they are, are much more difficult to eliminate.'[23] When the girl does open her mouth in a film, her social status is not always revealed. Middle-class speech can be a jarring intrusion in supposedly working-class homes. If this does not apply to the Huggett films, the reason is in part because the family are not resolutely working class. The point is underlined by the girls' employment: Jane works in Boots' lending library, while Susan begins the series by commuting to an office job. By *Vote for Huggett*, she is working locally as a secretary.

The Huggetts' house is in accord with their transitional status. It is a modest semidetached property, typical of those found on the interwar speculative estates ringing every British town and which were occupied by the respectable working class and the lower ranks of the middle class. Neighbourliness is lacking, as an opening scene of *The Huggetts Abroad* makes clear. Ethel quarrels with the woman next door about Joe's garage, which was built without planning permission – the provisions of the Town and Country Planning Act 1947 came into force on 1 July 1948. Regulations are never far away in films set in the late 1940s. The neighbour also complains about Joe's chickens escaping into her garden. Keeping chickens and rabbits was rooted in preindustrial working-class life, but it assumed greater significance with the war, when eggs were difficult to obtain and rabbit meat helped to eke out rations – providing people could bring themselves to kill what had become family pets. Meat was rationed until 1954.

True to working-class custom, the front room of the Huggetts' house is reserved for special occasions and important visitors. Status is denoted by possessions. This is evident from the corner display cabinet and the ornate china bowl on the table. The front room is where Joe talks to his employer, Mr Campbell, in *Here Come the Huggetts*, and Ethel entertains the alderman's wife in *Vote for Huggett*. It is seen at its best as guests gather for Jane's wedding in *Here Come the Huggetts* and the piano, that status symbol of an earlier age, is pressed into service.

The back room is the living room. The kitchen cabinet, used for storing food, occupies the alcove beside the fireplace. In older houses of this type, a dresser was built in (the free-standing Welsh dresser was not as common in cramped working-class homes as set designers imagined). Food preparation takes place on the living room table. The kitchen is relegated to its traditional role in the working-class household as the scullery, where clothes are washed and the gas cooker and deep, Belfast-pattern sink are sited. The kitchen opens off the rear of the living room rather than being accessed from the hall as in most houses of the period. The range in the living room is an updated version of the Victorian black-leaded monster, but it is recognisably a range. The ground floor layout of the house provides one-room living, essentially the same as in Victorian working-class homes. Coincidently it provides the easiest arrangement for shooting family scenes: Annakin used different camera angles and techniques to suggest breakfast, midday and evening.[24]

The upper floor of the Huggetts' house is more recognisably of its period than the ground floor. Given that bedrooms were not used during the day and were rarely seen by visitors, more money and effort was normally lavished on reception rooms. When cousin Di arrives and the household includes four adolescent girls, lack of privacy still generates tensions as in *It Always Rains on Sunday*. At least Jane can lock herself in the bathroom to get away from the others in *Here Come the Huggetts*.

The film-makers attempted to minimise the gap between screen and audience by giving many of the characters the same forenames as the actors who played them. This makes it difficult to distinguish between Di and Diana Dors. The Dors persona was hardly established when the films were released; if anything, the Huggett films contributed to her reputation rather than drawing upon it. Much the same might be said of Petula Clark, who was condemned to a prolonged screen adolescence.

In each of the Huggett films there are characters who disrupt the smooth progression into lower-middle-class suburban cosiness. One is Harold Hinchley (David Tomlinson), a suitor for Jane in competition with her longtime fiance, Jimmy (Jimmy Hanley). In *Here Come the Huggetts*, Harold is presented as an intellectual, spurning conventions like marriage and forever pursuing Jane in the library. Ray Seaton and Roy Martin comment on how he presents her with an apple, that age-old symbol of temptation.[25] Jane has the opportunity to turn her back on conventional values; instead she signals her acceptance of them by marrying Jimmy. In *Vote for Huggett*, it is Harold's turn to accept them by standing for a seat on the council. He expects to take his place as of right, in spite of knowing nothing of the issues. For his class, power is taken for granted.

The most interesting of the aberrant characters is Ethel's niece, Di (Diana Dors), whose values are so at odds with those of the Huggetts. Her aim is to enjoy herself while doing as little work as possible – a philosophy out of step with austerity Britain, which puts her on the side of the spivs. Her primary asset is her sexuality. Seaton and Martin see Dors as bringing a new type to the British cinema: the office Salome, offending lower-middle-class mores and producing moral indignation. As they note, Annakin seems fascinated by her well beyond her nominal place in the scenario.[26] In *Here Come the Huggetts*, the object of Di's attention is Gowan (John Blythe). It is Gowan who takes Di to a West-End restaurant in Joe's car and who crashes it when driving home after drinking too much. By *Vote for Huggett*, she has married him.

Gowan is the third disruptive force. He is the wartime spiv evolving into the entrepreneur of the 1950s. His motives are

The British working class in postwar film

9 A woman's place: Ethel (Kathleen Harrison) serves breakfast for Joe (Jack Warner) in *Here Come the Huggetts* (1948)

always suspect, notably his hopes of making money out of a land deal in *Vote for Huggett*. His clothes are just too smart for the owner of a small garage, raising questions about how he makes his money. In *Vote for Huggett*, an angry Susan accuses him of 'under-the-counter business', but generally the family are content not to enquire too closely about his business affairs. His contact with the family is usually through Di. This means that the Huggetts' respectability is not compromised by his dubious deals, though as Di reminds him in *Vote for Huggett*, he is one of the family now.

The scenario of *The Huggetts Abroad* precludes any major disruptive acts by Harold, Di or Gowan. Instead, a new character, the diamond smuggler Bob McCoy (Hugh McDermott) is introduced. Though his activities precipitate the family's problems, Susan becomes fond of him, nursing him when he is injured. Effectively he is incorporated into the family, neutralising his disruptive potential, so that another outsider is needed. This is the driver of the second lorry, Starkey (Olaf Pooley), who insists on driving through a dust storm against Joe's advice. Joe is proved right and the lorry breaks down. It is Starkey who sabotages the Huggetts' compass in a fit of pique and who becomes the group's scapegoat. He is knocked out by Joe in a rare display of anger.

If the Huggetts' social status is transitional, *Here Come the Huggetts* can also be seen as transitional in incorporating the shift from the wartime emphasis on community to a narrower focus on the family. The royal wedding should exemplify the community spirit, with a single event drawing people together both metaphorically and physically. So it seems as the Huggetts join the other spectators in camping overnight on the Mall to get a good vantage point (with Ethel and grandma harking back to older habits by wearing hats). The procession is appearing when grandma declares that she is ill, causing the family to abandon their place at the front of the crowd and trail after her. Her illness proves to be a false alarm. The Huggetts' attempts to return to their position at the front of the spectators provokes a fight, the consequence being that the procession is never seen. Even at a royal wedding, community counts for little. The contrast is with Jane's wedding, where Pet sings for the guests as they wait for Jimmy to arrive.

In *Vote for Huggett*, attention turns to local politics. Joe wants to provide a garden for the community, but businessmen and local politicians see opportunities to make money from the deal. The prevailing mood of the film is cynicism with bureaucracy and the political process. Joe's electioneering is amateurish and dependent on Pet and her friends from the youth club, who produce and distribute his election posters. Although he manages to thwart the vested interests, his victory is a long time coming.

In *The Huggetts Abroad*, disillusion with life in Britain is explicit. In this strange amalgam of family drama and adventure story, the family are more than ever thrown onto their own resources by the barrier of language and the isolation of the Sahara. Emigrating is a bold step, but women settle into their traditional roles of cooking and tending the wounded, while men make decisions and take on the driving and shooting. With the prevailing mood of pessimism, it is fitting that the Huggetts fail to reach their promised land. Instead, they end their cinematic triptych by returning home to grandma's never-ending complaints.

For Richards, the Huggetts endorse such established values as family life, sexual responsibility and clearly-defined male and female roles.[27] Joe is never seen doing the shopping. As Ethel points out to grandma in *Vote for Huggett*, he never pushed the pram when the girls were young. Yet it is an evolving family, grappling with enhanced status and new technology. It is of its time.

The Huggett films might be expected to appeal to working-class audiences. In the sample Leeds cinemas, this was not the case (Appendix, Table 6). In southeast Essex, the films met with fair success (Appendix, Table 7). At the Gaumont, Sheffield, only *Here Come the Huggetts* and *The Huggetts Abroad* were screened. They were described as well received and ranked within the first and second quartiles of attendances respectively (Appendix, Table 5).[28] This runs counter to the notion that a regional factor was at work, with a London setting and London people failing to appeal to northern audiences, though the Huggetts' lack of popularity in Leeds after the success of *Holiday Camp* is surprising. High rental costs are an unsatisfactory explanation given that the Leeds cinemas could have afforded the films by 1950, if the demand was there.

A family seen under pressure are the McCabes in *Waterfront* (d. Michael Anderson, 1950). The film, from a novel by John Brophy, is set during the Depression. Peter McCabe (Robert Newton) goes to sea, leaving no money for his family and not communicating with them for years. His wife (Kathleen Harrison) has to bring up their son and two daughters alone. The older daughter, Nora (Avis Scott), hopes to marry ship's engineer, Ben Satterthwaite (Richard Burton), but he loses his job. Her sister, Connie (Susan Shaw), becomes friendly with the affluent but dubious Maurice Bruno (Kenneth Griffith). Peter returns home unexpectedly after walking off his ship. While drinking, he encounters the officer who turned the captain against him. Peter kills his adversary in a fight outside a pub. Without knowing of Peter's involvement, Ben Satterthwaite takes the officer's job. When Peter is charged with murder, Maurice Bruno distances himself from Connie, afraid that his reputation will be tainted. Peter McCabe is visited in prison by the son he does not know. When Ben discovers how he gained the job, he visits Nora, unsure how she will respond. He discovers that their relationship is secure.

Nora is the power in the family. It is Nora who orders her father out of their home when he reappears, expecting to resume his place as head of the family as of right. His wife is ready to forgive him. Peter has no authority outside the home. His lack of responsibility and his drunkenness are stressed, though the demotion from greaser to stoker which prompts him to leave the ship is the consequence of being 'insubordinate' and a 'thorough-going sea lawyer'. Whether his real crime is to challenge authority is not pursued, though he is one of a long line of inadequate fathers found in films about the working class.[29] Whether paternal weakness should be seen as the cause or effect of being working class is never pursued, though drink is often implicated.

The McCabes live in a Liverpool tenement where everybody knows each other's business. One of the neighbours tries to seduce Peter, which gives a measure of community feeling. The McCabes' home is plainly furnished, though the girls have separate beds. Quite how the family afford to let the son take up his scholarship to secondary school is not clear.

Unemployment and the debilitating effects of being in a pool of casual labour are stressed throughout the film. For Peter and his wife, it is a constant accompaniment to their lives. For the officer, Ben, it is harder to bear, affecting his relationship with Nora. Though Nora is working, marriage is out of the question until Ben can be the breadwinner. Only Maurice Bruno stands outside this cycle of poverty. Whether his business, which he describes vaguely as insurance, is entirely legal is something else which is left unexplored, though he is doing well enough to be smartly dressed and to run a car.

In compensation for the sketchy characterisation, location shooting gives the film much of its appeal. Liverpool rarely appears in feature films.[30] The dockland settings are fully exploited, with the overhead railway much in evidence, along with those pre-Beatles symbols of the city, the Liver Building, the Mersey ferry and the department stores Owen Owen and George Henry Lewis. Scouse voices are absent, though desultory attempts at a Lancashire accent are made by the girls. Kathleen Harrison sounds like a recent migrant from the East End of London, though she was born in Lancashire.

The male leads provide the other attraction of the film: Richard Burton for an early starring role and Robert Newton for the strength of his performance. Newton, who had his own struggles with alcohol addiction, portrays a feckless father from the rough working-class, who assumes a peripheral place in *The White Unicorn* and *Good Time Girl*. The prison scene in which Peter shows his pride in his son is impressive and moving. Asking the boy to put on his school cap and recite a poem in Latin reveals with a minimum of effort the pride of the working-class parent and the gulf which education might open between parent and child. Passing on to the boy the tobacco tin which belonged to Peter's own father emphasises the continuity between generations and holds out the possibility that the gulf can be overcome. The irony is that Peter will be probably hanged for murder.

The portentous music over the opening credits (Liszt's *Les Preludes*) promises a dramatic intensity which never materialises. Two weeks after *Waterfront* had its first run in southeast Essex, it reached an independent cinema in the area for a three-day showing before disappearing entirely (Appendix, Table 7). It received more bookings from independents in working-class Leeds, though it played for the same number of days (Appendix, Table 6). In Sheffield, the film was described as 'well received by all types of patrons', but appeared in the third quartile of attendances (Appendix, Table 5).[31] As with *The Gorbals Story* (d. David MacKane, 1950), considered in the previous chapter, there was little taste for reliving the Depression years in the cinema.

The films considered portray the working-class family in interwar, wartime and postwar situations. A contrast of the McCabes with the Huggetts reveals changes in family life over two decades. Joe Huggett is closer to his children than Peter McCabe, while unemployment becomes more an annoyance than a tragedy. The younger generation are gaining from education. The self-confident, articulate youngsters in *Vote for Huggett* have no place in *Waterfront*, where Nora's strength is achieved through struggle. Kathleen Harrison provides a link between both films. She is resolutely working class, subservient and home centred, both as Mrs McCabe and as Ethel Huggett. Change comes from those around her. This conservatism is likely to be the consequence of the scripts and typecasting rather than any limitations in Kathleen Harrison's performances: the character of Ethel was more positive in her later incarnation on the radio, when she was again played by Harrison.

The Colters' home might resemble that of the McCabes, but Jim and Tillie are closer in spirit to the Huggetts, looking forward to life together in suburbia. This is their dream. Film cannot resolve the question of what difference the war makes to their hopes. The problems which beset the Huggetts were familiar to audiences, from Joe's encounters with his cantankerous mother-in-law and Ethel's difficulties in finding any fish other than cod for the family dinner, to Jane's dilemma in choosing between two suitors. The Huggetts epitomise the working-class family making good. It is hard to find another family in postwar British cinema of which this may be said.

Notes

1 Guy L. Pearson, 'The world of celluloid', *British Film Review*, 1:1 (1948), 14.

2 For an analysis of the self-regarding elements in film, see Robert Stam, *Reflexivity in Film and Literature: From Don Quixote to Jean-Luc Godard* (Ann Arbor, MI: UMI Research Press, 1985).

3 Geoff Brown, *Launder and Gilliat* (London: BFI, 1977), p. 111.

4 Marcia Landy, *British Genres: Cinema and Society 1930–1960* (Princeton, NJ: Princeton University Press, 1991), p. 301.

5 Elizabeth Wilson, *Women and the Welfare State* (London: Tavistock, 1977), p. 64.

6 Brown, *Launder and Gilliat*, p. 111.

7 Raymond Durgnat, *A Mirror for England: British Movies from Austerity to Affluence* (London: Faber & Faber, 1970), pp. 20 and 50–1.

8 Richard M. Titmuss, *Problems of Social Policy*, History of the Second World War: United Kingdom Civil Series (London: HMSO and Longmans, Green, 1950), pp. 329–30.

9 A. M. Carr-Saunders, D. Caradog Jones and C. A. Moser, *A Survey of Social Conditions in England and Wales as Illustrated by Statistics* (London: Oxford University Press, 1958), Table 4.2, p. 35.

10 Antonia Lant, *Blackout: Reinventing Women for Wartime British Cinema* (Princeton, NJ: Princeton University Press, 1991), pp. 86–7.

11 Robert Murphy, 'Riff-Raff: British cinema and the underground', in Charles Barr (ed.), *All Our Yesterdays: 90 Years of British Cinema* (London: BFI, 1986), p. 293.

12 Richard Winnington, *Drawn and Quartered* (London: Saturn Press, [1948]), p. 30; Murphy, 'Riff-Raff', p. 293.

13 Julian Poole, 'British cinema attendance in wartime: audience preference at the Majestic, Macclesfield 1939–1946', *Historical Journal of Film, Radio and Television*, 7:1 (1987), Table 7, 26.

14 *Daily Film Renter* (24 January 1945), p. 19.

15 *Kinematograph Weekly* (1 April 1948), p. 34. This is at variance from the impression given by Jeffrey Richards that the Huggett films were a spin-off from *Holiday Camp*. Jeffrey Richards, *Film and British National Identity from Dickens to 'Dad's Army'* (Manchester: Manchester University Press, 1997), p. 143.

16 Dinah Sheridan stepped in when Jane Hylton was ill. Dinah Sheridan, interviewed in Brian McFarlane, *Sixty Voices: Celebrities Recall the Golden Age of British Cinema* (London: BFI, 1992), p. 199.

17 BFI Library, BBFC scenario notes, note 9, 7 February 1949.

18 Paul Donovan, *The Radio Companion* (London: Grafton Books, 1991), pp. 174–5.

19 Robert Murphy, *Realism and Tinsel: Cinema and Society in Britain 1939–49* (London: Routledge, 1992), p. 215; Sarah Street, *British National Cinema* (London: Routledge, 1997), p. 67; Richards, *Film and British National Identity* p. 143; Landy, *British Genres*, pp. 317–18.

20 A. H. Halsey, 'Leisure', in A. H. Halsey (ed.), *Trends in British Society since 1900: A Guide to the Changing Social Structure of Britain* (Basingstoke and London: Macmillan, 1972), Table 16.9, p. 551.

21 BT Archives, 'Telecommunications statistics 1952'.

22 For a similar suspicion of the telephone by a working-class housewife, see Raymond Briggs, *Ethel and Ernest: A True Story* (London: Jonathan Cape, 1998), p. 74.

23 James Laver, 'Fashion and class distinction', in Charles Madge (ed.), *Pilot Papers: Social Essays and Documents* (London: Pilot Press, 1946), pp. 65 and 72.

24 *Kinematograph Weekly* (8 April 1948), p. 34.

25 Ray Seaton and Roy Martin, 'Gainsborough in the forties', *Films and Filming* (June 1982), p. 17.

26 *Ibid.*, p. 17.

27 Richards, *Film and British National Identity*, p. 143.

28 CTA, weekly returns for Gaumont, Sheffield, 22 January 1949 and 1 October 1949.

29 John Hill, *Sex, Class and Realism: British Cinema 1956–1963* (London: BFI, 1986), p. 162.

30 Exceptions are two other 1950 films, *The Clouded Yellow* (d. Ralph Thomas), in which Liverpool docks provide the location for the denouement, and *The Magnet* (d. Charles Frend) (see Chapter Eleven).

31 CTA, weekly returns for Gaumont, Sheffield, 30 September 1950.

6 Going up in the world: goodbye to the working class

If portraying a working-class community poses structural problems in holding together disparate storylines, no such difficulties arise in charting the social advancement of one character. The enduring power of the theme is apparent from the Dick Whittington legend, while the implied element of self-help was beloved of Victorian novelists. In films, a rapid change of class position is often the consequence of winning or losing money. This was a popular story line in the 1930s.[1] It slipped from favour as extremes of poverty and wealth became less evident after the war. Instead, treatments of social mobility came to focus as much on what was lost as what was gained.

Class position is crucial in two Boulting brothers films, though neither does much to illuminate social mobility in postwar days. *Fame is the Spur* (d. Roy Boulting, 1947) charts the rise of Hamer Radshaw (Michael Redgrave) from child of the Manchester slums to Labour cabinet minister. In achieving his ambition, he is distanced from the people whose cause he championed. The film stands apart from those so far discussed in being a political biography, consciously contrasting working-class poverty in the late nineteenth century with subsequent affluence.

Raymond Durgnat interprets the film as an attack on Attlee's administration.[2] Jeffrey Richards and Anthony Aldgate make a convincing case for seeing it as a warning to the Labour government not to repeat the mistakes of the past.[3] The point of agreement is that the work is about the betrayal of socialist principles. The figure of Hamer Radshaw might be found in any Labour administration.

Three sources of power are represented in the film: politics (Hamer), finance (entrepreneur Tom Hannaway) and status (Lady Lettice, upon whose land Hamer once trespassed, but whose social circle increasingly attracts him). The three are not mutually exclusive: Hamer gains status and wealth, while Hannaway becomes a peer. The balance shifts throughout the film, interacting with two more personal forms of power: the power of love, which is denied to Hamer when his wife dies, and the power of youth which slips away over the course of the film, leaving him an old and lonely man who has to be helped to bed.

By the 1970s, television was the home of the rags-to-riches saga. This was more than opportunism on the part of television producers. The television serial is the natural successor to the nineteenth-century serialised magazine story. Leisurely character development and a host of subplots can be accommodated. By comparison, the compression necessary in translating Howard Spring's novel into a film leads to an unrelenting focus on Hamer.[4] The consequence is that ordinary people attending meetings and demonstrations become little more than cyphers. Though dramatically unsatisfactory, this is appropriate in the sense that it is how Hamer comes to see them. As he complains to Lady Lettice (Carla Lehmann), 'Trying to show wider issues to a crowd of working men is like trying to show a picture to a blind man.' The film is a rags-to-riches odyssey which reveals more about the rulers than the ruled.

The Cinema considered the film 'Outstanding entertainment of absorbing interest to all patrons'.[5] The Rank card was more circumspect in recommending it 'for good class houses'. In the event, the film was not a commercial success. As the director later admitted, 'After five years of death, destruction and austerity, *Fame is the Spur* was far too grim for an audience now seeking escapism and peace. It flopped.'[6] Bernard Miles (who played Tom Hannaway) considered that Redgrave was not a popular star, while the role was unsympathetic – a view with which Richards and Aldgate concur.[7] In the sample Leeds cinemas, the film managed a single three-day run (Appendix, Table 6). It did better in southeast Essex (Appendix, Table 7), though it was hardly a box-office hit.

The other Boulting film is *The Guinea Pig* (d. Roy Boulting, 1948), in which tobacconist's son, Jack Read (Richard Attenborough), attends a public school. This is a working out of the recommendations contained in the Fleming Report, which aimed to reduce disparities between education in the state and private sectors. The strategy was not to improve the former, but to fund placement of children from less affluent backgrounds in fee-paying schools. Although Walthamstow in northeast London is an appropriately proletarian location, the father's occupation locates the boy as lower middle class rather than working class. A more serious drawback noted by Richards and Aldgate is that the film adopts the form of the standard public school story familiar from Thomas Hughes' novel *Tom Brown's School Days* (1857), with the unhappy newcomer adapting to his surroundings.[8] Jack's previous life is only revealed indirectly though the reactions of Jack and his parents. Both generations come to accept the values of the school. The social gulf between Jack's father (Bernard Miles), a former sergeant major, and the old housemaster, Hartley (Cecil Trouncer), is bridged by their common belief in team spirit and the virtues of fitting in.

The Boultings saw the film as 'of value domestically because it helps people to understand some of the issues and problems involved in social change,' and to show the world how Britain was 'endeavouring to adjust itself to changing conditions and new ideas'.[9] This implies a reformist agenda which is hard to discern. The film's one concession to progressive thought is when Hartley admits to feeling out of step with the times. Durgnat takes a typically astringent view: 'Isn't Guinea Pig strategy the Trojan Horse which the um-class offer their middle-middle-class antagonists, to separate them from the lower orders?'[10] He neglects to mention that the Trojan horse only contains men. The less partisan Richards and Aldgate compare the responses of critics who had attended public schools and those who had not. Both groups were generally well disposed towards the film.[11]

The Guinea Pig did well at the box office nationally (Appendix, Table 3). Richard Attenborough's boyish charm probably attracted female audiences. The film was successful in southeast Essex, though it gained minimal exposure in working-class Leeds (Appendix, Tables 6 and 7). What audiences there made of it must remain a matter for conjecture.

Once a Jolly Swagman (d. Jack Lee, 1948) fixes the working-class origins of its hero more securely. Bill Fox (Dirk Bogarde) grows discontented with his dead-end job in a factory. Set in 1937, the opening factory scene brings to mind *Saturday Night and Sunday Morning* (d. Karel Reisz, 1960), though Durgnat prefers to draw parallels with *This Sporting Life* (d. Lindsay Anderson, 1963).[12] When Bill is sacked, he ignores his mother's misgivings and becomes a speedway rider. He is encouraged by old hand, Lag Gibbon (Bill Owen), while becoming attracted to Lag's sister, Pat (Renee Asherson). Bill does well, taking over as star of the show after Lag is injured during a race. A rise in income accompanies this rise in status. Bill moves in a new social circle, but he cannot feel at ease there. His discontent is increased by the return of his brother, disillusioned from fighting with the socialists in the Spanish Civil War, and a visit to a nursing home to see Lag, now suffering from depression. In a speech made at his wedding to Pat, Bill declares his intention of fighting for the rights of speedway riders. The other riders are wary of supporting him, suspecting self-interest. As Bill's discontent grows, Pat urges him to give up racing. His response is to leave her and begin a new life in the army. After the war, lack of alternative employment forces him back to the speedway, but his heart is not in it. Finally he is reconciled with Pat.

The differences between the film and Montagu Slater's novel, first published in 1944, are significant.[13] In the novel, Bill is one of seven children. His father is a dustman. The family home in Kentish Town, north London, is precisely located in the neighbourhood around Lismore Road and Maldon Road.[14] A traditional working-class community is evoked:

There are about twenty streets on the side of the hill ending in a little circus of trees. Nobody left the place much except to go to work; and there were plenty of women who knew less about London than people do in Manchester. The local pubs and the flea-pits, ... the billiards-hall, the open-air market gave them all they wanted. The men get about because their work takes them.[15]

The circumscribed background makes the contrast with Bill's fame all the greater. His geographical horizons are further expanded by a speedway tour of South America which is omitted from the film.

The novel focuses on Bill's family relationships and his increasing disgust with himself: 'I was trying to forget the figure I had seen in the mirror, the figure I had become that wasn't really me.'[16] This is translated into increasing risk-taking as he works on a wall of death and eventually joins the commandoes during the war – aspects of his life which again do not figure in the screen version.

The film was targeted at speedway fans: as the poster proclaims, '12,000,000 speedway fans ... will jampack this smashing film [original ellipsis].' Speedway scenes occupy around half the running time, though they only receive passing mention in the novel. Bill's background is moved up the social scale. He is one of three children in a family from the respectable working class. Home is in a 1930s block of council flats in southwest London – far from Kentish Town and not the sort of place where Bill's motorbike would be the only one in the street, which the novel is at pains to emphasise.[17] All this diminishes the extent of Bill's social climb, as does Bogarde's performance. He never convinces as a working-class lad, either in his bearing or his voice. His rise in income is signalled by his choice of clothes and his pencil moustache – an unsettling premonition of his appearance in *Death in Venice* (d. Visconti, 1971) – yet this is never more than Bogarde in a better suit. Thora Hird fits more convincingly into the working-class milieu as Bill's mother.

A sherry party given by Bill's sophisticated girlfriend, Dorothy Liz (Moira Lister), epitomises the shift of emphasis between novel and film. In the latter, Bill is annoyed by the shallowness of her pretentious, art-loving companions and orders her to get rid of them. When she refuses, he makes a petulant exit, leaving his fellow rider, Tommy Possey (Bonar Colleano), to move effortlessly between the social groups. In the novel, Bill's disgust is internalised: 'I saw my smart alec suit and my way of wearing it, my way of standing and swaggering about: and I knew why none of those people were taking any notice of me. I was just another of the wide boys, and not quite wide enough.' [18]

Marcia Landy comments on the orgiastic effect of speedway on female audiences shown in the film, though she omits to mention their youth.[19] Their numbers support Ross McKibbin's contention that women found speedway racing more attractive than rugby or football.[20] Within ten years they changed their allegiance, with similar scenes greeting rock and roll films. The militaristic quality of the speedway scenes is also worthy of note. Before the racing begins, mechanics and St John Ambulance Brigade members parade around the track, marching in step to music blaring from the speakers. This is solidarity to gladden the heart of any dictator.

The novel ends in wartime; the film grafts on postwar scenes. Bill's interview at a labour exchange after his demobilisation points up the reversal of his social mobility. It also offers a clash of perspectives as the lower-middle-class bureaucrat pigeonholes Bill as lacking in workplace skills, only to be disconcerted when Bill reveals his prewar earnings. Less satisfactorily, the postwar additions include a stereotyped ending: happiness is being married to a good woman.

The novel's translation to screen emphasises the thrills of the speedway, the cost being some loss of characterisation. The omission of Bill's plunge into the classless world of the commandoes, where action is all, is probably deliberate given the public's lack of interest in war films at the time (see Chapter Three). The novel's first person exploration of the costs of social mobility is replaced by an overt socialism which seems out of character. The overall impression is of unease about dealing with class by the director, who co-scripted the film. This leaves the actors to stake out their own

10 'You're going on with it': Mrs Fox (Thora Hird) worries about Bill (Dirk Bogarde) as he tells of his divorce in *Once a Jolly Swagman* (1948). A council flat from the interwar years

class positions with varying degrees of success. Durgnat interprets this as middle-class moralising, in spite of his admiration for the film.[21]

Of the country's twelve million speedway fans, most of those living in southeast Essex must have seen the film, judging by its success there (Appendix, Table 7). At the Gaumont, Sheffield, the supporting feature was a Canadian documentary, *The Connors Case* (1948). The pairing was described as 'a poor programme' which received 'a mixed reception' and came in the third quartile of attendances (Appendix, Table 5).[22] Neither the 1947 nor the 1949 issue of the Post Office *Classified Directory* for Leeds, Bradford and York lists a speedway in Leeds; with this lack of interest, the film's single run of three days in the sample cinemas there is unsurprising (Appendix, Table 6). This variable response mirrors the patchy popularity of speedway, which was centred in working-class areas of London and the southeast and was probably past its peak by the time the film was released.

Like *The Gorbals Story* (d. David MacKane, 1950), *Floodtide* (d. Frederick Wilson, 1949) is set in Glasgow, though it focuses more explicitly on social mobility. Orphan David Shields (Gordon Jackson) leaves the family croft to work in a Glasgow shipyard. He makes friends with another apprentice, Tim Brogan (Jimmy Logan), sharing his room before taking up lodgings of his own. The owner of the shipyard, Mr Anstruther (Jack Lambert), notices David's potential and promotes him to the drawing office while encouraging him to take evening classes. David's progress is such that he is allowed to design a ship for a client, Senor Arandha. David's social contact with his employer means that he sees a lot of Mr Anstruther's daughter, Mary (Rona Anderson). The evening before the launch, Mr Anstruther entertains Senor Arandha. Mary is put out when David tells her that he cannot attend because he has already promised to go to Tim Brogan's engagement party. In a storm, a barge breaks free and threatens to damage the ship's propellor. Mary tries to warn David, but he has left the party. After scouring Glasgow, she finds him with Judy, a girl from the party whom he met on first coming to the city. David saves the ship, but fails to appear at the launch. Mary knows his haunts. She seeks him out and they resolve their differences.

Paternalism and Calvinism permeate the film. Paternalism is evident on the part of Mr Anstruther. (Jack Lambert's characterisation makes Anstruther look disconcertingly like J. Arthur Rank.) David's lodgings are recommended by the company and his fees for evening classes are paid by the company. Loyalty is expected – and given – on both sides. This extends to David being accepted in his employer's house more or less as a social equal.

Calvinism is often evident in prickly Scots characters, Richard Todd's Corporal Lachlan McLachlan in *The Hasty Heart* (d. Vincent Sherman, 1949) being a notable example. In *Floodtide* it is exemplified not only in David's devotion to his work, but in the horror of his landlady, Mrs McTavish (Molly Weir), when she returns home to find him entertaining his friends in the parlour. Alcohol, dancing and playing the piano all come in for her disapproval. She threatens to tell Mr Anstruther what has happened in her report on her tenant – another paternalistic touch. David's insistence on keeping his promise to attend Tim Brogan's engagement party in the face of Mary Anstruther's displeasure may be seen as an example of Calvinism; more convincingly it can be interpreted in class terms as a choice between social groups, or in personal terms as a clash of loyalties. The same range of interpretations can be brought to his choice between the sensuous Judy (Elizabeth Sellars) and the rich, clean-living Mary Anstruther. The film sides with Mary.

Exterior shots of Glasgow are all too brief, providing little opportunity to share the wonderment of a country boy encountering

11   Home on the tram: Tim Brogan (Jimmy Logan) tries on the 'wee hard hat' which signals that David Shields (Gordon Jackson) is going up in the world in *Floodtide* (1949)

city life. Mrs McTavish's parlour is seen to advantage. As befits the home of a lower-middle-class widow, it is furnished in Edwardian style and is markedly larger than Tim Brogan's tenement room with its bed-recess behind the door. The lowest rung of the social ladder is represented by Judy's comfortless room. The comparison is with the spaciousness of the Anstruthers' home.

Status is determined by age as much as class. David's friends defer to Mrs McTavish. In the shipyard, the sheds are presided over by older men, their status signified by suits and bowler hats. David has to buy a bowler when he is promoted from the plating shed to the drawing office. He tries unsuccessfully to hide it from Tim Brogan as they travel home on the tram. In his new post, David comes into conflict with the manager, though eventually the older man admits his grudging admiration for David's design.

The film betrays an ambivalence towards the working class. Getting on is seen as a good thing by David's grandmother and his uncle, Joe Drummond (John Laurie), who in another example of paternalism knows Mr Anstruther and is instrumental in getting David the job. Equally, loyalty to a workmate, Tim Brogan, is presented as an admirable quality. The message is that working-class life can be left behind by a combination of hard work and knowing the right people, but friends are still friends. Though the two strands hold the potential for conflict, it comes too late in the film. Only the final scenes grip the attention, as the spurned Judy attacks David with a bottle before he battles to control the drifting barge.

Floodtide was released as a main feature on the Gaumont circuit, supported by the American semidocumentary *Canon City* (d. Crane Wilbur, US 1948). At the Gaumont, Sheffield, this coupling attracted the lowest weekly attendance in the four years examined (Appendix, Table 5). The film found little favour among the independents in either Leeds or southeast Essex (Appendix, Tables 6 and 7). Nor has it received any subsequent critical attention, the exception being George Perry, who singles out the use of actuality footage.[23] This is the film's glory. In its evocation of Glasgow shipyards after the war, *Floodtide* is unique among feature films and undeserving of neglect.

Another regional film which fared badly at the box office was *Blue Scar* (d. Jill Craigie, 1949). The action takes place in a south Wales mining valley in the late 1940s. Olwen Williams (Gwynneth Vaughan), wins a scholarship to music college in Cardiff. She is congratulated by Alfred Collins (Anthony Pendrell), an industrial psychologist who visits her office and is attracted to her. Her boyfriend, Tom Thomas (Emrys Jones), is a miner who loves the valleys and knows that he will lose her if she goes away. His fears prove well founded.

While Olwen is away, her father is brought home from the pit after an accident – the film gets its title from the characteristic blue tinge which coal dust brings to cuts. When he dies, Olwen returns for the funeral. She reveals to Tom that she is marrying Alfred as the best way of helping her mother.

Tom witnesses a dispute in which a miner strikes a deputy who puts output above safety. Tom's dilemma is that in testifying against the deputy, his promised promotion to under manager is jeopardised. The consequence of following the deputy's orders is a roof fall in which Tom is injured. He is sent to a convalescent home where his physiotherapist is Glynis, whom he knew before his relationship with Olwen.

The deputy is pressured into admitting that he provoked the miner, so that Tom's evidence is no longer needed. When Tom is promoted to management, he goes to see Olwen in London, where she is establishing a career as a singer. Glynis is afraid that she will lose him, but does not try to dissuade him. He urges Olwen to go back to Wales, but she refuses. The world of her new friends is alien to Tom and he returns to the Welsh valleys and to Glynis.

The love–hate relationship between the miner and his work is summed up by Olwen's father as he looks down on the valley: 'I've cursed this place many a long year. Today I'm thinking it's beautiful.' The photography hardly offers a nostalgic view of the terraced houses clustered under belching factory chimneys. The scenery dwarfs the inhabitants, most noticeably when the ant-like figures are seen climbing the hillside to a football match. The image reappears in *Hell Is a City* (d. Val Guest, 1960).

The men's clothes are little changed from D. H. Lawrence's day, but material changes in the life of the miner such as pit baths are acknowledged. When Olwen's father is brought home in an ambulance, a neighbour remarks that 'They bring them in lovely these days – all washed and cleaned.' At the same time, traditional values are stressed. When Olwen's brother misses his shifts at the pit, their father puts in extra shifts so that the family will not get a reputation for absenteeism. For grandma, waiting for the football results on the wireless so that she can check her coupon, 'Everything's something for nothing, these days – a five-day week, holidays with pay. That's what comes when the God-fearing goes out of people.' She does have the grace to feel guilty about doing the pools.

In spite of the conservatism, change is at the heart of the film – change which does not always proceed as anticipated. There is social change as the pits are nationalised, albeit with misgivings on both sides. On telling Tom of his impending promotion, the manager declares that 'Nationalisation, ideals and business don't go together.' The miners feel that all the public wants is cheap coal, irrespective of the human cost. There is also personal change. Olwen breaks free of the valleys and acquires upper-middle-class friends and acquaintances, as well as discovering the limits of her talent. Tom announces early in the film that he will 'get a job that people respect. Something with a cup of tea in the middle of the morning. Adding up figures – that's what they like.' Yet he too compromises his socialist principles in becoming an under manager, distancing himself from the men he worked alongside at the coalface.

Class is presented in simplistic terms, middle-class characters being depicted as shallow, out of touch with working people and self-obsessed. When the industrial psychologist is asked why he does not respond to the lack of secretarial support by typing his own letters, he explains, 'Well if I did that, how would anyone know I was important?' By contrast, working-class people derive solidarity from working at the pit, following their football team and

– this being Wales – from singing. This gives an irony to Olwen's radio broadcast of 'Home Sweet Home' at the end of the film: she sang 'Bless This House' with her family at the beginning.

The film attempts to offer a realistic view of working-class people. In this it was out of the run of feature films, but novelty alone was not enough to ensure commercial success. *Kinematograph Weekly* judged the film 'Doubtful booking ... for the general run of halls'.[24] The Rank card was scarcely more enthusiastic, concluding that the film 'Will appeal to the thinking types who like natural realistic drama.' Not many of these turned out in Leeds, which was a coal-mining area. The film only managed a three-day run in the sample cinemas there (Appendix, Table 6). It ran as a second feature in southeast Essex, which makes its apparent success misleading (Appendix, Table 7).

Blue Scar was unusual in being directed by a woman and being made away from London – a disused cinema in Port Talbot was used as a studio.[25] Durgnat lumps the film among the documentaries, dismissing it as dreary and stilted.[26] More charitably, the miner in the film was probably correct in his summing up of British society: people were content to forget his kind now that nationalisation should have resolved their grievances. *Blue Star* offers little relief from the dourness of the mining, while the documentary style and socialist stance give the film the feel of a Labour Party polemic from the 1930s. A decade was to pass before industrial landscapes became fashionable in the new wave of British realist films.

Rags to riches was not a popular theme in contemporary film drama of the 1940s, though its use in costume dramas including *Blanche Fury* (d. Marc Allégret, 1948) and *The Reluctant Widow* (d. Bernard Knowles, 1950), together with the success of *The Guinea Pig*, suggest that the problem lay less in the theme per se than how it was treated. Following the struggles of a star to overcome obstacles had an appeal to audiences which was lacking if the subject was treated in a documentary style. *Once a Jolly Swagman* had Bogarde, but he was not yet a star. Only *The Guinea Pig* could offer a star, albeit a minor one, in Richard Attenborough.

Floodtide, *The Guinea Pig*, *Fame is the Spur* and *Blue Scar* emphasise the importance of education in getting on, as opposed to luck, birth, looks or talent. Though the cinema industry was hardly an exemplar of its own dictum, the message was in accord with the egalitarian principles of the Welfare State. Reality was different. War threw the education system into disarray. Working-class children from inner city areas had their schooling disrupted by evacuation, teachers entering the services, bomb damage (20% of school buildings were damaged or destroyed) and breakdowns in administration leading to truancy and failure to take up scholarships.[27] Richard Titmuss noted the deterioration of spelling, reading, history, geography and arithmetic among pupils of thirteen and fourteen in 1943 when compared with their counterparts in 1924 – a deterioration which was confirmed when boys entered the army in 1946 and 1947 – though Richie Calder took the optimistic view that teachers were tested as imagination and improvisation replaced set course work.[28] Butler's Education Act 1944 was not necessarily an advance. Selection for grammar school places under the new system depended on the eleven-plus examination. This was predicated on a conceptual approach to knowledge which accorded with Basil Bernstein's elaborated speech code and disadvantaged working-class children. In Middlesbrough grammar schools, the allocation of manual workers' sons dropped from 58 per cent in 1939–44 to 54 per cent in 1948–51; there was a smaller reduction in southwest Hertfordshire according to the same London School of Economics study.[29] Of entrants to two Wiltshire grammar schools in 1952, 65 per cent had been coached for the entrance examination, which gave them an average rise in IQ of 14 points.[30] This undermined the assumption behind the eleven-plus examination that intelligence was innate. Reassessments of the evidence have given a more optimistic picture, but how much the working class really gained from the reforms in education remains an open question.[31]

This litany of educational failures, proven or unproven, is predicated on the assumption that the values of a middle-class educational system were desirable. It might be argued that they were antithetical to working-class culture, separating working-class children from their cultural roots. The much-vaunted secondary education for all only amounted to an extra year at school, reinforcing a distrust for authority among children who went unwillingly to secondary modern schools teaching a syllabus seemingly irrelevant to everyday life. Going to the cinema provided an opportunity for these working-class adolescents to choose how they spent their time before employment and marriage restricted their options. Studies showing that secondary modern school pupils went to the cinema more than their counterparts in grammar schools bear reassessing from this viewpoint.[32] Perhaps secondary modern pupils were being realistic about their life chances. *Look Back in Anger* (d. Tony Richardson, 1959) and *Billy Liar* (d. John Schlesinger, 1963) were to demonstrate that education alone did not necessarily bring liberation from the confining effects of a working-class background.

Notes

1 Stephen C. Shafer, *British Popular Films 1929–1939: The Cinema of Reassurance* (London: Routledge, 1997), ch. 6 and 7.

2 Raymond Durgnat, *A Mirror for England: British Movies from Austerity to Affluence* (London: Faber & Faber, 1970), pp. 67 and 234.

3 Jeffrey Richards and Anthony Aldgate, *Best of British: Cinema and Society 1930–1970* (Oxford: Basil Blackwell, 1983), pp. 75–8.

4 Howard Spring, *Fame is the Spur* (London: Collins, 1940).

5 *The Cinema* (24 September 1947), p. 19.

6 Roy Boulting, interviewed in Brian McFarlane, *Sixty Voices: Celebrities Recall the Golden Age of British Cinema* (London: BFI, 1992), p. 34.

7 Bernard Miles, interviewed in *ibid.*, p. 167; Richards and Aldgate, *Best of British*, p. 84.

8 *Ibid.*, p. 89.

9 Roy and John Boulting, 'Why we made *The Guinea Pig*', *Cinema Studio* (supplement to *The Cinema*) (14 April 1948), p. 11.

10 Durgnat, *A Mirror for England*, p. 34.

11 Richards and Aldgate, *Best of British*, pp. 95–7.

12 Durgnat, *A Mirror for England*, pp. 151–2.

13 Montagu Slater, *Once a Jolly Swagman* (London: John Lane, The Bodley Head, 1944).

14 *Ibid.*, pp. 53–4.

15 *Ibid.*, p. 8.

16 *Ibid.*, p. 50.

17 *Ibid.*, p. 10.

18 *Ibid.*, p. 47.

19 Marcia Landy, *British Genres: Cinema and Society 1930–1960* (Princeton, NJ: Princeton University Press, 1991), p. 265.

20 Ross McKibbin, *Classes and Cultures: England 1918–1951* (Oxford: Oxford University Press, 1998), p. 365.

21 Durgnat, *A Mirror for England*, pp. 51–2.

22 CTA, weekly returns for Gaumont, Sheffield, 19 March 1949.

23 George Perry, *The Great British Picture Show from the 90s to the 70s* (London: Hart-Davis, MacGibbon, 1974), pp. 146–7.

24 *Kinematograph Weekly* (14 April 1949), p. 20.

25 *Kinematograph Weekly* (15 April 1948), p. 7, and (24 June 1948), p. xxxiii.

26 Durgnat, *A Mirror for England*, p. 122.

27 Richie Calder, 'The school child', in Richard Padley and Margaret Cole (eds), *Evacuation Survey: A Report to the Fabian Society* (London: Routledge, 1940), p. 153; H. C. Dent, *Education in Transition: A Sociological Study of the Impact of War on English Education 1939–1943* (London: Kegan Paul, Trench, Trubner, 1944); Richard M. Titmuss, *Problems of Social Policy*, History of the Second World War: United Kingdom Civil Series (London: HMSO and Longmans, Green, 1950), pp. 404–9; Paul Addison, *Now the War Is Over: A Social History of Britain 1945–1951* (London: BBC and Jonathan Cape, 1985), p. 145.

28 Titmuss, *Problems of Social Policy*, pp. 408–9; Calder, 'The school child', p. 152.

29 J. E. Floud (ed.), A. H. Halsey and F. M. Martin, *Social Class and Educational Opportunity* (London: Heinemann Educational, 1956), p. 38.

30 *Times Education Supplement* (1 February 1952), cited in H. C. Dent, *Growth in English Education 1946–1952* (London: Routledge & Kegan Paul, 1954), pp. 71–2.

31 Jean Floud, 'Social class factors in educational achievement', in Maurice Craft (ed.), *Family, Class and Education: A Reader* (London: Longman, 1970), pp. 31–48; Alan Little and John Westergaard, 'The trend of class differentials in educational opportunity in England and Wales', *British Journal of Sociology*, 15 (1964), 301–16; Geoff Payne, *Mobility and Change in Modern Society* (Basingstoke and London: Macmillan, 1987).

32 For a full listing, see Philip J. Gillett, 'British feature films and working-class culture 1945–50', Ph.D. thesis, University of North London, 2000, Appendix 2.

7 The wrong side of the law: who were the criminals?

Three groups of criminals make regular appearances in postwar British films. The first are the spivs. These black market traders are young, opportunistic and distinguishable by their clothes. Their adroitness in keeping a step ahead of authority stands them in good stead for evading conscription. The second group have served in the forces, but cannot adjust to civilian life. Many are officers down on their luck. The skills acquired in the services are turned to criminal purposes, though often the film-makers are at pains to emphasise that these men are not inherently bad. The third group are career criminals. The films in which they appear may make no reference to the war, so that the stories can take on a timeless quality. The three groups of criminals may interact, adding the conflict of competing perspectives to the drama of crime and its detection. Waiting in the wings was a fourth group – juvenile delinquents. These came to the fore in the 1950s and will be considered in the next chapter.

The spiv arose from a working-class subculture on the fringes of the underworld. He was a new phenomenon for the British cinema. What made him cinematic was his clothing. The well-cut suit with its wide lapels was the antithesis of the ill-fitting suit presented to every serviceman on demobilisation. Shirts were coloured or striped rather than the conventional white. Ties were ostentatious. Accessories such as a handkerchief in the breast pocket were favoured. To complete the image of conspicuous consumption, the hair was carefully tended and longer than the regulation short back and sides of service life. The effect was often complemented by a pencil moustache. As Bill Naughton explained, 'It's just that bit of style and poise, that knowing you're different

from the ordinary run of fellows – that's what makes a spiv.'[1] Thus
Tommy Swann in *It Always Rains on Sunday* (d. Robert Hamer,
1947) is a spiv, while the gang who steal roller skates in the same
film are petty criminals. Not that a spiv would be averse to stealing
roller skates, given the opportunity. In Naughton's words, 'He'll
swindle at cards, on a dog-track, or anywhere. He'll do anybody.
And he ain't ashamed of it. One point is he'll not moan if somebody
does him. And his motto is: "Get all I can for myself."'[2]

Forty years on, Trevor Blackwell and Jeremy Seabrook's bottom-
up perspective has the benefit of hindsight:

The spiv, and the yearning for prohibited luxuries which he embodied,
was a symbol to those who might see their way to making big money
out of the long history of privation and poverty of so many working
people. He is also a reminder that many working-class pleasures have
been illicit, and that the majority of working-class people have proved
much more adept at learning to play the system rather than to
transform it.[3]

By this interpretation, the spiv belongs in the working-class community and hones his skills there. It contrasts with Ross McKibbin's
contention that black marketeers were objectionable to the working class because they infringed the principles of fair play.[4] Whose
principles McKibbin is invoking is not clear. Alan Jenkins may be
more anecdotal, but his assessment, based on first-hand knowledge, is that fiddling was a way of life after the war.[5] Miki Cogswell
echoes this: 'Nobody thought of it as breaking the law. We
thought ... we were clever in beating the government.'[6]

Naughton saw the spiv as coming from the East End of London.[7]
Though the black market was not an exclusively metropolitan
affair, what remains unclear is whether the spiv was primarily a
London phenomenon – or how much London-based film-makers
fostered this notion in other parts of the country. Equally difficult
to gauge is his economic importance. By its nature, the black
economy eludes accurate measurement. From a study of five towns,
Edward Smithies concludes that Britain survived the 1940s
without a serious black market developing, though other towns
might yield a different picture.[8]

Though spivs rarely take a leading role in films, an exception who
cannot be ignored is Pinkie in *Brighton Rock* (d. John Boulting,
1947), produced by Roy Boulting. Pinkie Brown (Richard Attenborough) is a youth heading a protection racket in Brighton.
Colleoni is a gangster on a grander scale who offers to take over
his business. When Pinkie spurns the offer, his face is slashed as a
warning. A more immediate problem is his involvement in the

death of Hale, a journalist who was unwise enough to return to Brighton as part of a publicity stunt after exposing the gangs in the press. Two people can incriminate Pinkie. One is the oldest member of the gang, Spicer (Wylie Watson), who is losing his nerve; the other is Rose (Carol Marsh), a naive waitress who noticed Spicer in the cafe where she works, where he was leaving Hale's card as a alibi. Pinkie's solution is to kill Spicer and marry Rose, so that she cannot testify against him. He reckons without Ida (Hermione Baddeley), who works in an entertainment troupe. She befriended Hale in his final hours and becomes convinced of Pinkie's involvement in his death, though the police treat it as a heart attack. She tries to warn Rose of Pinkie's motives, but the girl refuses to listen. To free himself, Pinkie talks Rose into a suicide pact on the pier, in which she will be the first to kill herself. Ida alerts the police. As they close in, Pinkie jumps into the water and drowns.

A caption at the start of the film assures the audience that the action could not take place in present-day Brighton. This might have placated the residents of Brighton who objected to the adverse publicity, but Tim Pulleine doubts the veracity of the assurance.[9] He does not cite Pinkie's clothes as evidence. Similarly, Jeffrey Richards ignores Pinkie's clothes in placing him among the first of the juvenile delinquents.[10] Aside from the fact that heading a criminal gang puts him in a league above the petty and opportunist thieving of the delinquent, Pinkie's clothes are those of the postwar spiv in all his finery. By comparison, the Pinkie of the novel, first published in 1938, is a seedy character spawned by the Depression years. He lives by his wits in true working-class fashion, but Greene stresses his shabbiness, particularly his frayed tie.[11] In the film, Pinkie's involvement in protection rackets rather than the black market betrays his prewar origins. Whether Greene sanctioned the updating or whether this was instigated by the director and costume designer is not clear.

The novel ends with Rose confessing to a priest that she wants to be damned like Pinkie. The film ends with Rose telling a nun of her love for Pinkie. She plays the record which he made for her in a booth. It is faulty and all she hears is Pinkie endlessly repeating 'I love you.' She never discovers that he goes on to reveal his contempt of her. With this theatrical device, the repeated words can be juxtaposed against Rose's seraphic expression and the image of the cross on the wall. Visual symbolism is used in a way which would be hard to achieve using Greene's literary approach. It allows 'anyone who wanted a happy ending to feel they had a happy ending', in Greene's enigmatic words, though Attenborough recalls that Greene was unhappy with the change.[12] Richard Winnington was among those who criticised the revised ending, but Pinkie's fate in the novel would be unacceptable on screen: the bottle of vitriol he is holding is broken by a policeman's truncheon and spills over his face, making him stumble in agony and fall to his death over a cliff.[13] Whichever ending is preferred, beyond it loom the unanswered questions posed by Greene: is there a God and does hell exist? Pinkie seems to be testing both propositions to their limits.

Marcia Landy ignores the religious dimension. Instead, 'Rebellious, youthful behaviour has to be "explained" in psychological terms, contained through therapeutic strategies, and, when the therapy fails, corrected. The excessiveness of the affect embodied in Pinkie and Rosie's relationship raises questions ... about the film's motive for linking sexuality and criminality.'[14] This is a curious reading which is difficult to reconcile with what appears on screen, particularly as Landy never clarifies what she means by 'therapeutic strategies'. Sexuality and criminality are linked more explicitly in the novel – certainly more than film censors would allow – while Pinkie's lack of sexual experience is repeatedly stressed. Something different and equally disturbing appears on screen. Taking a cue from the dialogue, Greene is reworking the Faust legend as Pinkie makes a pact with the devil. Catholicism is less prominent than in the novel: it is not mentioned during the first third of the film. Shorn of the solace of redemption, the audience is left with an unrelenting focus on the nature of evil embodied in Pinkie. As Pulleine puts it, there is an increasingly intense sense of being trapped within the malign protagonist's psyche.[15]

Greene's exploration of evil is echoed in the photography of Harry Waxman. From Pinkie's underworld, the camera peers up at faces, allowing glimpses of ceilings, which are rarely seen on film sets and which heighten the sense of claustrophobia in interior scenes. The element of distortion caused by the camera angle brings a grotesque quality to the faces. Allied to this are the deep shadows achieved by lighting scenes predominantly from one side, usually from a higher level and often through a window – a device used in Pinkie's room. In the police station, the inspector is first seen from shoulder height. When Pinkie appears, the camera adopts a lower level as he draws the policeman into his world. The unrelenting focus on Pinkie is enhanced by long takes, notably as he leaves the inspector's office along a corridor, passing Ida on the way. The camera seems mesmerised by him.

For Winnington, 'The girl (Carol Marsh), plump and nice instead of peaked and tortured, scrapes by except in moments of grief when suburbia breaks relentlessly through her voice.'[16] If Marsh's performance lacks something in expression, she does convey innocence. Nor is niceness inappropriate if it contrasts with Pinkie's malevolence. But it is Attenborough who continually draws the eye. The pity is that in a long acting career, he played so few villains.

The film might be expected to fall foul of the censors. As James Robertson makes clear, it was passed uncut after the Boulting brothers and Greene made amendments to the script, though Greene later considered that the script was 'slashed'.[17] Little violence appears on screen. Hale's murder takes place on a fairground ride, with a sequence of grotesque masks substituting for violence. The racecourse scene in which Spicer is to be killed by Colleoni's gang begins in menacing fashion, with men converging on the camera which is at ground level, but the fight develops into a lighthearted free-for-all as an evangelist carrying a placard proclaiming 'The wages of sin is death' breaks it over his opponent's head. Nor is there much low-life dialogue to upset the censors, though its absence does not detract from the seedy milieu or the atmosphere of depravity which the film evokes. A few dropped consonants and the unmistakable working-class tones of Hermione Baddeley and William Hartnell are enough.

Nationally, *Brighton Rock* did well at the box office (Appendix, Table 3). This success was emulated in southeast Essex, though not in working-class Leeds, probably because high rental costs limited bookings (Appendix, Tables 6 and 7). Since then, Greene's cinematic collaboration with Carol Reed has overshadowed *Brighton Rock*, yet rather than being a prentice piece, the film ranks with *The Third Man* (1949) as a study of evil. They are progenitors of a clutch of unsettling British films, notably *Peeping Tom* (d. Michael Powell, 1959), *The Sorcerers* (d. Michael Reeves, 1967), *Witchfinder General* (d. Michael Reeves, 1968) and *The Wicker Man* (d. Robin Hardy, 1973). The Boultings' middle-brow reputation has not helped *Brighton Rock*, but it should not be allowed to overshadow their achievement in bringing to the screen a working-class character in all his psychological complexity, however malign.

Demobilisation spawned several films in which the protagonist leaves service life to take the path to easy money. *Night Beat* (d. Harold Huth, 1948) contrasts the careers of two wartime comrades, one of whom joins the police, while the other goes to the bad. A similar device is used in *Dancing with Crime* (d. John Paddy Carstairs, 1947), to be considered in Chapter Nine. In *The Flamingo*

Affair (d. Horace Shepherd, 1948) a former army captain works as a garage mechanic until he comes under the spell of a female black-marketeer.[18] Another of these figures is Clem Morgan in *They Made Me a Fugitive* (d. Cavalcanti, 1947).

Clem (Trevor Howard) is an RAF officer who finds civilian life monotonous and turns to drink. He finds work with a gang of black marketeers headed by Narcey (Griffith Jones), whose cover is a funeral director's business. Clem changes his mind when he discovers that Narcey deals in drugs, but he has already agreed to take part in a robbery. This goes ahead and in the getaway, Narcey orders Soapy (Jack McNaughton) to drive at a policeman who attempts to stop their car. When Clem tries to wrest control of the wheel, the car crashes, killing the policeman. Narcey drags the unconscious Clem into the driver's seat before fleeing. As the only member of the gang to be captured, Clem is sent to Dartmoor Prison for fifteen years.

Sally (Sally Gray) is Narcey's girlfriend. In a fit of jealousy, she visits Clem in prison to tell him that his girlfriend is seeing Narcey. She also reveals that Soapy might be willing to testify against Narcey. Clem escapes, returning to London in a bid to find Soapy, who has gone into hiding. The police recapture Clem, but the inspector is unhappy with Clem's conviction and shows more interest in discovering the gang's new hideout. He releases Clem, using him as bait to lure the others into the open. Meanwhile, Narcey tortures Cora (Rene Ray) into revealing where Soapy, her boyfriend, is hiding. Soapy is killed before Clem can get to him. Narcey also kidnaps Sally, knowing that Clem will turn to her for help. The place which Clem is sure to visit is the funeral parlour. Narcey sets a trap there, but with Sally's help Clem overcomes the gang. There is a rooftop confrontation between Narcey and Clem in which Narcey falls to his death.

At first sight, Narcey's activities mark him as a spiv. Sally calls him 'Cheap, rotten, after-the-war trash', though his association with Clem suggests that he is more interested in social climbing than most of his kind. His justification for having Clem in the gang is that 'He's got class. We need a bit of that in our business. Not that I ain't got it meself, but he was born with it.' Touches such as the cigarette holder and the monogram of a narcissus on his shirt, ring and handkerchief confirm his social aspirations (his nickname is an abbreviation of narcissus). Nor do spivs generally involve themselves in drug dealing when a quick profit can be made from nylons, alcohol and cigarettes.

The other members of the gang are distrustful of what they call an 'ama-ture', though it is debatable whether their real concern

Who were the criminals?

is Clem's lack of expertise or his class. The only woman in the gang is the mother figure, Aggie (Mary Merrall), who constantly warns Narcey not to go too far. She tries to keep up standards, admonishing the men, 'I haven't stooped to wiping my nose on my shirttails, mentioning no names.' Narcey's speech is working class and recognisably London-based in its inflexion (the gang's hideout is in Lambeth, south London, in the arch of a railway viaduct). Narcey is proud of his achievement. As he explains to Clem, 'I ain't a amateur [prounced 'ama-tewer'] mucking about for the fun of it. I built up this business from nufink and I'm the boss.' On taking the drugs from the coffin loaded with nylons, he boasts, 'That's the stuff that builds bonny, bouncing babies, my boy. There's more mazuma in that there packet than you'll see in a month of foggy Fridays.' This is a literary and dated form of cockney speech which drew criticism to Gordon Harker in the 1930s.[19] It accords with the look of the film, which has the trappings of the 1940s, but belongs in a Victorian underworld of gas-lit alleys, chorus girls and London characters, all lovingly shot in deep-focus photography. The opening scene of a horse-drawn hearse stopping outside the funeral parlour would not look out of place in Cavalcanti's *Nicholas Nickleby*, released four months earlier. Similarly, the extended stage scene in *They Made Me a Fugitive* recalls *Champagne Charlie* (1944), which revealed the Brazilian director's fascination with Victorian music hall. The excuse for its inclusion is that Sally earns her living as a dancer and is demonstrably not dependent on Narcey.

The most likeable character is the amiable and middle-class Inspector Rockliffe (Ballard Berkeley), who never loses his temper and who never seems surprised by the ways of the underworld. When Clem escapes, the inspector anticipates that Narcey will use Sally as bait and is waiting outside her door when Narcey arrives. The two men exchange banter:

INSPECTOR: I say, how's the undertaking business these days?
NARCEY: Booming. I wish I could interest you in one of our new models.
INSPECTOR: Utility?
NARCEY: From you, we wouldn't ask dockets.
INSPECTOR: I'll bear it in mind.
NARCEY: Don't forget to tell your friends.
INSPECTOR: Since when did a detective have friends?

The audience cannot doubt that a detective with Rockliffe's assurance will get his man.

Though Denis Gifford classifies *They Made Me a Fugitive* as a crime film, in many respects it is a black comedy akin to *Kind Hearts and Coronets* (d. Robert Hamer, 1949). In the visual effects and the dialogue, Cavalcanti and his scriptwriter Noel Langley repeatedly signal that the film should not be taken seriously. This is evident in the final scenes as the gang prepare for Clem's visit to the funeral parlour. A falling sign announces that 'It's later than you think.' Bert (Cyril Smith) hides in a coffin. Narcey knocks on the lid, prompting an exchange worthy of a music-hall routine:

BERT: Who's there?
NARCEY: Arthur.
BERT: Arthur who?
NARCEY: Ar-thur-mometer.
BERT: You've been listening to the Third Programme.

As they wait in silence, there is a close-up of another sign: 'Death is always around the corner. Insure against accident.' To underline the ironic tone, the fight between Clem and Narcey takes place around the letters 'RIP' on the roof.

No evidence is available for assessing the work's popularity with audiences generally, though it proved fairly popular in working-class Leeds and southeast Essex (Appendix, Tables 6 and 7). Robert Murphy cites *They Made Me a Fugitive* as an example of the films which critics attacked for not celebrating the New Jerusalem of the postwar world.[20] One of these was Patrick Rice, who came to the film with high hopes, given Cavalcanti's reputation. His hopes were dashed:

But purporting to be factual and contemporary, it paid no attention to the facts or the time. Its characters were anything between pronouncedly mad or cheaply caricatured, never in the round, never, in fact, treated as characters in a human story; … But where *They Made Me A Fugitive* was really debased was in its highly undocumentary fantasising of a real theme, its complete lack of any moral sense.[21]

Rice caught the film's ambiguity of period and its lack of characterisation, but he saw at its centre an opposition between two thugs rather than what he termed the 'proper' conflict between thugs and the wider world.[22] An alternative approach is to treat the film as an entertainment in which the middle-class characters – Clem, Sally and Inspector Rockliffe – triumph at the expense of the criminal and the working class. Though Cavalcanti had left Ealing, Balcon's ethos permeated his work. Law and order cannot be thwarted.

Narcey in *They Made Me a Fugitive* is a spiv attempting to move into a higher league. The same might be said of Harry Fabian (Richard Widmark) in *Night and the City* (d. Jules Dassin, 1950), loosely adapted from Gerald Kersh's 1938 novel.[23] Harry is an American hustler living in London. He is initially seen conning three visiting Americans and trying to talk singer Mary Bristol (Gene Tierney) into giving him money for a greyhound racing venture. On the strength of meeting an elderly wrestler, Gregorius (Stanley Zbysko), Harry decides to become a wrestling promoter, in defiance of Gregorius's son, Kristo (Herbert Lom), who controls the sport in London and whose new star is the Strangler (Mike Mazurki). Harry needs money for his venture. He tries to persuade nightclub boss, Phil Nosseross (Francis L. Sullivan), to back him. Phil does not take Harry seriously, but is prompted by his wife, Helen (Googie Withers), to put up half the money if Harry can raise the rest. Harry tries without success to borrow the balance from black marketeer Anna and from Figler (James Hayter), who runs a gang of beggars. It is Helen who comes up with the money on condition that Harry helps her to leave her husband and open her own club. Phil discovers her plans, but in an act of apparent generosity keeps his side of the bargain and gives Harry the agreed share of the money.

Harry tricks Gregorius into fighting the Strangler. Gregorius wins, but the strain kills him. Kristo seeks revenge, scouring London for Harry. Harry flees to Anna's houseboat, but again she refuses to help. Mary finds him there, but she has led Kristo to him. Harry is killed.

The mood has changed from *They Made Me a Fugitive*. Gangs might still be robbing warehouses, but the emphasis is on entrepreneurial skills – a shift foreshadowed by Nigel Patrick's Bar Gorman in *Noose* (d. Edmond T. Greville, 1948). Anna calls herself a hard-headed businesswoman. Harry is intent on establishing himself as a wrestling promoter – he gazes with pride at the metal plate on which is engraved 'Harry Fabian, Managing Director'. Kristo controls a monopoly. Phil runs a nightclub; his wife has aspirations to do the same. Yet the facade of commerce conceals a murky world. Harry is willing to steal, lie and cheat to make his enterprise successful. Kristo is not above using a crooked lawyer to threaten Harry, or enlisting underworld contacts in the search for him. Helen explains to the hostesses in the club how to extract as much money as possible from customers by such ploys as enticing them to buy expensive boxes of chocolates as presents, which the club later buys back. Lou, the fixer in *It Always Rains on Sunday*, would be comfortable with these values; the difference is that here they are adopted by all the protagonists.

The lower class are those who are not successful in business. As Phil says to Helen as she is about to leave him, 'Go. Get out.

But you'll end up back where you started, back on the streets. Then you'll come crawling back to me.' She betrays her origins in her speech. As she talks to the hostesses about her husband's rules, she explains, 'What you do outside is none of his business, but in here we take it from them legitimate.' Yet success can be a matter of luck. When Helen does come back after discovering the club licence which Harry obtained for her is a fake, she finds that Phil is dead and has willed everything to Molly, the disreputable flower-seller who haunts the club.

There can be ambiguity between looking successful and being successful. Anna's appearance belies her flourishing black market activities. More interesting is Figler, who, like Fagin before him, regards his gang of beggars as his family. His advice to Harry is to settle down: 'Get hold of a few good beggars and put 'em on the street. I'll give you all the supplies you need – legs, eyes, stumps. You can make a nice living out of it, Harry.' This is hardly a postwar image and owes nothing to Kersh, though it accords with the interest in Dickens apparent in films of the time (see Appendix, Tables 1, 2, 5 and 7). Hayter was to play Mr Pickwick in *The Pickwick Papers* (d. Noel Langley, 1952).

In common with *It Always Rains on Sunday*, betrayal runs through *Night and the City*. Phil is betrayed by his wife. Harry survives by deceiving everybody, but gradually the tide turns against him. Phil betrays him by setting him up in opposition to Kristo in full knowledge of what will happen. When Kristo puts a price on Harry's head, Figler is willing to betray his friend. In a scene recalling the earlier film, Harry's searches Mary's bag for money, hitting her when she gets in his way. It is Mary, his staunchest friend, who finally gives him away, though whether intentionally or unintentionally is never made clear. In contrast to this catalogue of deceit, the film does portray genuine feeling in two relationships. The first is Phil's love for Helen – love which is not reciprocated. She cannot bear to be touched by him. Buying her a silver fox fur does not win her over; neither does talk of selling the club and going on a cruise. When he predicts that Helen will come back to him, he adds, 'And I'll want to take you back.' The second relationship is between Kristo and his father. It is this love, apparent as the old wrestler is dying, which makes Kristo's revenge on Harry inevitable.

The film was released in the same year as *The Blue Lamp* (d. Basil Dearden), which seems stolid by comparison. Any sense of community is absent from *Night and the City*. The police might be upholders of societal values, but their viewpoint is excluded from the film. This is a society where money rules. The police are the service of last resort, for use when there is trouble at the club. Yet there is also deference to their authority. When an inexperienced constable visits Helen's new club and discovers that the licence is forged, she accepts unquestioningly his decision to refer the matter to his superiors.

The look of the film is more important in evoking the atmosphere of London than the dialogue, with location shots of Piccadilly Circus, Trafalgar Square, St Martin's Lane and the Thames bridges. More unusual are the scenes on what was to become the Festival of Britain site beside Waterloo Bridge, with Harry evading his pursuers among the debris of an industrial complex. In true noir fashion, Harry's world is the night. London is a place of flashing neon signs and basement drinking clubs. In daylight, there is nowhere to hide.

The use of two American leads and a Hollywood director, not to mention the lush score, suggest that the production was made with an eye to the American market, though cliches like the sound of Big Ben have been avoided. Internationalisation with a strong American flavour was the film industry's response in the face of declining audiences. *Night and the City* was financed by 20th Century Fox. The same year, 1950, saw the release of such British-registered offerings as Korda's *State Secret* (d. Sidney Gilliat), starring Douglas Fairbanks jr, Walt Disney's *Treasure Island* (d. Byron Haskin), 20th Century Fox's *The Black Rose* (d. Henry Hathaway), MGM's *The Miniver Story* (d. H. C. Potter), starring Walter Pidgeon and Greer Garson, and David Selznick's *Gone to Earth* (d. Michael Powell and Emeric Pressburger), starring Jennifer Jones. McCarthyite witch-hunts accelerated this trend. American stars slotted happily enough into mythical countries and mythical pasts; the problem was incorporating them convincingly into contemporary British dramas. A string of films in the 1950s and 1960s had American engineers passing through London, diplomats working at the American embassy, or American policemen seconded to Scotland Yard. The solution adopted in *Night and the City* is not to offer any explanation for the presence of American leads. Instead, the opening attempts to brush aside the incongruity by universalising the film's theme. Over location shots of London at night, a voice-over intones: 'Night and the city. The night is tonight, tomorrow night or any night. The city is London.' The city, too, could be anywhere. The middle class can exist in any urban environment – the skills of a doctor can be practised in London, Paris or New York. By comparison, the working class, from the miner to the farm labourer, are tied more closely to the local economy and are marginalised in a commercial film intended for an international market. Most obviously, accents have to be understandable by audiences with no knowledge of slum life or its humour. Harry could not be the working-class Londoner of the novel. A caricature of the cockney like Figler is more acceptable, even if this is a literary conceit.

The nightclub was remote from the experience of most working-class people. It is only in the final section of *Night and the City*, when Kristo searches for Harry, that something of the feel of working-class London begins to enter the film in scenes reminiscent of the hunting of Tom Riley in *The Blue Lamp*. The people searching for Harry are the working class, who cheer at the wrestling match and the greyhound stadium, and sell newspapers on the streets. They are omnipresent, yet always peripheral. The image which lingers in the memory is of Harry, the eternal optimist, living on his wits and always running, running – until his luck runs out.

Though the three films present different facets of the criminal, they should not be seen as charting his evolution from spiv to business-man over so short a period. A more useful approach is to see them as highlighting societal concerns of the time. The spiv faded into history once rationing eased and his services were no longer in demand, but the serviceman seduced into criminality lingered into the 1950s with *The Intruder* (d. Guy Hamilton, 1953) and *The Good Die Young* (d. Lewis Gilbert, 1954). National service kept the issue alive. The professional criminal never went away, though the distinction persists between the working-class criminal with an eye to an opportunity and Mr Big who controls a criminal empire while taking no risks himself. The former found a new home on television; Mr Big survives in the James Bond films, where the budgets match his ambitions.

Notes

1 Bill Naughton, 'The spiv', in Charles Madge (ed.), *Pilot Papers: Social Essays and Documents* (London: Pilot Press, 1946), p. 100.

2 *Ibid.*, p. 107.

3 Trevor Blackwell and Jeremy Seabrook, *A World Still to Win: The Reconstruction of the Post-War Working Class* (London: Faber & Faber, 1985), p. 69.

4 Ross McKibbin, *Classes and Cultures in England 1918–1951* (Oxford: Oxford University Press, 1998), pp. 202–3.

5 Alan Jenkins, *The Forties* (London: William Heinemann, 1977), p. 185.

6 Miki Cogswell, *Ready to Wear*, BBC TV (18 May 1999).

7 Naughton, 'The spiv', p. 100.

8 Edward Smithies, *The Black Economy in England since 1914* (Dublin: Gill & Macmillan, 1984), pp. 7 and 110.

9 Richard Attenborough, interviewed in Brian McFarlane, *An Autobiography of British Cinema as Told by the Filmmakers and Actors Who Made It* (London: Methuen, 1997), p. 15; Tim Pulleine, 'Spin a dark web', in Steve Chibnall and Robert Murphy (eds), *British Crime Cinema* (London: Routledge, 1999), p. 32.

10 Jeffrey Richards, *Film and British National Identity from Dickens to 'Dad's Army'* (Manchester: Manchester University Press, 1997), p. 146.

11 Graham Greene, *Brighton Rock* (Harmondsworth: Penguin Books, 1971), pp. 26, 86 and 90.

12 Quentin Falk, *Travels in Greenland* (London: Quartet Boooks, 1984), p. 63, cited in McFarlane, *An Autobiography of British Cinema*, p. 244; Richard Attenborough, interviewed in *ibid.*, p. 15.

13 Richard Winnington, *Film Criticism and Caricatures*, ed. Paul Rotha (London: Paul Elek, 1975), p. 73; Greene, *Brighton Rock*, pp. 242–3.

14 Marcia Landy, *British Genres: Cinema and Society 1930–1960* (Princeton, NJ: Princeton University Press, 1991), p. 444.

15 Tim Pulleine, 'Spin a dark web', p. 32.

16 Winnington, *Film Criticism and Caricatures*, p. 73.

17 James C. Robertson, 'The Censors and British Gangland', in Chibnall and Murphy (eds), *British Crime Cinema*, p. 19; Graham Greene, *Reflections* (London: Reinhardt Books, 1990), p. 204.

18 The significance of the ex-serviceman is examined in Andrew Clay, 'Men, women and money: masculinity in crisis in the British professional crime film 1946–1965', in Chibnall and Murphy (eds), *British Crime Cinema*, pp. 51–65.

19 *Picturegoer Weekly* (5 November 1932), p. 29, cited in Stephen C. Shafer, *British Popular Films 1929–1939: The Cinema of Reassurance* (London: Routledge, 1997), p. 43. 'Mazuma' was North American slang for money. The expression has Yiddish origins.

20 Robert Murphy, *Realism and Tinsel: Cinema and Society in Britain 1939–49* (London: Routledge, 1992), p. 168.

21 Patrick Rice, 'When sadism becomes British', in John E. Cross and Arnold Rattenbury [eds], *Screen and Audience* (London: Saturn Press, [1947?]), p. 40.

22 *Ibid.*, p. 40.

23 Gerald Kersh, *Night and the City* (London: Brainiac Books, 1993).

Going to the bad: the treatment of the young offender   8

The bottom-up approach to the spiv adopted by Trevor Blackwell and Jeremy Seabrook was introduced in the previous chapter. The mirror image is embodied in the work of the American social scientists Clifford Shaw and Henry McKay, dating from the 1940s:

> The automobile, motion pictures, magazine and newspaper advertising, the radio and other means of communication flaunt luxury standards before all, creating or helping to create desires which often cannot be satisfied with the meagre facilities available to families in areas of low economic status. The urge to satisfy the wishes and desires so created has helped to bring into existence and to perpetuate the existing system of criminal activities.[1]

Viewed from this middle-class perspective, relative deprivation, aided and abetted by the mass media, fuels working-class crime. The conundrum is that the ideal solution would be to eliminate deprivation, reducing the relative advantages of being middle class in the process. This is unlikely to tempt a middle-class electorate seeking a reduction in crime. The mass media make an easier scapegoat.

Working-class youth presents a particular challenge to authority. Stephen Humphries detects two traditions conceptualising their behaviour: the mass culture theory – malleable youth being led astray by the media – and the deprivation theory premised on faulty socialisation.[2] But there need be no distinction between the two theories: when taken in its entirety, Shaw and McKay's work straddles both camps. Humphries own approach, which he does not acknowledge as belonging to a third tradition, is derived from Gramsci: 'The behaviour that I contend can be regarded as resistance is the persistent rule-breaking and opposition to authority characteristic of working-class youth culture that has traditionally been viewed as indiscipline or delinquency.'[3] From this viewpoint, minor crime is a symbol of class and inter-generational conflict, which puts Humphries in the same camp as Blackwell and Seabrook.[4]

J. G. Bagot's Liverpool study of 1935–36 goes some way to supporting Humphries' contention that teenage crimes are generally minor and opportunist. Most of the items stolen had been left unattended, or were taken from open shop counters, with 68 per cent being valued at less than a pound and 15 per cent less than a shilling.[5] In 1955, 73.7 per cent of stolen goods were valued at under £10.[6] What evidence of this kind cannot do is challenge the implication of Humphries' approach: if such crime is inherent in the structure of working-class life, then the search for solutions becomes meaningless without fundamental changes in society. And who should arbitrate on what is right?

Was juvenile delinquency an increasing problem after the war? The makers of *Cosh Boy* (d. Lewis Gilbert, 1952) had no doubts. The film opens with an on-screen announcement:

By itself, the 'Cosh' is the cowardly implement of a contemporary evil; in association with 'Boy', it marks a post-war tragedy – the juvenile delinquent. 'Cosh Boy' portrays starkly the development of a young criminal, an enemy of society at sixteen. Our Judges and Magistrates, and the Police, whose stern duty is to resolve the problem, agree that its origins lie mainly in the lack of parental control and early discipline. The problem exists – and we cannot escape it by closing our eyes. This film is presented in the hope that it will contribute towards stamping out this social evil.

Whether this interest indicated prurience or a genuine sense of social responsibility is a moot point, given that the film's X certificate was likely to attract audiences looking for sensation rather than a social critique.

Crime statistics are seldom unambiguous. In Hermann Mannheim's words, 'Statistics of Juvenile Delinquency do little more than indicate the varying degrees of willingness on the part of the public and the Police to bring this category of delinquents before the Juvenile Courts.'[7] With the Second World War came a plethora of new regulations to transgress and new opportunities for delinquency with truancy, the blackout, looting from bombsites and less supervision of children where fathers were called up and mothers were working. Table 8 in the Appendix indicates the scale of the problem in England and Wales during the 1940s. The culprits were predominantly boys. The increase in delinquency was stepwise and came with the war rather than during the subsequent peace. This reprised the pattern noted with the First World War, though without the rapid decline.[8] Juvenile crime declined during the early 1950s, though changes in data collection and the greater use of cautions may have distorted the figures. If films are implicated in inciting delinquency as the mass culture theory posits, it must be demonstrated that their message became antisocial early in the Second World War, when rates of delinquency showed a marked increase. Given the stress on national unity which is more often detected, this seems a wilful reading of the film evidence.[9]

A Workers' Educational Association study conducted in Lincoln in 1942–43 sheds light on the age and social origins of offenders.[10] Obvious limitations are that Lincoln may be atypical and the findings not necessarily applicable to postwar Britain. The 'dangerous age' for boys according to this research was twelve, which accords with government figures for 1947 and 1948, though it was to rise to fourteen or fifteen in the following year.[11] The class dimension was also considered. The father's occupation in 35 per cent of all Lincoln households was semiskilled or unskilled. During the war years, 84.3 per cent of juvenile offenders came from these groups, compared with 67.3 per cent in prewar days. In spite of this, the authors concluded that poverty was not a factor in juvenile crime, their argument being that the proportion of offenders coming from homes where the weekly income was at least £1 per head increased from 2 per cent before the war to 13.2 per cent during the war.[12] This contrasts with studies made in Glasgow and London, which showed adolescent criminals coming from crowded homes and larger families.[13] Though adolescent unemployment was no higher than in the general population, adolescents were more likely to commit crimes during spells of unemployment.[14]

The scale of the official response hardly supports the view that postwar delinquency reached endemic proportions. The number of police officers in England and Wales declined from 63,800 in 1938 to 62,629 in 1951, while the hours they worked per 1,000 of the population declined from 3,595 to 3,144. The number of officials in the probation and aftercare service remained steady at 1,004 in 1938 and 1,006 in 1950.[15] G. Prys Williams ascribes the postwar increase in crime to the seventeen to twenty-one age group, despite cases of theft by this group declining in the late 1940s.[16] To keep things in perspective, Frank Musgrove concludes that youth was generally conservative and most young people, for better or worse, were adjusted to their position in life, with fewer than 4 per cent being at risk of criminal deviation.[17]

A central problem is that delinquency may be defined culturally as well as in narrow legal terms. An impoverished community in which pilfering makes up for low wages may take a different view of antisocial behaviour from those who police them.[18] The working out of this difference represents a struggle for power between a subordinate group and the dominant group. For those who have already reached an accommodation with the dominant group, this oppositional state need not prevail: as John Barron Mays points out, fiddling employers is not the prerogative of the working class and arouses little moral indignation.[19] This cannot be said of juvenile delinquency. It might have exercised the minds of film-makers in 1952, but as John Davis notes, researchers discovered another delinquent generation in the late 1950s. Their work became outdated when a new generation displayed higher crime rates in the 1960s.[20] As well as being an easy target, delinquency is a recurring target.

In considering how delinquency is portrayed on film, the question for the researcher is whose viewpoint is being offered: that of the dominant (hegemonic) group or a dissident (subordinate) group. Offering a dissident view implies being sympathetic towards the behaviour of that group. In the age of the spiv and the delinquent, this could prove unacceptable to some sections of the public, not to mention the censors. One way of evading the problem while keeping to a dissident view is to set the action safely in the past or within a comedy. Both apply in the case of *Cardboard Cavalier* (d. Walter Forde, 1949). The solution adopted in *Waterloo Road* (d. Sidney Gilliat, 1945) is to frame the action by using a middle-class narrator. Another tactic is to make the dissident an upper-class character, which is somehow more acceptable. *The Wicked Lady* (d. Leslie Arliss, 1945) adopts this approach – and sets the action in the past for good measure. More equivocal is *Kind Hearts and Coronets* (d. Robert Hamer, 1949). With its sympathetic viewpoint towards a mass murderer, the film is dissident, though leavened by being set in the past – albeit a past within memory – and by being ostensibly a comedy – albeit a black comedy. It is also framed by having the story told in flashback, but the narrator is the central character, Louis Mazzini, who occupies an uncertain class position. On the film's release, a critic judged that 'Essentially literary in conception, its poker-faced fun can be appreciated only by people with a good working knowledge of English language and the English people.'[21] Presumably it was aimed at middle-class cinemagoers, who might be expected to take the received (dominant) view even if they comprised a minority of cinema audiences. Little wonder that the audience at the Venice Film Festival were mystified, though less explicable is why their counterparts at Cannes received the film with delight.[22] Ultimately the dominant view triumphed. It was, after all, an Ealing film and in Charles Barr's words, 'As *The Blue Lamp* soon confirms, Ealing is *for* established moral convention, and believes that it can be practised [original emphasis].'[23]

Crime is generally presented in British films as a battle of wits between the police and the criminal. At least until the 1960s, the police were on the winning side. A few films such as *Cosh Boy* and *The Boys* (d. Sidney J. Furie, 1961) examine how wrongdoers embark on the path which brings them into conflict with the police. Others such as *Scum* (d. Alan Clarke, 1979) and *Scrubbers* (d. Mai Zetterling, 1982) examine how the penal system deals with offenders. In practice the two aspects are often conflated, with the story of the individual in an institution being presented in flashbacks, a distinguished example being *The Loneliness of the Long Distance Runner* (d. Tony Richardson, 1962). Earlier films were often prescriptive as well as descriptive, showing that in the end the system worked, whatever its inadequacies. *I Believe in You* (d. Basil Dearden, 1952) and *The Weak and the Wicked* (d. J. Lee Thompson, 1953) exemplify this trend.

Offenders are usually working class. In *The Weak and the Wicked*, a middle-class character played by Glynis Johns does stray into this world, but as the opening scenes are at pains to make clear, she is the victim of a deception. Mindless crime is working-class crime. Middle-class crime is planned, from *Dear Murderer* (d. Arthur Crabtree, 1947) to *The League of Gentlemen* (d. Basil Dearden, 1960).

Early examples of delinquents appear in *The Blue Lamp* (d. Basil Dearden, 1950). Near the beginning of the film, PC Andy Mitchell is seen in a tenement flat, taking details about the missing Diana Lewis from her mother. This dissolves to an night scene, with Diana walking jauntily past an amusement arcade and a cinema showing an Anna Neagle film. A bebop soundtrack sets the mood. The scene cuts to two youths loitering by a subway entrance. A voice-over gives a documentary tone to both outdoor sequences:

The case of Diana Lewis is typical of many: a young girl showing the effect of a childhood living in a home broken and demoralised by war. These restless and ill-adjusted youngsters have produced a type of delinquent which is partly responsible for the postwar increase in crime. Some are content with pilfering and petty theft. Others with more bravado graduate to serious offences. Youths with brain enough to organise criminal adventures and yet who lack the code, experience and self-discipline of the professional thief, which sets them as a class apart, all the more dangerous because of their immaturity. Young men such as these two present a new problem to the police: men as yet without records, for a natural cunning and a ruthless use of violence has so far kept them out of trouble. The small, exclusive circle which represents the underworld does not accept them and they are avoided by the regular criminals, for they are a liability even to their associates.

The social problems of the day, including the increase in crime, are ascribed to the war, which prevented youngsters from becoming properly socialised. Real thieving is elevated to the status of a profession, conducted according to rules accepted by both sides. The trouble with the new generation of criminals is that they have not learned the rules. Their youth constitutes part of the problem, making them unpredictable and a nuisance to everybody. This distinguishes them from spivs, who know the rules and play the system rather than rebelling against it.

The Blue Lamp was released at a time when juvenile crime was a topical issue. The solution offered in the film – a strong police force and the support of the community – might be simplistic, but at least it was a contribution to the debate. The salient point is that delinquency became defined as a working-class problem. To what extent it stemmed from the war rather than from the nature of working-class society was left vague, though the message was clear that, for whatever reason, working-class socialisation had failed. Yet this same working-class community had to contribute to the solution by its coherence in the face of disruptive forces like crime and by providing a recruiting ground for the police. Quite how this transformation should take place remained unexplained. Eugenics was rendered unacceptable by the war. Instead, the British chose socialism at the ballot box. By 1950, the limitations of socialism in a capitalist world were showing, but what was to take its place had yet to become apparent. Ealing presented the problem; the solution was beyond Ealing's remit. Other films supplied more specific answers. One was a good belting, as in *Cosh Boy*. Another was conscription, which supposedly instilled self-discipline and had the incidental virtue of keeping young men off the streets. *Carry on Sergeant* (d. Gerald Thomas, 1958) was one of the last films to emphasise the melding of disparate individuals into an efficient fighting unit. A stumbling block for its proponents was Williams' conclusion that juvenile crime dropped when conscription ceased in 1960.[24]

Those who committed mindless crime were young as well as being working class. Not only did this admit the possibility that they would settle into a better life by learning more acceptable ways, but it allowed miscreants to be guided by somebody older, wiser and in a position of authority. This was usually a (middle-class) probation officer, governor or matron.

In *The White Unicorn* (d. Bernard Knowles, 1947), Lucy (Margaret Lockwood) is matron of a remand home, euphemistically called a mission for girls. One inmate, Lottie (Joan Greenwood), is involved in a fight. As Lucy reasons with her, their stories are revealed. Lottie comes from a large family with a violent father. She left home to work in a department store. There she met a wealthy customer, Paul (Paul Dupuis), who seduced her, only to abandon her when she became pregnant. She was forced into cheaper and cheaper accommodation until she was reduced to living in the damp cellar where she tried to gas herself and her baby.

Lucy's story is that she became disillusioned with her marriage to barrister Philip Templar (Ian Hunter). A baby did not bring them any closer, for Philip hired a nanny, leaving Lucy with little say in her daughter's upbringing. She met Richard Glover (Dennis Price) at a party and their relationship deepened as she became estranged from her husband. Matters came to a head when the child was involved in a road accident, for which Philip blamed Lucy. Following the couple's divorce, Lucy married Richard in Finland, but their happiness was short-lived: Richard drowned when the ice on a lake broke under him during their honeymoon. Lucy was urged to give something back to life, which was why she took the post of matron.

Lucy's intention in recounting her story is to show that her own life has not been easy. Working-class audiences might have disagreed. The problems Lucy faced in her marriage – her failure to assert her own wishes and taking Richard as a lover – were of her own making and contradictory in their motivation. More cynically, audiences could have interpreted the tribulations of the two women as plot devices, with each character trying to trump the other in the bathos of her story.

At her trial, Lottie pleads guilty to attempted infanticide. The judge is Philip Templer. When Lucy appears as a character witness, pleading for leniency, Philip accepts her plea. He uses the occasion to heal his rift with her, allowing Lucy to see her daughter after years of denying access.

Lottie's response on becoming pregnant reveals a working-class ordering of priorities: 'I'll lose my job. What will people say?' Her attempt to survive by her own efforts shows working-class pragmatism. She progresses from addressing envelopes to buying a sewing machine, so that she can earn more money from dressmaking. The noise of the machine provokes complaints from other tenants and she loses her lodgings. When the baby falls ill, she can do less work and the downward spiral becomes inexorable. Unfortunately the bulk of the film is devoted to Lucy's story, leaving

Lottie a sketchy character. The inference is that all Lottie's troubles stem from poverty. With the promise of a job and an allowance for the child (paid by Lucy), her difficulties will be resolved. There is no hint that this is a problem for society at large. The other girls in the home never appear after the opening scene. Allied to the studied avoidance of Lottie's social situation is a melodramatic portrayal of her home life which would not look out of place in a silent film, with Joan Greenwood unconvincing as a slum girl. The result is a showcase for Margaret Lockwood yoked to a sentimentalised view of the poor. The Welfare State never figures in the story, adding to the sense of unreality.

The White Unicorn met with fair success both in the sample Leeds cinemas and in southeast Essex (Appendix, Tables 6 and 7). Unusually, there was no supporting feature on its circuit release, in spite of a running time of only ninety-seven minutes, suggesting that this was intended as a prestige production. At the Gaumont, Sheffield, the film attracted the second biggest audience over four years, though it was programmed with the film of the royal wedding, which on the evidence from other areas was probably the real draw (Appendix, Tables 5, 6 and 7). Subsequently, The White Unicorn has been ignored even by feminist critics.

In Good Time Girl (d. David Macdonald, 1948), the wiser, older person is the chair of the juvenile court, Miss Thorpe (Flora Robson). Here, the problems of Lyla (Diana Dors), the girl she is trying to help, are left unexplored. Instead, Miss Thorpe recounts the cautionary tale of Gwen Rawlings (Jean Kent), who leaves home after being beaten by her father. She takes a room in Mrs Chalk's boarding house. A fellow tenant is Jimmy Rosso (Peter Glenville), who finds Gwen a job in the club where he works. When he hits her, the club's owner, Max (Herbert Lom), sacks him. Jimmy takes revenge by knifing Max and contriving to have Gwen convicted for stealing jewellery from Mrs Chalk. The girl escapes from approved school, taking up with rich but crooked Danny Martin (Griffith Jones). After causing a fatal accident while driving Danny's car, she abandons him. In partnership with two American deserters, she is involved in a string of robberies. During the gang's attempt to steal a car, the driver is shot. He is revealed to be Red Farrell (Dennis Price), a musician who befriended her at the club. Gwen is caught and sentenced to be detained for fifteen years. Her fate is enough to make Lyla return home, determined never to get into trouble again.

Like It Always Rains on Sunday (d. Robert Hamer, 1947), Good Time Girl is based on a novel by Arthur La Bern.[25] The film was

12   While dad's asleep: Gwen Rawlings (Jean Kent) and her mother
            (Beatrice Varley) enjoy a moment's peace in *Good Time Girl* (1948).
                                                    A lower-working-class flat

scripted by Muriel and Sydney Box, together with Ted Willis. Not
unexpectedly, the socialist trio take a sympathetic view of Gwen.
Jean Kent considers that the character was more balanced in the
book, though as Robert Murphy points out, La Bern had already
remoulded a 1944 murder case to make Gwen a victim of her
environment.[26] The films retains this focus on a young woman
trying to escape from poverty, even if her domestic life is sketchily
represented. She shares a bed with her sister (as so often, the shared
iron bedstead signifies impoverishment), though being in bed
proves no bar to being hit by her father. The incident prompts her
to leave home. She is shown as wanting a better life, but being
unwilling to work for it – that classic working-class character
defect. Like other working-class girls, she has to rely on her looks.[27]
As Pearl Jephcott put it, 'the "poor" girl's personal appearance is
her main stock-in-trade. Her face is literally her fortune: and a girl
can more quickly be a success through this than by her job.' [28] In
her lodgings, the cycle of violence begins again when Jimmy Rosso
hits her. Her looks are damaged, which is what annoys Max.

Domestic violence, overcrowding and poverty appear not to
bother Miss Thorpe greatly. What scandalises her is that a girl of

sixteen should spend a night in Red Farrell's flat without his wife being there. Her priority is that Lyla should return home rather than live independently. A more liberal view is expressed at a board meeting of the approved school where Gwen is sent. As the matron pleads for more staff, she explains that the girls have suffered from 'bad upbringing, bad companions or plain bad luck'. This is a transformation of the matron in the book, who is described as a suppressed sadist.[29]

Murphy is certain of his readers' exasperation with middle-class busybodies and their sympathy for a girl who just wanted to have a good time.[30] Whether audiences of the 1940s concurred is something which he does not pursue, though evading the issue risks divorcing the film from its social context. Other aspects of the film worried critics. Gavin Lambert observed that 'To judge from the popular British cinema, the pursuit of luxury in everyday living is either criminal or disastrous.'[31] *Good Time Girl* was one example which he cited.

Muriel Box recalls that the film fell foul of the censors.[32] The changes demanded failed to satisfy some local authorities: *Good Time Girl* was banned to cinemagoers under sixteen in Manchester, while Leeds City Council sought to ban it outright.[33] Putting the film in the same category as *No Orchids for Miss Blandish* (d. St John L. Clowes, 1948) hurt J. Arthur Rank, who regarded it as one of his personal 'darlings'.[34] Doubtless he discerned a moral in Lyla's response to Gwen's fate. If so, he would not have appreciated Marcia Landy's verdict that 'While the film identifies Gwen's struggles as economic, this is belied by the film's preoccupation with the disruptive and violent nature of sexuality set in motion by the female quest for pleasure.'[35] The economic origins of Gwen's problems should not be dismissed too lightly, however. Her female quest for pleasure is initiated by 'borrowing' a brooch from her pawnbroker employer – an act which may equally well be attributed to her low wages. Once she leaves home and has to pay for her lodgings, taking a job at Max's club becomes an economic necessity. At this stage, she is still portrayed as an innocent abroad. Even when she escapes from the approved school, she rejects the overtures of the man who gives her a lift to London (Garry Marsh). It is not until she meets Danny Martin that she explicitly uses her sexuality. This is a toning down of the book, in which she lives with Red Farrell and later with a lorry driver.

The film is rich in criminal types, from Jimmy Rosso's spiv-on-a-budget, through the semi-respectable Max to the wealthy Danny Martin, who is involved in race-fixing and makes little attempt to conceal his activities. Men's clothing becomes more conservative as they ascend the social ladder: wealth is shown, not flaunted. By contrast, the immature Gwen parades her newly-acquired status when she is with Danny by wearing furs.

Viv Chadder is illuminating on the contradiction between the middle-class, reformist stance of the school and the staff's tacit support for an underground power structure in which senior girls exploit the younger ones. The message, she concludes, is that the pretence of conformity pays dividends.[36] Honesty is relative, or as Nigel Gray puts it, 'To "them" it means not telling lies. To "us" it means not being a hypocrite. Not playing the middle-class game of adopting role and living behind a facade of illusions.'[37] Chadder's approach to the routine of the school is gender based: 'The girls are shown dutifully at work on that most fulfilling of female activities – mopping; they are compulsorily dressed in the most functional, unfeminine utility dress; inflammatory literature (such as Red's love letters to Gwen) is carefully censored.'[38] An interpretation predicated on class rather than gender has equal validity. Mopping is a low-status rather than a specifically feminine activity – in films of service life, it is the province of the humblest recruits such as Brian Rix's cleaner in *The Night We Dropped a Clanger* (d. Darcy Conyers, 1959). This film serves as a reminder that dress is linked to status: when Rix's character impersonates an officer, his clothing signifies the change, even if his behaviour belies it. The censoring of letters in *Good Time Girl* may also be interpreted as an issue of power rather than gender: there is no indication that these are love letters and given Red Farrell's brief and circumspect relationship with Gwen in the film, the conclusion that the couple had an affair is difficult to sustain.

The film's trailer proclaims that 'Whether you Like it or Not, YOU are Responsible for the 'GOOD TIME GIRL!' Chadder sees this as an appeal to a male audience to take up the paternal role rather than a straightforward challenge to audiences to accept blame.[39] Yet Gwen's father does exercise his paternal role – by using his belt. If his response fails, should he administer more of the same medicine? Accepting the option which Chadder rejects opens the way to seeing in the film a more radical approach to crime in which society assumes responsibility for the situation of Gwen's family and the behaviour of her father.

The attempt to ban *Good Time Girl* in Leeds failed, though notoriety hardly made the film a runaway success there (Appendix, Table 6). It proved more popular in southeast Essex (Appendix, Table 7), though after two weeks in Rank cinemas, it only played for twelve days in the independents. Once controversy abated, demand was not strong enough to justify repeated runs. Why *Good*

Time Girl was less successful than *The White Unicorn* is unclear. Aside from the possibility of high rental costs, parents might have been deterred from allowing their offspring to see the film, given its reputation, but intrinsic factors also counted against it. Apart from lacking romance and the star appeal of Margaret Lockwood, *Good Time Girl* has no sympathetic lead characters with the exception of Red Farrell who is absent for half the film. Gwen becomes steadily less appealing as the film progresses.

A year later, delinquent boys came under scrutiny in *Boys in Brown* (d. Montgomery Tully, 1949). Jackie Knowles (Richard Attenborough) is already on probation when he is arrested for being involved in a robbery. He is sent to borstal for three years. His intention is to seek an early release for good conduct. Another inmate, Bill Foster (Jimmy Hanley), is being released and promises to tell Jackie's girlfriend, Kitty (Barbara Murray), that Jackie is well. Bill becomes attracted to Kitty, though his feelings are not reciprocated. He repeatedly loses jobs when his past is discovered and ends up in borstal again, embittered and willing to take part in an escape. Jackie is persuaded to join in. He is discovered stealing clothes for the breakout and fractures a master's skull in the ensuing struggle. The boys escape, but are soon recaptured. Both Jackie and Bill are shocked by what has happened and resolve to mend their ways.

Montgomery Tully both wrote the script (from a stage play by actor Reginald Beckwith) and directed the film. He had to achieve the delicate balance of providing entertainment without glamorising crime. One way of allowing audiences to relate to unsympathetic characters is to use established stars. In addition to Attenborough and Hanley, the film sports Dirk Bogarde as Alfie Rawlins, an inmate with an unlikely Welsh accent, and an avuncular Jack Warner as the governor. The credo of social responsibility is maintained by the statistics which appear in the final frames. These are intended to show the success of borstals in rehabilitating offenders, though by the time they appeared on the screen, most of the audience were probably heading for the exit.

Jackie's working-class credentials are established by his home. It is an early Victorian town house which has declined in status. The few location shots place it in the East End of London. The former grandeur is belied by the interior shots which show the front door opening directly into the living room where the range is situated – its normal location in a house of this size would be in the basement. As so often, impoverishment is denoted less by the quality of the furnishings than the fact that they are out of date.

Most of the action takes place within the borstal. The governor is at pains to point out to the new inmates that it is not a prison. There is nothing to stop them leaving, he assures them, even if the message is belied by the bars across his office window. This inconsistency runs through the film. The panopticon layout and the emphasis on keys create the atmosphere of a prison, yet the staff are elderly masters rather than uniformed warders. The escape is planned and executed with the precision of a prison breakout – and prompts a comparable response from the police.

As at the approved school encountered in *Good Time Girl*, work means mopping. This allows plenty of opportunities for the boys to talk among themselves. They are working class, the possible exception being Alfie Rawlins, who also happens to be the most complex character. His responses have a sexual undercurrent unusual for the time. 'If you have a pal, it makes it a bit easier,' he explains to Jackie on their first encounter. 'I could look after you.' Later in the dormitory as Bill talks of getting a job, Alfie tells him, 'I reckon you could get anyone to do anything for you – anything you wanted. Without work.' Superficially he is friendly, but he is also devious, tricking Jackie into joining the escape by intimating that Kitty has switched her affections to Bill. Alfie is the planner of the group. The others defer to him, though his relationship with them is always uneasy. When they suspect him of a doublecross, they turn against him.

For the governor, home conditions are seen as contributing to the boys' problems. He carries this belief as far as tracing Bill's natural mother in the hope that she will provide a home for the son she gave away as a baby. Now married, she lives in a large, detached house in a leafy suburb. She refuses to cooperate, not wanting her family to discover her shameful past.

Quite how home circumstances have contributed in Jackie's case is not made explicit. He appears to have no brothers or sisters and his mother (Thora Hird) is caring, though no father is in evidence. The audience is left to decide whether the problem is the absence of a father, or simply being working class. Jack Warner's governor takes the middle-class standpoint: the borstal is intended to make failures into good citizens. It is Alfie Rawlins who voices the unthinkable: 'Of course, those that fail, fail because of something wrong with their character. Something borstal did to their character, I suppose.'

The actors playing the boys were in their mid to late twenties. They look ill at ease in the shorts which form part of the school's uniform. For Landy, 'The age of the actors, consonant with the film's ending, reveals that, though the pretext of the film may be juvenile delinquency, the film is not concerned with the issue of their youth per se so much as with its disruptiveness and its containment. In this respect, the film betrays that realism often takes a back seat to ideology.' [40] Where Landy writes of youth, being working class might be substituted. The focus in the film is on Attenborough and Hanley, neither of whom convince as working-class delinquents, They are portrayed as being basically decent, but easily led by the rougher elements. The inmate who fails to be contained is Casey (Andrew Crawford), forever refusing to work for nothing more than pocket money and being put in solitary confinement for his stand. He is presented as the least sympathetic character in the film, in contrast to Alfie's pretence of conformity. The moral seems to be that middle-class deviousness is more attractive than working-class rebellion.

A fascination with crime in the late 1940s and an awareness of the problem of juvenile delinquency did not necessarily translate into success at the box office. With *Miss Pilgrim's Progress* (d. Val Guest, 1950) as supporting feature, *Boys in Brown* came in the third quartile of attendances at the Gaumont, Sheffield (Appendix, Table 5). The manager reported that 'This programme was received with mixed feeling [*sic*] by most patrons, in most cases the 2nd feature was considered the best.' [41] An indifferent circuit performance almost exhausted the film's commercial potential. It fared worse than *Good Time Girl* among independents in southeast Essex as well as in the sample Leeds cinemas, though there may have been further runs after 1950 (Appendix, Tables 6 and 7). In the verdict on the Rank card, the film was good entertainment 'where heavy dramatic fare is wanted'. This target audience proved elusive. The middle-class sympathies of the film deterred working-class audiences, yet the subject matter hardly appealed to the middle class.

Though few girls figure in statistics on delinquency in the late 1940s, this is not the impression given by films. Membership of the working class is associated with an acceptance of violence; in the case of the girls in *The White Unicorn* and *Good Time Girl*, it is endemic in their home circumstances. Violence leads inexorably to conflict with the law and, as Bill discovers in *Boys in Brown*, to being stigmatised with a criminal record. This scenario might get away from the notion of crime being attributable to individual pathology, but it is not necessarily more useful in changing public opinion, if that is the aim. The use of a middle-class authority figure as a narrator to put forward a model of desired behaviour in *The White Unicorn* and *Good Time Girl* leaves hanging in the air the implication that the real crime is belonging to the working class, even if the message is sugar coated in the case of *The White Unicorn*. A variant of this device is used in *No Room at the Inn* (d. Daniel Birt, 1948). In an opening sequence not found in the original play, a girl who has made good watches a shop-lifter being taken away. This allows her story to be presented as an extended flashback, showing how she might have taken the same route. In *Boys in Brown*, casting as much as narrative helps to convey a similar message: only characters played by stars masquerading as working-class delinquents can be redeemed and reliable old Jack Warner is on hand to ensure that it happens. Real working-class characters like Casey are different.

Many British films of the late 1940s involving middle-class crime were set in the past, including *Uncle Silas* (d. Charles Frank, 1947), *The Mark of Cain* (d. Brian Desmond Hurst, 1948), *The Spider and the Fly* (d. Robert Hamer, 1949) and *Madeleine* (d. David Lean, 1950). If this signalled that times had changed and now there were other ways of getting what you wanted, the message had yet to permeate to delinquents in the lower strata of society.

Notes

1 Clifford R. Shaw and Henry D. McKay, *Juvenile Delinquency in Urban Areas: A Study of the Delinquents in Relation to Differential Characteristics of Local Communities in American Cities* (Chicago: Chicago University Press, 1942), cited in John Barron Mays, *Growing Up in the City: A Study of Juvenile Delinquency in an Urban Neighbourhood* (Liverpool: Liverpool University Press, 1954), p. 12.

2 Stephen Humphries, *Hooligans or Rebels? An Oral History of Working-Class Childhood and Youth 1889–1939* (Oxford: Basil Blackwell, 1995), pp. 1–26. A similar emphasis is found in John Westergaard, 'About and beyond the "underclass": some notes on influences of sociological climate on British sociology today', *Sociology*, 26 (1992), 575–87.

3 Humphries, *Hooligans or Rebels?*, p. 1.

4 The various approaches, including those of American social scientists, are examined in David M. Downes, *The Delinquent Solution: A Study in Subcultural Theory* (London: Routledge & Kegan Paul, 1966).

5 J. G. Bagot, *Juvenile Delinquency: A Comparative Study of the Position in Liverpool and England and Wales* (London: Jonathan Cape, 1941), pp. 36–7.

6 F. H. M. McClintock, N. Howard Avison and G. N. G. Rose, *Crime in England and Wales* (London: Heinemann Educational, 1968), Table 2.12, p. 53.

7 Hermann Mannheim, *Social Aspects of Crime in England between the Wars* (London: George Allen & Unwin, 1940), p. 18.

8 WEA, *A Study in Delinquency: Who Has Offended?* (London: WEA, [1945]), p. 3.

9 For the stress on unity, see Antonia Lant, *Blackout: Reinventing Women for Wartime British Cinema* (Princeton, NJ: Princeton University Press, 1991); Anthony Aldgate and Jeffrey Richards, *Britain Can Take It: The*

British Cinema in the Second World War (Edinburgh: Edinburgh University Press, 2nd edn, 1994).

10 WEA, *A Study in Delinquency*.

11 *Ibid.*, p. 5; Home Office and Ministry of Education joint circular, *Juvenile Delinquency*, HO 99/1953 and Min. of Ed. 265/1953, 20 July 1953, p. 7.

12 WEA, *A Study in Delinquency*, pp. 10 and 12.

13 T. Ferguson, *The Young Delinquent in His Social Setting: A Glasgow Study for the Nuffield Foundation* (London: Oxford University Press, Geoffrey Cumberlege, 1952), Tables 3 and 4, pp. 19 and 21; W. Norwood East, with Percy Stocks and H. T. P. Young, *The Adolescent Criminal: A Medico-Sociological Study of 4,000 Male Adolescents* (London: Churchill, 1942), pp. 113–26.

14 *Ibid.*, p. 166.

15 Nigel Walker, 'Crime and penal measures', in A. H. Halsey (ed.), *Trends in British Society since 1900: A Guide to the Changing Social Structure of Britain* (Basingstoke and London: Macmillan, 1972), Tables 15.10 and 15.11, pp. 535–7.

16 G. Prys Williams, *Patterns of Teenage Delinquency in England and Wales 1946–61* (London: Christian Economic and Social Research Foundation, 1962), pp. 8 and 34.

17 Frank Musgrove, *Youth and the Social Order* (London: Routledge & Kegan Paul, 1964), p. 20.

18 Dick Hobbs, *Doing the Business: Entrepreneurship, the Working Class and Detectives in the East End of London* (Oxford: Oxford University Press, 1988), pp. 147–54.

19 Mays, *Growing Up in the City*, p. 117.

20 John Davis, *Youth and the Condition of Britain: Images of Adolescent Conflict* (London: Athlone Press, 1990), pp. 89–90.

21 Campbell Dixon, 'The year's work in the feature film: a personal impression', in Roger Manvell (ed.), *The Year's Work in the Film 1949* (London: Longmans, Green, for British Council, 1950), p. 23.

22 *Ibid.*, pp. 23–4.

23 Charles Barr, *Ealing Studios* (London: Studio Vista, 2nd edn, 1993), p. 133.

24 Williams, *Patterns of Teenage Delinquency*, p. 34.

25 Arthur La Bern, *Night Darkens the Street* (London: Nicholson & Watson, 1947).

26 Jean Kent, interviewed in Brian McFarlane, *Sixty Voices: Celebrities Recall the Golden Age of British Cinema* (London: BFI, 1992), p. 149; Robert Murphy, *Realism and Tinsel: Cinema and Society in Britain 1939–49* (London: Routledge, 1992), p. 91.

27 La Bern, *Night Darkens the Street*, pp. 16–17.

28 Pearl Jephcott, *Rising Twenty: Notes on Some Ordinary Girls* (London: Faber & Faber, 1948), p. 63.

29 La Bern, *Night Darkens the Street*, p. 106.

30 Murphy, *Realism and Tinsel*, pp. 91–2.

31 Gavin Lambert, 'Film and the idea of happiness', *Contact*, no. 11 (1949), 61.

32 Muriel Box, interviewed in McFarlane, *Sixty Voices*, p. 42.

33 *Daily Film Renter* (10 June 1948), p. 9 and (10 May 1948), p. 3.

34 Jympson Harman, *Evening News* (29 April 1948). Contained in BFI Library, 'Rank films 1945–48' cuttings file.

35 Marcia Landy, *British Genres: Cinema and Society 1930–1960* (Princeton, NJ: Princeton University Press, 1991), p. 453.

36 Viv Chadder, 'The higher heel: women and the post-war British crime film', in Steve Chibnall and Robert Murphy (eds), *British Crime Cinema* (London: Routledge, 1999), pp. 69–70.

37 Nigel Gray, *The Silent Majority: A Study of the Working-Class in Post-War British Fiction* (London: Vision Press, 1973), p. 219.

38 Chadder, 'The higher heel', p. 69.

39 *Ibid.*, p. 70.

40 Landy, *British Genres*, p. 447.

41 CTA, weekly returns for Gaumont, Sheffield, 18 March 1950.

The young offender

9   The Janus faces of the dance hall

A recurring image in British films of the postwar years is the dance hall or palais de danse – a foreign name hints at something exotic beyond the swing doors. In 1946, dance halls in Britain were visited by an estimated three million people per week paying an average of 2s 0d for admission.[1] By comparison, cinema admissions averaged thirty-one million per week at a price of 1s 5d.[2] A quarter of the six million people in the sixteen to twenty-four age group went dancing each week, with more interest being shown by girls.[3] Whether dancing was a class-based activity is more difficult to determine. A pointer is Wilfrid Harper's wartime study conducted in industrial Lancashire and based on 721 diaries and 892 questionnaires: elementary school pupils and working adolescents spent four times as much time in dancing on Saturdays as their grammar school colleagues, who were more likely to be middle class.[4]

The dance hall was an urban phenomenon. In smaller population centres, dances were held in the more prosaic surroundings of church halls and similar multipurpose buildings. By comparison, the dance hall operated six days a week, offered greater comfort and was likely to attract better bands. This could only enhance its mystique for girls unable to sample its pleasures.

The appeal of the dance hall is evident in two Scottish films. In *Floodtide* (d. Frederick Wilson, 1949), considered in Chapter Six, it is where Tim Brogan takes newcomer David Shields as an introduction to Glasgow nightlife. There they meet Tim's future fiancee, Rosie, and her friend, Judy, who later tries to seduce David. In *The Gorbals Story* (d. David MacKane, 1950), considered in Chapter Four, Johnnie recounts events after his humiliation at the hands of Peter Reilly: 'I went to where there was something of youthful happiness, spontaneous gaiety. It was a dance hall – good band, rhythm, rhythm, cleanliness, light, life, light and colour. My senses fell on someone – whom, I don't know – but I kept on searching for sympathy, affection, love.'

The dance hall embodied contradictions. It was a place for enjoying company and finding intimacy away from an over-crowded home, for breaking relationships and making new friends. Though it offered an escape from the workaday world, it was run as a business, satisfying a demand for leisure pursuits in the same way as the cinema. It promised enjoyment, but this was sanctioned pleasure. Because the dance hall had no alcohol licence and dancers were strictly supervised, it was a venue which met with the approval of the Quaker, Seebohm Rowntree.[5]

The ambivalence between pleasure and profit goes deeper. In films, the superficial glamour of the dance hall can conceal something distinctly unpleasant. In *Waterloo Road* (d. Sidney Gilliat, 1945), discussed in Chapter Five, the Alcazar dance hall is a place for illicit trading, where a spiv like Ted Purvis can take a girl for the afternoon. When it is raided by the police, a host of dubious characters tumble out of a back window. *Appointment with Crime* (d. John Harlow, 1946) explores this darker side in greater depth. According to the publicity material, the film was 'as typical as the morning paper headlines and was made as a deterrent to crime'.[6]

John Harlow is a forgotten figure. He was a prolific director, making nine low-budget films between 1944 and 1950. The British Film Institute's SIFT database contains no information on him. The only reference work to mention him reveals that he was born in 1896 and worked as a music hall artist before turning to films.[7] *The Dream of Olwen* (first released in 1947 as *While I Live* and retitled for its 1950 reissue) is his only work to be remembered, and then not for the film itself, but for the theme music by Charles Williams – a pastiche piano concerto in the grand romantic style popularised by Richard Addinsell's Warsaw Concerto. Working for British National was the nearest Harlow came to directing for a major production company.

In *Appointment with Crime*, Leo (William Hartnell) takes part in a smash and grab raid on a jeweller's shop. The organiser is Gus Loman (Raymond Lovell), with Hatchett as getaway driver. A shutter comes down as Leo breaks the shop window, trapping his hands. His companions escape, but Leo is captured and undergoes surgery on his wrists.

Aftercare on Leo's release from prison is limited to the governor's comment that 'If you should require assistance, you may apply to the Discharged Prisoners' Aid Society. It's in the phone book.' Instead of following this advice, Leo survives by committing petty robberies. When he seeks help from Loman, now managing a dance hall, his old boss pulls a gun on him. In the ensuing struggle, Leo takes the gun, using it later to kill Hatchett. Carol Dane (Joyce Howard), a hostess at the dance hall, unwittingly provides an alibi. Loman looks for support from his own boss, the wealthy, foreign art dealer Gregory Lang (one of Herbert Lom's shudderingly sinister gallery of villains), who is the registered owner of the gun. Lang's response is to have Loman killed. The task is assigned to Jonah Crackle (Ivor Barnard), a printer with a sideline in torture and murder. But Lang still needs to discover where the gun is hidden. He has Leo kidnapped by Crackle's gang. Leo breaks down when threatened with having his hands crushed in a printing press. He agrees to steal a diamond for Lang. The robbery is successful, but when Leo returns with his haul, he demands more money. In the ensuing fight, Lang is shot dead. Leo makes his getaway by train on the first stage of his journey to the continent, only to discover that Carol has revealed his plans to the police. As he tries to escape, he is trapped by his wrists again, this time in the window of the train door.

William Hartnell regularly appeared in British films of the 1940s and 50s. His voice and body language marked him as working class, though he often found himself in a supervisory role which isolated him from his fellow characters, making him something of a loner. As Billy Hartnell, he was a sergeant in *The Way Ahead* (d. Carol Reed, 1944). Using his full forename hardly changed his status: he presided over the bar where the hunted gunman sought refuge in *Odd Man Out* (d. Carol Reed, 1947). In 1949, Hartnell was a sergeant again in *The Lost People* (d. Bernard Knowles and Muriel Box). A decade later, he was still training recruits in *Carry on Sergeant* (d. Gerald Thomas, 1958) and *The Night We Dropped a Clanger* (d. Darcy Conyers, 1959). Shirley Eaton, who worked with him, portrays a man whose abrasive screen persona was at odds with his own personality, and who talked frankly about his discharge from the army with a nervous breakdown.[8] His final major role as Doctor Who marked an abrupt change of direction.

Whatever contributed to Hartnell's screen portrayals, working-class fatalism had no place. In *Appointment with Crime*, the pent-up anger is palpable in his strident voice. Leo may be afraid, but he is never cowed. This contributes to the frisson of his scenes with Loman, the dance hall manager, where middle-class superiority buckles in the face of working-class resolution. A more worthy opponent is the wealthy Lang. Loman calls him 'sir'; Leo does not.[9]

Clothes help to delineate the characters' status. Though Leo begins the film dressed in stylish clothes, by the time of his release from prison he is a colourless figure who merges into the London crowds. As so often in films of the period, men's suits have their own range of gradations. This applies to the detectives: the smartly-dressed Inspector Rogers (Robert Beatty) and the lower-status sergeant, Charlie Weeks (Cyril Smith), who inhabits his baggy suit rather than wearing it. The bustling and obsequious little printer-cum-murderer, the Dickensian Jonah Crackle, wears a bowler with his suit and has the neat, old-fashioned demeanour of a small businessman. Loman wears a suit in keeping with his position as dance hall manager, yet it looks creased and ill-fitting when he confronts the immaculate and wealthy Lang. When Lang is killed, he is wearing a tailored, brocade jacket which contrasts with Leo's zipped jacket. Zips were a novelty in the 1940s. For men, they were used by the lower classes, except when leather clothes were worn by flyers and sports car enthusiasts.

Psychiatry came of age during the war, with a bastardised form often helping to shore up an ailing film plot, *Madonna of the Seven Moons* (d. Arthur Crabtree, 1944) and *The October Man* (d. Roy Baker, 1947) being notable British examples. The damage to Leo's wrists in *Appointment with Crime* is reminiscent in its effect to James Mason striking Ann Todd's hands in *The Seventh Veil* (d. Compton Bennett, 1945), if more unusual in that the victim who suffers the subsequent psychological trauma is working class. Though not overemphasised, the psychological effect of the damage to Leo's wrists is established in a series of montage shots early in the film as he lies sedated in hospital. This hints that Leo earned his living by playing in a dance band, which makes his injuries all the more poignant. The panic recurs at two key moments: his breakdown when Jonah Crackle threatens to crush his hands and his final capture by the police when he is again trapped by his wrists. His repeated cry of 'My wrists!' is genuinely chilling.

The dance hall is as central to the film as Hartnell himself. Its commercialism becomes evident on his first visit, when Carol explains that for each dance with her, he needs to buy a sixpenny ticket from the cashier. Carol is alone in London. Like Gwen in *Good Time Girl* (d. David Macdonald, 1948), she lives off her looks, waiting for a man to choose her in preference to another hostess. She confides to Leo that the other girls call her Chastity Ann. As her relationship with him deepens, she comes to accept his view of events to the extent of visiting Scotland Yard to support his alibi. This makes her rapid conversion to the official view unconvincing when the inspector calls at her lodgings during the murder hunt.

Surprisingly for a film released in 1946, there is no reference to the war and no bomb damage is shown in the few location shots. The only indication of the date is the air raid shelter where Leo hides Hatchett's body. Stylistically, the noir elements are of their time. When Leo attempts to rob a garage, the camera lingers on his shadow stretched across the brightly-lit entrance. The world of officialdom represented by prison and Scotland Yard operates during the day. Leo's world – of crime and the dance hall – belongs to the night, the brightly-lit interiors contrasting with the surrounding darkness. In this respect the film foreshadows *Night and the City* (d. Jules Dassin, 1950).

Lang's colleague, Noel Penn (Alan Wheatley), is described in the press book as 'an effeminate, simpering dandy'. His role in the story is as ambiguous as his character, which suggests that some of his scenes may have been cut. His voice betrays an upper-class education. He has a business relationship with Lang, insisting on a higher fee for arranging Loman's murder. 'Expenses are increasing by leaps and bounds,' he explains as he sketches a glissando on Lang's grand piano. Yet he is at home in Lang's flat, particularly in the final scenes as the two men await Leo's return with the stolen diamond. Lang is on edge; Penn plays Tchaikovsky. Any explicitly sexual relationship between the two men would have fallen foul of the censors – there are no extant records to indicate what changes to the script were demanded after it was initially turned down.[10]

Appointment with Crime is ambiguous in its morality. The focus is on Leo. Because he is the victim of a double cross and because the characters he confronts are, with the exception of Carol, uniformly unattractive, the audience is on his side even though he is a robber and a murderer. The synopsis in the press book is less sympathetic. In the film, the scene in which Lang is killed emphasises his double cross of Leo; according to the press book, 'the greed of the criminal comes to the fore and he [Leo] tries to extract more money from Lang.' The emphasis may have changed during shooting and editing. Leo has his own moral standards based on group loyalty. What angers him is not so much that his colleagues abandoned him when the robbery went wrong, but that Loman 'failed to redeem his pledge' when asked for help. Leo emphasises this on their second encounter after his release from prison, when he has disarmed Loman and is twisting his wrists:

LEO: But what you did to me then was nothing to what you did to me a few days ago.
LOMAN: I didn't do anything.
LEO: No, that's just it – you didn't do anything. But you told me I was

washed up, that I couldn't do another job with these wrists of mine, that I bungled things. There was no room for me in your organisation. That hurt me more than anything else.

Leo's values have little to do with the law. The amorality of those above him fuels his bitterness. Yet in holding to his own values, he shows a kind of integrity. He may be seen as a thug and a murderer who is using Carol. This is the way in which she comes to regard him. He may also be seen as a misused individual, intent on making a new life. This is how he represents himself to her. Whether he really has any feelings for her is left unresolved.

As Robert Murphy notes, critics' responses varied according to their attitudes to violence.[11] On the BFI's copy of the press book, an unknown hand has written 'Slow by Hollywood standards, but what does it matter. This is London calling, & calling in her own authentic accent.' This seems a fair assessment. More succinct is the verdict on the Rank card: 'Saturday entertainment for strong stomachs'. Perhaps there were few of these in Leeds and southeast Essex, where the film met with modest success (Appendix, Tables 6 and 7).

The girls interviewed by Pearl Jephcott 'not only chat about last night's picture at work but will discuss it at a deeper level with a particular and intimate friend. Two girls at camp retold each other the story of *The Sullivans*. Although they normally never talk about ideas they fumbled to discover the values that this picture had for them.'[12] If Jephcott's girls saw *Appointment with Crime*, they had plenty to discuss the following morning.

There are no moral ambiguities in *Dancing with Crime* (d. John Paddy Carstairs, 1947). A demobbed Ted Peters (Richard Attenborough) works as a taxi driver. He meets an old friend, Dave Robinson (Bill Owen), who lives on the fringes of the law. Ted drives him to Marsh Lane in southeast London. It is not until later that he discovers Dave's body in the back of the cab. Ted is dissatisfied with the speed of the police enquiry. He suspects that Dave was visiting a dance hall in Marsh Lane. When Ted goes there with his girlfriend, Joy (Sheila Sim), she encounters a show-business friend, Annette (Diana Dors in an early character part), who is working as a dance hostess. In confirmation of his suspicions, Ted recognises another hostess, Toni (Judy Kelly), from a photograph in Dave's room. Joy takes a job alongside Annette in the hope of discovering information. Toni becomes jealous when the master of ceremonies, Paul Baker (Barry K. Barnes), pays Joy too much attention. The crooked manager, Gregory (Barry Jones), poses as a police inspector to discover what Ted knows. Sub-

13 Old friends: Ted (Richard Attenborough), Joy (Sheila Sim) and Dave (Bill Owen) are reunited in *Dancing with Crime* (1947). Dave's clothes mark him as a spiv

sequently, Gregory arranges for Ted to be killed and for the gun used to kill Dave to be planted on him. Ted is lured to a warehouse, but escapes.

In the dance hall, Joy overhears a plot to raid an Oxford Street store. She has time to telephone Ted and the police before her true identity is revealed to the gang by Toni. Ted goes to the store, still believing that Gregory is a policemen, only to be captured by him. When the police arrive, Gregory escapes. He returns to the dance hall, taking Joy hostage, but Ted rescues her in the final shootout.

Dancing with Crime is a variation on the well-worn theme of the amateur sleuth who rushes in where the police fear to tread. The audience can either groan at his foolishness, or bite their nails as he imperils himself. The war is not long over: Ted still wears his army uniform. The point is reinforced in the opening conversation between Ted and Dave, in which they catch up on what they have been doing since serving together at Tobruk. No location shots of bombsites are needed to enhance the sense of period.

Dave's clothes proclaim that he is a spiv if his truculent manner does not give it away. Joy wants Dave to get a proper job, but she does not press the point and she shows no hostility towards him.

When Ted and Dave are alone, Dave makes his source of income clear:

DAVE: Do you want to do yourself a bit of good?
TED: It all depends.
DAVE: Well this thing I'm in now is money for jam.
TED: Yer? What is it?
DAVE: This and that. Nice connections, though. Everything the rich man wants and can't get. No cheques, no questions, no coupons. And a very nice sideline in jewellery.

Dave is the loveable rogue rather than a career criminal. The audience is on his side – something which is not the case with spivs who had dodged call-up, like Ted Purvis in *Waterloo Road*. Dave's chosen path is attributable to the war. This is made clear when the police interview Ted and Joy after his death:

JOY: Dave was never hard up.
TED: He could think of more ways to earn a couple of bob.
INSPECTOR: Civvy street seems pretty strange to some of the boys.
JOY: Yes – when they come out, they don't know what to do.
TED: Well, sir, it isn't only that. But the job he did before the war seems sort of small after six years.
JOY: Besides, it costs so much more to live now.
INSPECTOR: And Robinson couldn't wait to save the half.
TED: No sir. Whatever old Dave wanted, he had to have. He usually got it, too.

Ted's deference to the middle-class inspector is evident. None of them sees Dave as intrinsically bad. Dave's wish to have whatever he wanted is perceived as an example of the working-class preference for living for the present, or, from the inspector's middle-class viewpoint, a desire for instant gratification. This is what led him into crime.

Bill Owen sounds a convincing working-class Londoner, with a tang of Shepherd's Bush rather than the flatter vowels of south London later immortalised by Michael Caine. Richard Attenborough assumes an all-purpose working-class accent which at least contrasts with the middle-class accent and demeanour of the master of ceremonies at the dance hall. Though Joy, Ted and Dave were childhood friends, Sheila Sim's Joy is a more classless creation than the male characters, both in her speech and in her attitude to the middle-class inspector. In mitigation, Joy's career in show business may have given her a middle-class veneer. Toni and Annette, the other hostesses, show no signs of being anything other than middle class. If Carol in *Appointment with Crime* has reservations about the status of her work, these girls do not share them. Nor does Ted, who positively encourages Joy to become involved.

The Janus faces of the dance hall

143

As in *Appointment with Crime*, the dance hall is a den of crime involving everyone from the manager to the barman, with control being exerted downwards through the social scale. In common with other films about criminal gangs, dirty work is delegated to working-class characters. The manager, Gregory, literally has life or death power over his gang – the penalty for Sniffy, who fails to kill Ted, is to be killed himself – though this power does not extend to controlling the middle-class master of ceremonies, Paul Baker, who is nominally a subordinate. It is Baker who shoots Dave in the alley beside the dance hall, despite Gregory's pleading. No sanctions are applied in this case. The middle class do things differently.

Dancing with Crime did well in southeast Essex, but was seen less in the sample Leeds cinemas (Appendix, Tables 6 and 7). This is likely to be another case where high rental costs put a popular film beyond the reach of the Leeds independents. Casting is one reason why *Dancing with Crime* proved more popular at the box office than *Appointment with Crime*. Neither film had box-office draws of the calibre of James Mason or Anna Neagle, but Hartnell was an actor's actor, while Attenborough was a rising star. Crucially, Ted is likeable, which cannot be said of Leo in *Appointment with Crime*. The relationship between Ted and Joy is uncomplicated, in contrast to the bitter taste left by the relationship of Leo and Carol. There was more for audiences to relate to, or want to relate to, in *Dancing with Crime*, particularly as Attenborough and Sim were husband and wife. The audience also knows a crucial fact denied to Ted, Joy and the police: Gregory, the manager of the dance hall, masterminds the criminal gang in which Dave was involved. This adds a frisson to the scenes in which Ted accepts Gregory as a policeman: when will the villain show his true colours? For all its simplicity of characterisation and plot, *Dancing with Crime* hooked audiences in a way which eluded *Appointment with Crime*.

The third of the trio of dance-hall films is *Dance Hall* (d. Charles Crichton, 1950). This has received more critical attention than its predecessors, not only on the strength of its place in the Ealing canon, but because of the range of female characters portrayed.[13]

The film follows the fortunes of a group of factory girls whose social lives centre on the Chiswick Palais. The story resembles a repressed version of Max Ophuls' *La Ronde*, released in the same year. Eve (Natasha Parry) has to decide between her dancing partner, the philandering Alec (Bonar Colleano), and the jealous and work-centred Phil (Donald Houston). Georgie (Petula Clark) and her dancing partner, Peter (Douglas Barr), are intent on winning the dancing championship. Carol (Diana Dors) seeks the man of her dreams and finds him in the silent giant, Mike (James Carney).

Eve and Phil marry, but Phil does not change his ways. Eve tires of being left alone in the evenings and drifts back to the dance hall. Phil comes looking for her and picks a fight with Alec, who is paying her too much attention. Meanwhile, Georgie and Peter fail to win the championship, but become engaged, as do Carol and Mike. Eve and Phil finally make up.

In *Dance Hall*, the benign side of the palais is portrayed. Dancing and the kaleidoscope of the dancers' relationships are at the core of the film. Most of the action takes place in the classless surroundings of the dance hall with its incessant background of dance music – location shooting took place at the Hammersmith Palais. These scenes are counterpointed by the family-centred life in the tenement blocks and the girls' work in a factory. At work they are subservient to the machines, their conversation restricted by the noise and the glares of the patrolling overseer. Overalls emphasise their working-class status. Only Carol shows any hint of rebellion.

The tenement rooms are old-fashioned and overcrowded by comparison with the uncluttered, curving lines of the dance hall. Eve has her own bed, though she shares the room with her two sisters who sleep in an iron-framed double bed. No bathroom is shown. This is a traditional, communal world, in which girls do the washing up and look after younger siblings. It is also a world without formality. Carol greets Georgie's parents through the window beside the walkway – and enters the flat by the same route.

A telling incident is when Georgie's parents buy her a dress for the championship. The dance hall manager has already hired a far more lavish dress for the night, but Georgie cannot hurt her parents by telling them. Though the suitability of the dress is a generational issue, it is also a class issue: by implication, her parents have inappropriate standards of what is suitable and a level of income which is associated with restricted horizons.[14]

For Melinda Mash, '[the dance hall] is . . . the site through which the characters enter into new patterns of consumption. Yet the desire to escape from a world bounded by "austerity" is tempered by another boundedness: the lack of means ever to fully escape.'[15] Austerity is certainly in evidence as Eve bewails Phil's profligacy in using up food which is on points (a system of supplementing rationed goods by accumulating points). Yet Mash implies escape in a wider sense: from economic circumstances, class, or their subordinate status as women. What the girls escape to is less

14   Eve (Natasha Parry) gets ready for a Sunday dancing class
in *Dance Hall* (1950). A shared bedroom in a tenement flat

clear. It might entail coming to terms with new constraints, such
as a demanding job or higher material expectations which cannot
be fulfilled. *Dance Hall* offers several escape routes, even if they are
hardly innovative. Eve can achieve middle-class status through her
marriage to the aircraft engineer, Phil, though the film demonstrates that this route may cut her off from her friends. Georgie has
her talent as a dancer; marriage may constrain or liberate her.
Carol has her sexuality: whether she lives happily ever after with
Mike remains unknown. The fourth girl, Mary (Jane Hylton), who
harbours a hopeless love for Phil, is the only member of the quartet
with no obvious means to change her life. She seems destined to
be everyone's auntie, forever dispensing sensible advice as she
matures into a Flora Robson figure.

A weakness of the film is the lack of consistency in its class
images. Aside from Georgie, there is little attempt to anchor the
girls in their class by exploring their home lives. The presence of
Gladys Henson as Georgie's mother signals that this is respectable
working-class territory. Among the girls, only Diana Dors' insou-
ciance is convincingly working class. No attempt is made to adopt
working-class speech idioms; both Petula Clark and Natasha Parry
sound resolutely middle class.[16]

15   Living room set from *Dance Hall* (1950). The furniture and
ornaments were dated by the 1950s

16   Kitchen set from *Dance Hall* (1950). The shallow sink gave way to
the deep Belfast pattern sink in the early years of the century, but
was still a common sight in 1950

Alec is the disruptive character in what might otherwise be a cosy drama. He brings American ways and American sexuality to complement the exoticism of the palais. He is smartly dressed and independent – a man who is sure of himself. He can take Eve back to his lodgings and dance with her as they talk of their feelings – something which Phil would never do. Though Alec has contacts with the black market – he supplies the fish for Phil's breakfast – he is a man for the 1950s, less concerned with mere sartorial display than the spiv of austerity years. Instead, enjoyment is coming to the fore, including ownership of a car.

Dance Hall was released in June 1950. It was never shown in the sample Leeds cinemas by the end of the year. In southeast Essex it did well, given that the release date was late in the period studied (Appendix, Table 7). At the Gaumont, Sheffield, the film was 'Well received by [the] younger generation many of whom were disappointed that better use was [not] made of the Bands.' [17] The comment is surprising given the number of times the action is held up for musical numbers, though complainants may have been indicating that they wanted better integration of music and action. The film ranked in the third quartile of attendances (Appendix, Table 5).

Segregation by seat price meant that the cinema was not truly egalitarian. No such distinctions applied in the dance hall. This classless arena might have been exploited in film with a Romeo and Juliet inspired plot involving a boy and girl from different social backgrounds. For an era when social differences were supposed to be dissolving, this theme received scant attention. Instead, the superficial allure of the dance hall was contrasted with the criminal activities which, in the eyes of film-makers, underpinned it. While working-class innocents (usually girls) were seduced by the glamour of the palais, working-class villains (usually male) carried out crimes and shouldered the risks. Middle-class figures spanned both worlds, exercising control and taking the profits. *Dance Hall* does at least acknowledge that not all dance hall managers ran criminal gangs, even if it fails to portray working-class life in any realistic sense. It was also one of the first films aimed specifically at the youth market.

The decline of the palais was to mirror that of the cinema and the music hall. *Dance Hall* celebrates its heyday. Jympson Harman saw the film as a slice of life. [18] In its attempt to eavesdrop on ordinary people rather than to resolve a story are elements of the working-class soap opera which began on television with *Coronation Street* (Granada TV, 1960–current). The difference a decade made was that by 1960, working-class characters could be presented without self-consciousness.

Notes

1 Mark Abrams, 'Britain off duty', *Contact*, no. 6 (1947), 2.

2 Calculated from BFI, British Film Producers' Association, 'The film industry statistical digest', no. 1 (1954), p. 9.

3 Abrams, 'Britain off duty', 2; University of Bristol, *The Welfare of Youth: A City Survey* (Bristol: University of Bristol, 1945), pp. 20–2.

4 Wilfrid Harper, 'The leisure activities of adolescents. An investigation of the psychological function of the various leisure activities of adolescents in a particular town with some special references to the cinema and reading', MA thesis, Victoria University of Manchester, 1942, Tables 1 to 10.

5 B. Seebohm Rowntree and G. R. Lavers, *English Life and Leisure: A Social Study* (London: Longmans, Green, 1951), p. 281.

6 BFI Library, press book for *Appointment with Crime*.

7 Leslie Halliwell, *Halliwell's Filmgoer's and Video Viewer's Companion* (London: Grafton Books, 9th edn, 1988), pp. 322–3.

8 Shirley Eaton, *Golden Girl* (London: Batsford, 1999), pp. 77–8.

9 An unknown hand has written in the BFI's copy of the press book that this is a cliché.

10 For details see James C. Robertson, 'The censors and British gangland', in Steve Chibnall and Robert Murphy (eds), *British Crime Cinema* (London: Routledge, 1999), pp. 17–18.

11 Robert Murphy, *Realism and Tinsel: Cinema and Society in Britain 1939–49* (London: Routledge, 1992), p. 152.

12 Pearl Jephcott, *Rising Twenty: Notes on Some Ordinary Girls* (London: Faber & Faber, 1948), p. 156.

13 One example is Melinda Mash, 'Stepping out or out of step? Austerity, affluence and femininity in two post-war films', in Christine Gledhill and Gillian Swanson (eds), *Nationalising Femininity* (Manchester: Manchester University Press, 1996), pp. 257–63.

14 Clothes are considered in more detail in Pat Kirkham, 'Dress, dance, dreams and fantasy: fashion and fantasy in *Dance Hall*', *Journal of Design History*, 8:3 (1995), 195–214.

15 Mash, 'Stepping out or out of step?', p. 260.

16 The same point as been made elsewhere. See Peter Stead, *Film and the Working Class: The Feature Film in British and American History* (London: Routledge, 1991), p. 164. It is not completely true, as Stead suggests, that this was only perceived by later critics – the Rank card for *Dance Hall* notes the unreality of the leading characters.

17 CTA, weekly returns for Gaumont, Sheffield, 25 August 1950.

18 Edgar Anstey, Roger Manvell, Ernest Lindgren and Paul Rotha (eds), *Shots in the Dark: A Collection of Reviewers' Opinions on Some Leading Films* (London: Allan Wingate, 1951), p. 197.

10 Echoes of applause: from music hall to celluloid

As a latecomer to the entertainment scene, the film industry drew on established traditions and expertise. For comedy, this meant reliance on the music hall, even though the crucial interaction between audience and performer could not be emulated on screen. Because the cinema assumed its dominant position slowly, the conventions of both forms of entertainment were known to audiences and were used interchangeably by film-makers. Stars like George Formby and Gracie Fields were schooled in the music-hall tradition and continued appearing on stage at the height of their fame as film stars. Just as pantomime seasons have come to form a regular part of the schedules for television personalities, so curiosity prompted fans to see film stars in person, reinforcing their popularity – a symbiosis of stage and screen which deserves more academic attention.

The music hall reinvented itself as variety with sufficient success for new theatres to be built in the 1930s.[1] After the Second World War, the fortunes of the two forms of entertainment were similar. Both experienced an initial boom – two northern entrepreneurs set about converting cinemas into variety theatres.[2] Both forms experienced a reversal in the 1950s, the difference being that, for the music hall, the decline proved terminal. The last rites were administered in *Charley Moon* (d. Guy Hamilton, 1956), *Davy* (d. Michael Relph, 1957) and *The Entertainer* (d. Tony Richardson, 1960). The cinema's debt to its older partner did not go unacknowledged. The early days of the music hall were evoked nostalgically in *Champagne Charlie* (d. Cavalcanti, 1944) and a string of films which followed.

A fitful scholarly interest in the music hall became apparent in the 1970s, when it was seen as an early example of mass culture.

An emphasis on its role as a means of social control was modified in later literature.[3] Undeniably, the halls took on the characteristics of businesses during the late nineteenth century, becoming larger and more specialised. Their organisation into circuits foreshadowed how the cinema industry was to evolve.[4] But this did not preclude artists from using the halls as platforms for more subversive views – such an august institution as the BBC managed to accommodate the maverick talents of Tommy Handley, the Goons and Mort Sahl, not to mention punk rock.[5]

In the late 1940s, the cinema's debt to the music hall was evident in the Mancunian comedies and the Old Mother Riley series. Both were distinctive forms of British cinema, though their proletarian character means that they have received scant critical attention.

A dozen films and some forty photographs held by the North West Film Archive are the only tangible reminders of John E. Blakeley's grandly-named Mancunian Film Corporation. A generation of neglect came to an end with a television documentary in 1988. Aside from Jeffrey Richards' contributions, this contains reminiscences from former studio staff which also appear in a slim but comprehensive history of Blakeley's venture.[6]

The heyday for Mancunian came in the late 1940s, when the studio at Rusholme in Manchester was operating and Mancunian became its distribution arm. The studio's output consisted almost entirely of comedies. In the television documentary, Richards suggests that variety performers were used because they were adept at timing gags and working in single takes. When combined with the saving on props (items were often lent by staff and friends) and the low overheads achieved by working away from London, films could be made on shoestring budgets: a ninety-three minute feature, *Cup Tie Honeymoon* (d. John E. Blakeley, 1948), was made for £45,000 in fourteen weeks.[7] The claim is made in the television documentary that of more than twenty-five feature films made by Mancunian, none lost money. If true, this is something unique among British film production companies of the 1940s.

A roster of northern variety artists worked regularly for Mancunian, the most notorious being Frank Randle. Richards describes him as disreputable, subversive, lecherous, drunken and insubordinate – a man who recognised traits in ordinary people which were generally suppressed.[8] James Casey, a scriptwriter for Mancunian and the son of comedian Jimmy James, considers Randle to be an anarchist, beating authority.[9] The popularity of the stars was reinforced by their stage appearances – summer seasons at the seaside, notably Blackpool, and pantomimes in the major northern conurbations.

The scenarios of Mancunian films, the characters of the stars and the low production costs resulted in a unique style of filmmaking which appealed to northern, working-class audiences. Two Mancunian offerings, *Somewhere in Camp* (d. John E. Blakeley, 1940) and *Somewhere on Leave* (d. John E. Blakeley, 1942) drew the largest audiences at the Majestic, Macclesfield, in 1942 and 1943 respectively.[10] Although made at Riverside Studios in London, *Home Sweet Home* (d. John E. Blakeley, 1945) is a typical Mancunian product in its casting and scenario. It gives scope for stage business and music to be woven around a romantic storyline (there is an opportunity for the pianists Rawicz and Landauer to make an appearance playing Lizst). Dot Stimson, who worked as film editor for Blakeley, recalls that on another of his films, *Holidays with Pay* (1948), the script had blank pages headed BUS, indicating that stage business should fill the gap.[11]

In *Home Sweet Home*, Frank Randle works for Wright's Pianos as commissionaire and handyman. His wife is about to have a baby. An orphaned evacuee from the Channel Islands, Jacqueline Chantry (Nicolette Roeg), lodges with them and works as chauffeuse to the owner of the company, Colonel Wright (H. F. Maltby). The colonel's son, Eric (Tony Pendrell), wants to marry Jacqueline, but the colonel and his wife are against such an unequal social match. They dismiss Jacqueline while Eric is in the Channel Islands uncovering her background. When he discovers that she comes from an old French family and is an heiress, his parents have second thoughts. Mrs Wright pays Frank to find Jacqueline. By pretending to be a foreign prince, he gains access to the exclusive London nightclub where she works. He takes her to Eric's home, where the couple are reunited. Frank turns down an improved position at the works in favour of running his own business – charging the public to see the quadruplets to which his wife has given birth.

Class is central to the film, most obviously in the romance between Eric and Jacqueline. It underpins Randle's performance – he reprises his stage persona as the shambling, comedic drunk. To what extent his stage persona was carried into his private life is another matter. John Fisher sees strong connections.[12] Even as a commissionaire, Randle manages not to be subservient, handing Colonel Wright the morning post to take into the office. An employer is someone to be outwitted rather than feared or revered. This shows most clearly in the colonel's office, where Randle takes charge of their exchange, reading a book on the desk through the colonel's monocle before helping himself to a packet of cigarettes and a cigar. The obvious solution is to sack him, but as the colonel explains to the manager, 'I've been going to a score of times and then he says he forgives me and behaves as though he were the aggrieved person.' After a Home Guard reunion supper, Randle and the colonel go back to the latter's house to continue their drinking. This convivial occasion comes to an abrupt end when Randle insults his host, who finally recognises his companion.

Randle's clothes symbolise his attitude to convention. They might be ordinary, but he never wears them in an ordinary way. One pocket of his trousers hangs out, as does one side of his shirt tail; his tie is crooked and needs tightening; his waistcoat is folded in on itself at the back; his army cap is coming apart, with strands hanging down like ribbons. His bowler is respectable enough – except that he wears it at home when the vicar and the doctor visit his wife. Yet he is also a kindly family man, prepared to make breakfast for his wife and Jacqueline, to do the ironing and take in puppies which he is supposed to drown.

Randle is the working-class hero: living on his wits, disdainful of authority, hard-drinking, family-centred and with an eye to any opportunity which comes his way. Though he might be expected to inhabit a Coronation Street world of corner pubs and cramped terraces, his home in the film is a spacious, middle-class semi-detached house from the 1930s. Yet despite the trappings of affluence, this is still a traditional world where workmates live nearby, the policeman wakes residents by giving them an early morning knock and Randle can throw a bottle of milk at the cat. Similarly, the inside of the house abandons modernity in favour of the traditional northern pattern of a kitchen doubling as living room, though it does boast an electric cooker as well as a range.

In terms of attendance, *Home Sweet Home* ranked fourth out of fifty-one films screened at the Majestic, Macclesfield, in 1945.[13] It was moderately successful in working-class Leeds; surprisingly it was even more popular in southeast Essex, where it was the only Mancunian film to make any impact (Appendix, Tables 6 and 7). One reason for this must be that Randle rebels. In a short scene which sums up his attitude, he tears up his time card and throws the pieces in the air. Many members of the audience must have longed to emulate his gesture after six years of wartime regulations. In this, the timing of the film's release was fortuitous. Yet is this really a gesture of rebellion when he is anticipating promotion to a salaried job in which he does not have to clock on? Randle manages to side with the traditional working class while harbouring middle-class aspirations – a delicate balancing act confronting many working-class people. The other factor in the film's favour is the comforting familiarity of the location: houses in the mythical town of Redvale were similar to those cinemagoers passed on their way home. What cannot be easily explained is why other Randle films failed to find an audience in the south of England.

After five years of austerity came one of the last of the Mancunian films, *Over the Garden Wall* (d. John E. Blakeley, 1950). Distribution was aided by a loan from the National Film Finance Corporation.[14] The film was successful enough to be reissued in 1959, albeit with thirty-nine of its ninety-four minutes cut. This ability to undergo savage cutting underlines the episodic nature of Mancunian productions. Removing several scenes hardly makes the finished product any less comprehensible.

A telegram throws Fanny Lawton (Norman Evans) and her husband, Joe (Jimmy James), into confusion. Their daughter, Mary, who married a GI and lives in America, has had a baby and is to visit them. When the couple arrive, the 'baby' proves to be a dog. Mary visits the factory where her father works and where she was once employed. The owner's son urges her to stay in England, so that they might resume their relationship. His present fiancee is jealous. A rift also develops between Mary and her husband, but at the end of the film they are reconciled and return to the States.

The two stars, Norman Evans and Jimmy James, were well known on stage and radio. The film's title comes from Norman Evans' most famous sketch: a monologue in which he plays a housewife gossiping over the wall to an unseen neighbour. The sketch duly appears towards the end of the film (with Evans falling into the fish pond) and must have caused a ripple of recognition among audiences. Evans' role as Fanny Lawton is in the tradition of pantomime dames, down to the obligatory revealing of layers of underwear as she undresses at night, though the twin beds are an innovation. Norman Evans trying his hand at dentistry and Jimmy James as a drunk are other pieces of stage business inserted none too subtly into the scenario, along with the obligatory musical interludes. Some sections of the film, such as a drunken Joe Lawton drying plates by putting them through the mangle, hark back to the days of silent film comedy. Stimson recalls that the routines were the work of Bert Tracey, who wrote for Laurel and Hardy.[15] Tracey worked with Oliver Hardy in 1914 and was living in the Victoria Park area of Manchester in the late 1940s.[16]

In the factory scenes, the distinction between management and workers is apparent in clothing (clean suits rather than dirty overalls), accents (received pronunciation vies with northern accents) and the emphasis on time-keeping for manual workers. A timekeeper watches them clocking on. He is firmly in the management camp, reprimanding Joe and his pals for their late arrival. They retaliate by reminding him that they know of his pilfering and his affair with the canteen manageress. Like Frank Randle, these are not workers who are cowed by authority; if anything they exploit its weakness, calling a strike over an argument with the supervisor.

The stars belong among ordinary people; the film takes the viewpoint of ordinary people. A stereotyped working man's world of life on the factory floor is evoked, enlivened by drinking, betting, the closeness of workmates and with the prospect of being henpecked on returning home. Norman Evans' Fanny Lawton is a caricature, but the character contains enough elements of truth to be credible. 'What will Mrs Webster say?' she laments, conscious of the impression being made on neighbours as Joe comes home drunk after celebrating Mary's return. Yet as in *Home Sweet Home*, this is no traditional working-class environment. Home is a 1920s semidetached cottage of the kind which could be found in a private development or on a council estate influenced by the garden cities movement. The kitchen has a washing machine, which was a rarity in 1950, though water for washing up is heated in the kettle – an authentic touch given the cost of heating water. Nor should a bathroom be taken for granted in a house of this age and size – particularly a bathroom as luxurious as the one seen here. It is needed for several pieces of stage business, including Jimmy James falling fully clothed into a bath of water.

The film's release date of May 1950 means that its fortunes in the two areas can only be followed for a few months (Appendix, Tables 6 and 7). In southeast Essex, *Over the Garden Wall* ran for a week as main feature at a Rank cinema and was passed to independent cinemas in the area without further circuit screenings.[17] This suggests that Rank had little confidence in its drawing power.

Home Sweet Home and *Over the Garden Wall* celebrate the working class without eulogising it. Both contrast the warmth and solidarity of the working class with the duplicitous ways of authority symbolised by the family business – that most traditional means of organising capital and labour. Both show the aim as accommodation with authority rather than its overthrow, though along the way the pomposity of authority figures is punctured. In both films a young woman experiences social mobility, recalling Michael Powell and Emeric Pressburger's *I Know Where I'm Going* (1945). Powell and Pressburger might have developed the theme more elegantly, but for a populist approach, Mancunian takes the honours.

Female impersonation was staple fare for the music hall and Arthur Lucan's Old Mother Riley was its most enduring creation on film. For Andy Medhurst,

The Riley films offered perhaps the most honest solution to the problem of reconciling variety traditions and generic credibility: don't bother. The public that liked the act on stage would pay to come and see it on film, and it was the mass paying public that these films were made for. Fretting over their narrative flaws and absence of psychological credibility is, in the final analysis, a waste of time.[18]

Though it is hard to disagree with Medhurst's conclusion, his approach does preempt serious consideration of the films. Class offers a route which avoids his condescending view of the mass public.

Of the fifteen films in the Old Mother Riley series, *Old Mother Riley's New Venture* (d. John Harlow, 1949) was the only one to reach the West End of London.[19] As in the Mancunian films, the plot is little more than a device for introducing stage business and musical numbers. Old Mother Riley (Arthur Lucan) washes up in the hotel where her daughter, Kitty (Kitty McShane), is a receptionist. The owner is advised by his doctor to go abroad immediately. He entrusts the running of the hotel to the first member of staff who comes through his door. This happens to be Old Mother Riley. The bedroom which she chooses for herself is the one in which the other staff hide jewellery stolen from the guests. Meanwhile, the owner's nephew and his wife suspect Old Mother Riley of murdering their uncle. They have her arrested so that they can take control of the hotel. She escapes from jail and goes back to the hotel to clear her name. The owner returns at the same time and Old Mother Riley helps him to unmask the real thieves.

Economy is the watchword of the production, with a dozen basic sets and one location sequence in which Old Mother Riley makes her way to her tenement flat after escaping from prison.[20] The flat has heavily-patterned wallpaper in a style which was in vogue before the First World War, while the furniture is dark and heavy. By contrast, the hotel is modern, with wide staircases, large rooms and minimal furnishings in art deco style. Old Mother Riley's excitement on seeing her hotel bedroom is understandable.

Old Mother Riley's clothes give the film its old-fashioned air. The bonnet holding her wispy white hair in place and the shawl belong half a century earlier, when the music hall was in its heyday. The same may be said of the excessively long shoes, so like those of Chaplin. Clothing also helps to chart her changing social position. The apron is abandoned as she tries on new dresses, only to be donned again as her status declines. Her habits remain robustly proletarian throughout. A beer bottle and a mug stand on her bedside table at the hotel. Her money is kept beneath a loose floorboard. The dichotomy between status and habits is exploited in an extended sketch in which an Arab potentate and his party seek to adopt English eating habits by imitating her gestures. The humour might be simple, but it is also surreal.

Family is represented by Old Mother Riley and her daughter, Kitty. The only other family grouping is that of the hotel owner, his nephew and the nephew's wife. In contrast to the Riley's closeness, the middle-class couple are duplicitous, being more interested in gaining control of the hotel than their uncle's welfare. They resent Old Mother Riley's sudden promotion, as do other members of the staff. So upward mobility has its price. The moral of her adventure is that being poor but honest is the best policy.

The film revels in its own artifice, or in Robert Stam's terms, the reflexive element is marked.[21] There is a sense of playing with the medium, with a nod towards the interaction between performer and audience which is so much a feature of music hall and pantomime. As Old Mother Riley sets eyes on her room in the hotel for the first time, she tells Kitty, 'It's like a film star's. If I had my time again, I'd be a film star.' Later, as she examines a hair drier in a beauty parlour, she asks, 'What's this? Mine own executioner?' (Anthony Kimmins' film, Mine Own Executioner, had been released two years earlier in 1947.) Most intriguing of all is the closing scene in which everyone joins in throwing custard pies. There is a cut to the film studio, with Harlow himself demanding 'Give me more.' A cinema-literate generation had plenty to enjoy.

Old Mother Riley, Headmistress (d. John Harlow) was released a year later in 1950. The scenario by John Harlow and Ted Kavanagh allows for the usual quota of music and slapstick. A distant relative leaves Old Mother Riley the laundry where she is a not very efficient employee. When her daughter, Kitty, is sacked from her job as music teacher at a private school, Old Mother Riley confronts the headmistress, Miss Carruthers (Enid Hewitt). When Miss Carruthers confesses that she has to sell the school, Old Mother Riley offers to buy it, using the laundry as security for a loan. A group of businessmen put in a rival bid, believing that they will be offered generous compensation when a railway is put through the site. They are thwarted by Old Mother Riley and set fire to the school in the hope that she will resell to them. She does – only to discover that the railway is being routed through the laundry, meaning that she will receive the compensation.

Other than the interior of the laundry, where employees are

addressed by their numbers, the settings yield few clues to Old Mother Riley's working-class status. As in *Old Mother Riley's New Venture*, location shooting is minimal, being largely confined to the garden of Victorian mansion which houses the school. Most of the action takes place inside the school. The film received a loan from the National Film Finance Corporation for its production.[22] Wherever the money went, it was not on the rudimentary sets. Some might have gone into hiring the Luton Girls' Choir and George Melachrino and his orchestra for the musical numbers.

Like Randle and Will Hay, Old Mother Riley appears bumbling and out of her depth when confronting middle-class professionals. Like Randle and Hay, she uses her native shrewdness to win through by sowing verbal confusion. This is apparent in the opening scene, where customers at the laundry complain about her work. She uses the same strategy when the lawyer asks how she will raise the money needed to buy the school:

OLD MOTHER RILEY: I've got it all worked out. Now listen. We can pawn the mortgage debt to pay the deposit on the school. Then we can mortgage the school to pay back the deposit on the laundry. Six months after, we could raise more on the school to pay less on the laundry. Then we can do the bank. Then we can do a bunk.

Ted Kavanagh's hand is evident in the punning – he scripted the wartime radio series *ITMA* – yet rather than being merely a display of verbal dexterity, this speech illustrates a distinctively working-class approach to making ends meet which is sophisticated in its balancing of debits and credits. Something similar is encountered in working-class autobiographies of life earlier in the century.[23]

Allied to the working-class concern about money is the importance of hard-won material goods, especially for women, who were normally the buyers. When Old Mother Riley is wakened by the handyman calling that the school is on fire, her instinct is to save her possessions. The comic potential of the scene is exploited as she throws furniture, ornaments and a potted plant out the window, knocking out the arsonists who are standing below.

As with Randle, Old Mother Riley's working-class status is negotiable. She becomes rich enough to own a private school, though this is wealth acquired by luck – the only possibility open to most working-class people. By an inversion of Raymond Durgnat's principles, it is the middle class rather than the working class who are represented by a figure of fun (the lawyer) and criminals (the middle-class businessmen who have no qualms about taking a step beyond duplicity to committing arson). The female middle-class characters provide a respectable foil: the headmistress who is forced by lack of money to sell the school and the pupils who want to see fair play for Kitty. Women, including Old Mother Riley herself, are on the side of law, order and fairness. The exception is the French mistress – and in this world of stereotypes, the French are always duplicitous. When Old Mother Riley cheats in the egg and spoon race, she does so obviously.

For Marcia Landy, the Old Mother Riley films are a parody of female melodramas:

> By adopting the persona of an old woman, Lucan usurps cultural images that are threatening to both men and women – the elderly Irishwoman and the mother. He plays with the freedom that age and marginality grant to her to attack prevailing social practices. Since Mother Riley has too little invested in the social order, she can flout middle-class conventions and pretensions.[24]

Whether elderly Irishwomen and mothers are threatening figures is debatable. Given the popularity of Old Mother Riley among the Irish communities of Lancashire, the opposite might be true.[25] She is as incompetent in her work as Randle and displays a similar disrespect for authority, though without his contempt. This makes an emphasis on gender as a key to the humour questionable. The class position of Old Mother Riley is more important, as Landy acknowledges in the final sentence of the quotation.

An alternative approach to the Old Mother Riley films is to explore the familial relationship of mother and daughter. Fisher stresses the protective pride for Kitty, whose shortcomings make Old Mother Riley fierce, fretful and fidgety. He likens the love–hate relationship to that of Harold and Albert Steptoe in *Steptoe and Son* (BBC TV 1964–1973).[26] This raises the possibility that the Old Mother Riley role might equally well be played as Old Father Riley, though audiences' complicity with the actors in the gender disguise adds an extra dimension to the humour. The stage origins of the character are evident in this device. As a qualification to Fisher's view, the astringency of the mother–daughter relationship is re-placed in the later Old Mother Riley films by a closeness which is less interesting cinematically. Ironically, this happened as Lucan and McShane's marriage was deteriorating.

For Richards, Old Mother Riley is a 'comic heroine of titanic dimensions, exaggerated admittedly but rooted in truth'.[27] This is Ien Ang's psychological reality as distinct from external reality – musicals and opera are examples where believable emotions are portrayed in forms which are inimical to realism in the accepted sense.[28] A similar blend of exaggeration and truthfulness might be claimed for other music-hall characters who reached the screen. Working-class audiences found something to relate to in those stereotypes of the Irish washerwoman, the inebriated husband and the gossiping housewife. Middle-class patrons who strayed into cinemas where these films were showing would have had their prejudices confirmed. Had they persevered with this style of film-making, they might have discerned values which were not dissimilar to their own.

Unlike the Mancunian comedies, the appeal of Old Mother Riley was considered to be national. In 1944, Len England observed that 'Old Mother Riley is the biggest money-maker of all British films. In some parts of England cinemas that nothing else can fill are packed to the doors by Old Mother Riley.'[29] At the Granada, Tooting, an Old Mother Riley film in a double bill with *A Yank at Oxford* (d. Jack Conway, 1938) achieved a wartime box-office record.[30] According to the *Kinematograph Weekly*, *Old Mother Riley's New Venture* achieved excellent business on its London release on the Gaumont circuit, particularly in northeast London, while the management at Colchester, Essex, claimed that it gave them their best business for twelve months. The film also proved successful in Chester, Dover and Cardiff.[31]

Old Mother Riley's New Venture was released as a main feature by Rank. After a week at a first-run cinema in southeast Essex, there was little demand for the film from local independents (Appendix, Table 7). As a garrison town, nearby Colchester may have attracted a different type of audience, though the contrast with the film's success in northeast London (from where many Essex people had moved) is more difficult to explain. The film proved more popular among the sample cinemas in working-class Leeds (Appendix, Table 6), though by the end of 1950, *Old Mother Riley, Headmistress* had hardly reached subsequent-run cinemas after its release as a supporting feature. At the Gaumont, Sheffield, it ran as second feature to *A Ticket to Tomahawk* (d. Richard Sale, US, 1950) and came in the bottom quartile of attendances (Appendix, Table 5). The manager noted that 'It is so many months since we have had so many complaints from all types of patrons about the poor quality of this programme. The 2nd feature was considered by many Patrons as an insult to their intelligence.'[32] Audience's responses to Old Mother Riley were more varied than Len England allowed. Upwardly mobile audiences may have considered that this style of humour was beneath them, or else the changing age profile of cinema audiences was associated with a shift in taste as younger patrons turned to American styles of humour.

For critics of the Roger Manvell school, the very popularity of Frank Randle and the Old Mother Riley films counted against them, as did their rejection of the orthodoxy of realism. Distaste for such films on the grounds of their popularity is difficult to demonstrate. The most telling point is a negative one – critics ignored them. Yet judged by other criteria, the films have something to offer. For the historian they are testimony to the attitudes and interests of large sectors of the population. Culturally they are significant in their knowingness: artifice is glorified, most obviously by drawing on the tradition of the pantomime dame. This is an approach to film-making far removed from that of David Lean, but with equal validity.

The films discussed hark back to the music hall, while presaging new forms of comedy. Their surreal humour was carried into the 1950s by the Goons, brought to television in the 1960s by former Goons Michael Bentine and Spike Milligan, and achieved cult status in the 1970s with Monty Python. The homely settings were equally influential, with Richards claiming *Over the Garden Wall* as a proto-type sitcom.[33] Some variety performers made the transition into sitcom on radio and television, notably Ted Ray, Jimmy Clitheroe, Hylda Baker and Jimmy Jewell; older performers fell by the wayside. Though sitcoms have been earnestly pored over for their cultural significance, the proletarian comedies of the 1940s which provide a link between sitcom and variety are only now being accorded serious attention. This should not be allowed to obscure the fact that they were intended to make people laugh. It would be an irony if they were rescued from obscurity only to be revered as cultural artefacts.

Notes

1 G. J. Mellor, *The Northern Music Hall* (Newcastle-upon-Tyne: Frank Graham, 1970), pp. 189–94.

2 *Ibid.*, pp. 130, 154, 190 and 197–202.

3 Laurence Senelick, 'Politics as entertainment: Victorian music-hall songs', *Victorian Studies*, 19:2 (1975), 149–80; 'The working class and leisure: class expression and/or social control', *Society for the Study of Labour History Bulletin*, no. 32 (1976), 14; Bernard Waites, 'The music hall', in Open University, *Historical Development of Popular Culture in Britain 1* (Milton Keynes: Open University Press, 1981), pp. 41–76; Andy Medhurst, 'Music hall and British cinema', in Charles Barr (ed.) *All Our Yesterdays: 90 Years of British Cinema* (London: BFI, 1986), pp. 168–88.

4 Mellor, *The Northern Music Hall*.

5 For Mort Sahl, see Asa Briggs, *The History of Broadcasting in the United Kingdom*, vol. 5: *Competition 1955–1974* (Oxford: Oxford University Press, 1995), p. 359.

6 North West Film Archive, *Mancunian Presents ...* (Tyne Tees Television, 1988). Some of the material reappears in Jeffrey Richards, *Stars in Our Eyes: Lancashire Stars of Stage, Screen and Radio* (Preston: Lancashire County Books, 1994); Philip Martin Williams and David

L. Williams, *Horray for Jollywood: the life of John E. Blakeley and the Mancunian Film Corporation* (Ashton-under-Lyne: History on your doorstep, 2001).

7   *Mancunian Presents* . . . The Cinematograph Exhibitors Association estimated production costs at £40,000. *Kinematograph Weekly* (17 March 1949), p. 9.

8   *Mancunian Presents* . . .

9   *Ibid.* Casey later worked on radio with another Mancunian star, Jimmy Clitheroe, in the long-running *The Clitheroe Kid* – the last gasp of the Mancunian tradition.

10   Julian Poole, 'British cinema attendance in wartime: audience preference at the Majestic, Macclesfield 1939–1946', *Historical Journal of Film, Radio and Television*, 7:1 (1987), Tables 4 and 5, 22 and 24.

11   *Mancunian Presents* . . .

12   John Fisher, *Funny Way to Be a Hero* (London: Frederick Muller, 1973), p. 167.

13   Poole, 'British cinema attendance in wartime', Table 7, 26.

14   *Kinematograph Weekly* (20 April 1950), p. 32. The amount is not given.

15   *Mancunian Presents* . . .

16   A. J. Marriot, *Laurel & Hardy: The British Tours* (Blackpool: A. J. Marriot, 6 Gainsborough Road, 1993), p. 49, n. 8, and p. 72.

17   This is at variance from the assertion by Philip Martin Williams and David Williams that *Over the Garden Wall* was not shown in Rank cinemas. Williams and Williams, *Horray for Jollywood*, p. 105.

18   Medhurst, 'Music hall and British cinema', p. 177.

19   Fisher, *Funny Way to Be a Hero*, p. 77. Although the title is not given by Fisher, this was the only film in the series to be released in 1949.

20   Economy extends to the editing. At the opening of the film, stock library material is used for establishing shots of well-known London locations. In the National Film Archive's viewing copy one sequence is reversed, so that road vehicles appear to be travelling backwards.

21   Robert Stam, *Reflexivity in Film and Literature: From Don Quixote to Jean-Luc Godard* (Ann Arbor, MI: UMI Research Press, 1985).

22   *Kinematograph Weekly* (20 April 1950), p. 32. The amount is not given.

23   One example is Rose Gamble, *Chelsea Girl* (Bath: Chivers Press, 1980), pp. 58–64.

24   Marcia Landy, *British Genres: Cinema and Society 1930–1960* (Princeton, NJ: Princeton University Press, 1991), pp. 356–7.

25   Fisher, *Funny Way to Be a Hero*, p. 80.

26   *Ibid.*, p. 76.

27   Jeffrey Richards, *The Age of the Dream Palace: Cinema and Society in Britain 1930–39* (London: Routledge, 1989), p. 298.

28   Ien Ang, *Watching Dallas: Soap Opera and the Melodramatic Imagination*, trans. Della Couling (London: Methuen, 1985), p. 47.

29   University of Sussex, Mass-Observation Archive: FR 2120 'The film and family life', 13 June 1944, p. 2.

30   Guy Morgan, *Red Roses Every Night: An Account of London Cinemas under Fire* (London: Quality Press, 1948), p. 46.

31 *Kinematograph Weekly* (5 January 1950), p. 24.
32 CTA, weekly returns for Gaumont Sheffield, 21 October 1950.
33 Richards, *Stars in Our Eyes*, p. 31.

11 Think of the kids: the postwar child in films

One consequence of the Second World War was greater state investment in the next generation. Service life, directed work, displacement and evacuation meant an unprecedented movement of people during the war years, with sixty million changes of address in a population of some forty million.[1] This exposed the weakness of locally organised welfare provision with residence as a qualification, while the enforced mingling of the classes (including the appearance of middle-class patients in public assistance institutions after air raids) led to a greater awareness of social inequalities and the inadequacies of welfare provision.[2] The response was a shift to centrally financed services which included school dinners (provided for one in thirty children in 1940, but one in three by 1945), free school milk, National dried milk for babies, and orange juice and cod liver oil for young children.[3] Postwar Welfare State legislation consolidated and extended these improvements.

The emotional investment in children apparent in *The Way to the Stars* (d. Anthony Asquith, 1945) was noted in Chapter Three. This was associated with demographic and economic changes. Families were smaller than in the early years of the century. Despite the postwar baby boom, births in 1945–48 were 81 per thousand women, compared with 115 per thousand in 1900–1902.[4] Nor was this a phenomenon of the higher social classes. Using the Registrar General's five social classes, the standardised fertility rate showed increases in the birthrate of the two highest social classes between 1931 and 1951, but a decrease in the lowest class (Appendix, Table 9). Families were still larger in the lower social classes by 1951, but the gap was narrowing. Allied to the demographic change was a levelling up of wages. By Dudley Seer's calculations, the net incomes of the working class rose by over 9 per cent between 1938 and 1947, compared with a fall of over 7 per cent in middle-class incomes (subsidies and benefits included).[5] Rationing and price controls raised the standards of the poor relative to other groups.

The overall effect of these changes was to encourage a shift towards the home-centred nuclear family which had hitherto been the province of the middle class. One implication noted in Chapter Two was less social contact with neighbours. At the same time, contact between relatives was reduced by relocation to new towns and peripheral council estates, followed in the 1960s by inner-city redevelopment. However erratic these changes, working-class life was altered irrevocably. With fewer offspring came closer bonds between parents and children, who could share interests such as television programmes or Sunday outings in the car. The desire to escape from crowded homes was removed in many cases. Whether this signalled the adoption of a middle-class lifestyle (the embourgeoisement thesis) or an adaptation of traditional living patterns as proposed by John Goldthorpe *et al.* divided sociologists in the 1960s and 1970s.[6] Technology and increasing prosperity have continued to blur the distinctions between classes to the point where controversy can seem irrelevant.

In tandem with these changes, adolescents were evolving their own culture, derived in part from the music and mores of America. This is another contested topic. Mark Abrams sees the teenage consumer as a product of postwar prosperity, while David Fowler argues that a high teenage disposable income was apparent in the 1930s.[7] Working-class gang culture predated both periods: Stephen Humphries has detected it in the 1890s.[8] What cannot be contested is that the media gave youth a higher profile after the Second World War, while the targeting of young people as consumers of clothing, records and eventually cars made this group more noticeable. One effect was to make childhood and adolescence into separate and distinct phases of life. Youth culture also subverted the cosy, home-centred model promoted in countless TV advertisements, though both were reliant on a high level of disposable income. The youth market made an obvious target audience and film-makers responded from the late 1950s with a rash of films featuring pop stars such as Cliff Richard and Adam Faith. Solving the 'cosh boy' problem slipped down the agenda. Cultural trends are notoriously difficult to chart with any accuracy, but the arrival of rock and roll marked the point when tensions between the home-centred and youth-centred models became explicit. The change can be appreciated by comparing Pearl Jephcott's *Rising Twenty*, a study of a working-class girls published in 1948, with autobiographies of people who were working-class teenagers in the 1960s.[9]

Since its inception, the cinema industry had wrestled with a problem of how to satisfy a child audience without alienating older age groups, particularly adolescents who were leaving behind childish things. Westerns and swash-bucklers were well-tried solutions. An option promoted by Rank in the 1940s was to separate out the child audience and produce films specifically for Saturday morning screenings. Films starring children and produced for general audiences were less common. The problem for film-makers was finding children who could act convincingly and who were intelligible to a wide audience. Because working-class children were more likely to have strong regional accents and less likely to be prompted into acting by ambitious parents, they were doubly handicapped. The alternative was an older performer who could pass muster as a child, though these were few in number. The consequence was, with honourable exceptions, films in which an unrepresentative array of middle-class children were paraded on screen.

Heading the honourable exceptions is *Hue and Cry* (d. Charles Crichton, 1947). Joe Kirby (Harry Fowler) discovers that a story in a boys' comic, *The Trump*, is being used by a criminal gang to pass coded messages among its members. He tracks down the writer of the story, Felix H. Wilkinson (Alastair Sim), who concedes that it has been changed, but refuses to help in solving the mystery. Through befriending a boy who works for the publisher, Joe comes to suspect Rhona Davis (Valerie White) who opens the post at the publisher's office. With the help of his gang, Joe follows her to a house in St Johns Wood, where his suspicions are proved correct. When a plan to raid an Oxford Circus store is discovered, Joe tells his employer, fruit and vegetable wholesaler Jim Nightingale (Jack Warner). The children hide in the store, but the raid fails to materialise and they only succeed in capturing the detectives whom they have alerted.

To trap the gang, the children persuade Wilkinson to rewrite a story after it has been changed at the publisher's office. In the rewritten version, the villains are told to meet at Ballard's Wharf. Only then does Joe notice that the registration number of his employer's car corresponds with the one in the story: Jim Nightingale heads the criminal gang. Jim drives to Ballard's Wharf, with Joe hidden in the back of the van. Children from across London are alerted to the adventure by a variety of means including the telephone and an announcement on the radio. They converge on the site and overpower the criminals. Jim tries to escape, but Joe captures him.

The opening scene of a church choir practice belies the tone of the film – until the choirmaster removes a copy of *The Trump* which a boy is hiding behind his score. The practice is for the service which takes place in the final scene, when the bruised and bandaged boys sing angelically. The events in between are a child's fantasy.

Joe belongs to a gang, though whether this is enough to stamp him as working class is arguable. Steve Humphries *et al.* see the working-class gang or group friendships as characteristic of the early decades of the century, with the middle-class 'best friend' assuming prominence after the Second World War. Though ostensibly symbolising community, conformist and aggressive gangs could be territorial, victimising those from outside the neighbourhood.[10] Against this, there is a case for claiming that gangs or group friendships in children's stories have no class connotations. Much children's literature is predicated on the group, most obviously in school stories. The group features in Enid Blyton's Famous Five series and the William stories of Richmal Crompton, both of which are resolutely middle class. If one function of such works is to rehearse the problems of socialisation for children, the appearance of the group is hardly surprising. It also has the practical merit of externalising the subject matter, which can be expressed as dialogue or action. This becomes apparent in looking at the exceptions such as Frances Hodgson Burnett's *The Secret Garden* (1911) or Philippa Pearce's *Tom's Midnight Garden* (1958). Both are middle-class dramas involving solitary children. With this scenario, a device such as a narrator or an internal monologue is difficult to avoid.

Joe's social position is established by his home, which is a modest terraced house in Battersea, southwest London. The twin chimneys of the power station in the background are a reminder that this is working-class territory (the second pair of chimneys was added in the following decade). Children play in the street, to the accompaniment of the incessant clatter of trains. The voices may not owe much to Battersea, but they are never jarringly middle-class, the exception being the minor role of Joe's sister. The gang shows a wide age range, from a small boy in short trousers who displays an impressive talent for aircraft impersonations, to youths like Joe who are already working. The younger boys wear the ubiquitous grey flannel suits. Working youths can dispense with ties, which are inconvenient or impractical in some manual occupations. Territoriality is on display in the reluctance of gang members to accept the boy from the publisher's office into their hideout – he comes from Camberwell in southeast London – though the prospect of a big adventure is enough to deflect overt hostility. Clarry (Joan Dowling) is admitted grudgingly to the all-male preserve. As the same wariness towards women could be found in any gentlemen's club, this is not a peculiarly working-class misogyny. Dowling was eighteen in 1947 and made a speciality of playing girls younger than herself. She took a similar role in Daniel Birt's *No Room at the Inn* the following year.

Joe's home life is sketchily presented, emphasising that this is a world where life takes place on the streets. His father – a picture of respectability in his three-piece suit – is wary of Joe taking a job in a market because of the lack of prospects, though he has to concede that the money is good at thirty shillings a week. If Joe's mother has reservations, she keeps them to herself. She has little to do in the film other than supplying meals. Bread is delivered: the unwrapped loaf is left on the windowsill, from where Joe collects it on his way into the house. The only room seen in any detail is the kitchen-cum-living room, which is dominated by the kitchen table where the family have their meals. The Welsh dresser has runners on the shelves, so that the best china can be displayed to advantage. The shallow, glazed sink with its single tap is below the window. A washboard and copper are visible in the adjoining scullery.

As in other Ealing films, the authority of the police is stamped on the proceedings. Joe's first response on discovering that messages are being passed in *The Trump* is to contact the police, though the inspector does not take him seriously. The same applies when the plot to rob the Oxford Circus store is discovered, though the children make sure that they join in the fun. Their relationship with authority is uneasy – there is consternation when police visit their street – yet ultimately it is the children who thwart the criminals. Right triumphs, but the community of children is needed to achieve victory.

The glory of the film is the location photography of Douglas Slocombe. His evocation of a London rent by bombing is unique in its scope. Joe's terrace is incomplete; some of the remaining houses are derelict, though one is being repaired. The gang meet on a bombsite, climbing over the mounds of rubble and through gaps in lath and plaster walls to get to their hideout. This is a den which any boy would covet, irrespective of class. It is furnished with whatever comes to hand – one boy uses a portable bath as an armchair. The business area of the city is also pitted with bombsites. There is one opposite the publisher's office where the gang wait to trail Rhona Davis. Rebuilding is taking place – she walks through a site of several acres where council flats are under construction. The denouement takes place beside Cannon Street Station on the north bank of the Thames. The vast bombsite conveys the scale of the devastation and allows panoramic shots of children converging on the criminals from all directions. Nor should the film's incidental visual pleasures be overlooked: the ice cream sellers pedalling their barrows to the final showdown, Joe's attempts to balance wicker baskets of produce on his head like the other porters (one is seen carrying eight), or the boy repairing the inner tube of his bicycle in the middle of the street. He is using a chipped enamel bowl filled with water – until his mother demands her washing-up bowl back. Polythene bowls were a decade away. The film's only jarring notes are the children's attempts to hire a taxi – something working-class children would neither consider nor afford – and the unconvincing studio sets of Covent Garden market.

Denis Forman's verdict was that the story had 'an unsophisticated gusto which romped into the cinema like a tomboy into a cocktail party'.[11] The passing years have not dimmed this freshness. The tale is told economically and vividly, with a visual flair which holds an audience's attention. This is the adventure which the child in every adult dreams about, yet it is rooted in the reality of bomb damage, black-marketeering and manual work which lacks prospects.

Because the story was unconventional, Michael Balcon insisted on keeping to the budget.[12] The result was one of Ealing's most profitable productions (Appendix, Table 2). This success was apparent in southeast Essex, though not in working-class Leeds or at the Gaumont, Sheffield, where the film slipped into the bottom quartile of attendances (Appendix, Tables 5–7). This accords with Thorold Dickinson's comment that it proved difficult to sell.[13] The paucity of stars may have counted against it. Alternatively, the material may have been too London based for northern tastes, or perceived as the stuff of children's matinees, for which the running time of eight-two minutes was too long. Yet these are also the film's strengths. It never outstays its welcome and it appeals to all ages. A wonderland is conjured from the bombsites – something of its time, yet timeless in its appeal. This is a film to treasure.

Three years later, a very different film starring a child came from Ealing, again with T. E. B. Clarke as scriptwriter. This was *The*

Magnet (d. Charles Frend, 1950). Johnny Brent (William Fox) lives on the Wirral. He is away from school, in quarantine for scarlet fever. On the beach at nearby New Brighton, he tricks a younger boy into giving him a magnet in exchange for an invisible watch, running away when the victim's grandmother threatens to tell a policeman. Johnny feels guilty. When he tries to throw the magnet away, a policeman retrieves it. In an amusement arcade, Johnny encounters an older youth who uses the magnet to cheat on the pinball machines. Both boys flee when the ruse is discovered. The policeman is on patrol outside, which prompts Johnny to continue running. In the alley where he hides, he sees through a basement window what he thinks is a body. The policeman catches up with him and shows no surprise at the news, taking him inside the workshop to meet Mr Harper (Meredith Edwards). The 'body' is a wax model made by Harper, who is on the board of St Valentine's Hospital and is collecting for an iron lung. In a fit of remorse, Johnny gives him the magnet before running away. When Harper presents the iron lung to the hospital, he tells the story of the boy who donated his prized possession without leaving his name.

On a train journey, the grandmother of the little boy whom Johnny tricked tells her friend about the death of her budgerigar. Johnny is sitting opposite, hidden by a newspaper, and overhears part of what is being said. He assumes that it is the little boy who has died of pneumonia as a result of contracting scarlet fever from him. This compounds Johnny's guilt. His parents become worried about his disturbed sleep, his psychiatrist father (Stephen Murray) suspecting a deep-seated psychological problem. While shopping for his mother (Kay Walsh), Johnny is seen by the policeman and Mr Harper. Both men give chase and to evade them, Johnny stows away in a van which takes him from his home on the Wirral peninsula, through the Mersey Tunnel to Liverpool. There he encounters a gang of working-class boys. Although initially wary of him, they become more friendly when they discover that he is on the run from the police. They take him to a hideout on a derelict pier. Their leader, Spike (Keith Robinson), falls through the superstructure in a dare and is knocked unconscious. Johnny goes to his aid, preventing him from drowning. When Johnny visits Spike in hospital, the gang leader is being treated in the iron lung which the appeal helped to buy. Mr Harper finally corners Johnny to present him with a medal. When the little boy who originally owned the magnet is playing on the beach again, Johnny gives him the medal in exchange for the invisible watch.

As so often in Ealing films, the moral values being espoused are never in doubt. The police have a pervasive presence, while

Johnny's qualms of conscience are only salved when he receives the invisible watch back. A working-class boy would have rejoiced in his good fortune at getting the magnet in the first place. The presence of the tramp whom Johnny so admires (a cameo from James Robertson Justice) hints at a rebellion against middle-class values, but it is a small rebellion which is never pursued. The film's whimsy could veer into sentimentality were it not undercut by wry touches worthy of Bill Forsyth. After tricking the younger boy, Johnny's conscience is stirred by an evangelist whose sandwich boards proclaim 'Be sure your sins will find you out'. The boards are next seen propped outside a pub.

The film's attitude to psychiatry is muddled. Though Johnny's father is a doctor, Mrs Brent calls him a psychologist, who would not be medically qualified. After poking gentle fun at his Freudian interpretation of their son's problems, the film goes along with his strategy of encouraging his wife to show how much she relies on Johnny – an ambivalence which must have confused audiences. Fortunately humour breaks through: as Dr Brent explains to the parents of a young patient that children can associate the father figure with an animal, the film cuts to Johnny stroking a donkey.

As befits a professional family, the Brents' home is a detached Victorian villa. The postwar squeeze on middle-class incomes is affecting them, for Mrs Brent looks after the house herself, relying on Johnny to help with the shopping. Dr Brent does not own a car, though he tells Johnny that they will soon be getting one. This remark is prompted by the sight of a transporter loaded with bulbous Standard saloons which passes as the doctor sees Johnny off to a private school in Liverpool. Times cannot be too hard.

Like Mr Harper, Dr Brent is on the board of St Valentine's. As the film is at pains to make clear, the hospital is outside the newly-created National Health Service, or the iron lung could have been obtained without an appeal, with fatal damage to the plot. Perhaps Dr Brent is one of those consultants who opposed health service reforms. The Freudian analysis which he favours is time-consuming, which stops it from fitting readily into the state system.

As with *Hue and Cry*, the glory of the film is its location shooting, this time of New Brighton as a flourishing resort and Liverpool on the opposite bank of the Mersey. Within two decades, the trippers had abandoned New Brighton, while inner-city Liverpool was changed out of all recognition by a combination of inner-city redevelopment and the obsolescence of the docks. As in *Hue and Cry*, there are incidental visual pleasures. Johnny stows away in a Jacob's biscuits van loaded with metal boxes of cream crackers – biscuits were still sold loose from boxes. As Johnny escapes from the van, there is an image of industrial Liverpool worthy of *Things to Come* (d. William Cameron Menzies, 1936), with a road and the overhead railway dwarfed by the retaining wall behind them and the massive arches in the foreground.

In 1950, Liverpool only had an Anglican cathedral and that was still under construction, as the film shows. The cathedral provides the backdrop to Johnny's encounter with four working-class boys. In a typically English way, they are playing cricket and Johnny catches the ball. They are suspicious of this boy from across the river, mimicking his refined accent. As in *Waterfront* (d. Michael Anderson, 1950), considered in Chapter Five, a Lancashire accent replaces the more impenetrable Scouse, which remained hidden from national audiences until the Beatles made it acceptable in the 1960s. At least the boys' accents are authentic.

As might be expected, Spike, the leader of the gang, is the largest of the boys. He is also the shabbiest. His retort of 'You're a liar' to anybody who disagrees is enough to silence the others, though even he runs from a policeman – and stops when the officer calls the boys back to ask about Johnny. They deny having seen him. This is deferring to the police without helping them.

The other gang members are Perce, Mike and Chippo. Chippo (Geoffrey Yim) is from Liverpool's Chinese community which was located between the cathedral and the river. Acknowledgement of the community's existence makes the film unique for its period. Chippo obeys his mother as she calls him back for his tea in her own dialect. His disappointment at missing the adventure is palpable.

Although a common purpose seemingly dissolves class barriers, as in *Hue and Cry*, residual tensions remain. Spike turns down the hiding places which the other boys suggest and decides on the disused pier. The following morning, Perce, Mike and Chippo bring food for Johnny, who has slept in a divers' hut on the pier head. Perce has the idea of playing on the pier. Johnny goes one step further, suggesting that they break up the wrecked barge lying in the mud. This is when Spike arrives. Not to be outdone, he is wearing a tie.

SPIKE: Hey, what's the big idea? Who let him out?
PERCE: He wanted to come out.
SPIKE: I told you to wait for me. Where are you going?
CHIPPO: To smash that old barge up.
SPIKE: Who said so?
CHIPPO: Johnny did.
SPIKE I didn't say so.
PERCE: Johnny says so.

SPIKE: Huh, I've had the cops after me afore now hundreds of times.
JOHNNY: What's that got to do with the barge?
SPIKE: (*Pushing Johnny*) You shut up.
(*Johnny raises his hand and flicks Spike's hair.*)
JOHNNY: Why should I shut up for you?
SPIKE: (*Pointing to a beam across a break in the planking*) See that hole there?
JOHNNY: What about it?
SPIKE: Dare you to walk across it.
JOHNNY: Dare you.

Spike does, and with dire consequences as he falls to a platform at water level. When the rest of the gang run off, Johnny climbs down to prevent Spike from drowning.

Unlike the rest of the gang, Johnny does not defer to Spike. There is an almost Lawrentian struggle as working-class physicality encounters middle-class superiority, but the mood changes abruptly with Spike's fall. Then comradeship (or perhaps a middle-class instinct to do the right thing) takes precedence. When the two boys meet later in hospital, their friendship is secure.

The Magnet was a favourite of T. E. B. Clarke, who recalled that it won an award in Belgium.[14] Subsequently, the scant critical attention bestowed on the film has been negative. Charles Barr sees it as an example of Frend's unease with comedy and considers the story unworkable.[15] George Perry judges the film 'less than satisfactory' and finds fault with its middle-class attitudes.[16] It may be a minor entry in the Ealing comedy canon, but it is noteworthy for the location photography and for an early performance by William Fox, later to become better known as James Fox. Like *Hue and Cry*, the film confirms that the working-class gang was alive and well after the Second World War and still had dramatic mileage. It also demonstrates that the shared interests of children can transcend class.

The Yellow Balloon (d. J. Lee Thompson, 1953) keeps resolutely to its working-class milieu, though again it might be questioned whether this is a child-centred adventure story which could take place in any class. Frankie (Andrew Ray) lives with his parents in a London tenement block. He takes a balloon from his friend, Ronnie, who chases him through the remains of a bombed building. The mood changes abruptly as Ronnie is killed in a fall. Len (William Sylvester), a gangster hiding in the ruins, convinces Frankie that he will be blamed for Ronnie's death unless they make a pact to keep quiet. Frankie begins stealing food and money for Len and is unwittingly drawn into helping him rob a pub. During the robbery, the pub owner is killed in a fight. Len decides to kill

Frankie, whose evidence can incriminate him. He takes the boy to a disused underground station, but Frankie realises what Len has in mind. A cat-and-mouse game ensues through the passages and staircases. The driver of a passing train sees the boy being chased along the platform and alerts the police at the next station. As they close in, Len attempts to escape by climbing down a lift shaft, but he loses his grip and falls to his death.

As in other films of the period, the sights and sounds of a London street market establish the locale and the social position of the characters, though the barrel organ was an anachronism by the 1950s. Frankie is seen watching an escapologist from his window, until PC Chapman (Bernard Lee) orders the performers to move on – a frequent occurrence judging by the easy-going relationship between authority and transgressors. As in *The Magnet*, the recurring image of the policeman serves to prick the boy's conscience. This is community policing as espoused in Ealing films, even if this was an ABPC production and the constable is conspicuous by his absence when Len is around.

Len is Canadian, judging by his accent. In his belted raincoat he stalks the film as a malign presence, devoid of any personal history. If he has a home, it is never shown. His favourite haunt is a cafe. Here he encounters one of his lowlife companions (Peter Jones), a spiv who complains that 'The bottom's dropped out of the nylon racket.' Spivs were having a hard time as consumer goods become increasingly available and affordable – one sign of the times was the unprecedented demand for television sets in the run-up to the 1953 coronation. Government controls were not quite a thing of the past – rationing was not completely phased out until 1954 and Retail Price Maintenance lingered for another decade – but price was increasingly the arbiter of demand. Stockings were still expensive: in 1952, fifteen denier nylons were advertised at 17s 6d in the *Daily Mirror*, while print dresses were available for 16s 11d.[17]

There were still plenty of bombsites for adventurous children to explore in 1953 – a child's body is found on a bombsite in *Eight O'Clock Walk* (d. Lance Comfort) from the same year. Frankie and Ronnie play in the remains of a palatial building – a reminder that in London, affluence and poverty can coexist in the same street. The police are more interested in patrolling the streets than the bombsites, which were technically private property, though the dangers of bombsites are shown in both films as being of concern to mothers.

Frankie is the only child of working-class parents. The flat has no running water – Frankie fills a bucket from the tap on the half-landing – though there is a small sink beside the dresser for disposing of waste water. In 1951, 14 per cent of households had no water supply of their own.[18] A family of three are lucky to have a flat with a living room and two bedrooms. As in *Hue and Cry*, the Welsh dresser is prominent as a place to display crockery. In spite of these traditional touches, this is a postwar family in its attitudes, which cannot be classified neatly in class terms. Frankie's father, Ted (Kenneth More), works for London Transport. Father and son appear to have a close relationship, though like other working-class fathers, Ted uses his belt when he discovers that Frankie has stolen money from his mother, Em (Kathleen Ryan). Ted listens to Beethoven on the radio, which is enough to take him out of the normal run of working-class fathers. Nor is his speech pattern working class. Em is Irish, which sets her apart from English linguistic class distinctions. Not surprisingly, Frankie's speech is not distinctively class based. To find cockney voices means turning to the subsidiary characters, including the South African Sid James as a costermonger, though none of the speech is incongruous enough to jar.

The Yellow Balloon is at heart a suspense story and Jack Lee Thompson does not sell the audience short. In their concern about their only son, Ted and Em are not dissimilar to the Brents in *The Magnet*, with the exception of Ted's attitude to corporal punishment. Though Frankie plays in the streets and has adventures on bombsites like Joe in *Hue and Cry*, the family is characterised more strongly than in the earlier film. The evidence of two films made six years apart does not signal a decisive shift in working-class family relationships; it does demonstrate that there was sufficient change in attitudes for film-makers to acknowledge the fact.

Like Johnny in *The Magnet*, Frankie is a boy with a conscience and it is this which prompts him towards his chosen course. Both films focus on a loner. This throws the onus on one child actor to support a film, but it also allows for a psychological exploration of the child's mind which is a shift from the simplicity of *Hue and Cry*. If Joe in *Hue and Cry* has a conscience, the story does not allow him to display it. To reinforce the sense of inwardness in films, an inanimate object such as a magnet or a balloon can serve as a totem, substituting for the best friend. The most celebrated example is *The Red Balloon* (d. Albert Lamorisse, France, 1955). The gang can also come up against a loner, as in *Heathers* (d. Michael Lehmann, US, 1988), but here childhood has been left behind. The appeal of the earlier films is that they develop the notion fostered by Victorian writers such as E. Nesbit of childhood as a special world; the difference was that by 1953, the working class could play. A Fabian sympathiser like Nesbit would have approved.

Notes

1 Sheila Ferguson and Hilde Fitzgerald, *Studies in the Social Services*, History of the Second World War: United Kingdom Civil Series (London: HMSO and Longmans, Green, 1954), p. 4.

2 Richard Titmuss, *Problems of Social Policy*, History of the Second World War: United Kingdom Civil Series (London: HMSO and Longmans, Green, 1950), p. 501.

3 *Ibid.*, pp. 510–14.

4 Mark Abrams, *The Home Market* (London: George Allen & Unwin, 1950), p. 12.

5 Dudley Seers, *Changes in the Cost-of-Living and the Distribution of Income Since 1938* (Oxford: Basil Blackwell, [1947]), p. 65. For similar conclusions, see Guy Routh, *Occupational Pay in Great Britain 1906–79* (Basingstoke and London: Macmillan, 1980), p. 157.

6 John H. Goldthorpe, David Lockwood, Frank Bechhofer and Jennifer Platt, *The Affluent Worker in the Class Structure* (London: Cambridge University Press, 1969), p. 25.

7 Mark Abrams, *The Teenage Consumer* (London: London Press Exchange, 1959); David Fowler, *The First Teenagers: The Lifestyle of Young Wage-Earners in Interwar Britain* (London: Woburn Press, 1995).

8 Stephen Humphries, *Hooligans or Rebels? An Oral History of Working-Class Childhood and Youth 1889–1939* (Oxford: Basil Blackwell, 1981).

9 Pearl Jephcott, *Rising Twenty: Notes on Some Ordinary Girls* (London: Faber & Faber, 1948); Roy Greenslade, *Goodbye to the Working Class* (London: Marion Boyars, 1976); Ray Gosling, *Personal Copy: A Memory of the Sixties* (London: Faber & Faber, 1980).

10 Steve Humphries, Joanna Mack and Robert Perks, *A Century of Childhood* (London: Sidgwick & Jackson, in association with Channel Four Television, 1988), p. 118.

11 Denis Forman, *Film 1945–1950* (London: Longmans, Green, for British Council, 1952), p. 22.

12 T. E. B. Clarke, *This Is Where I Came In* (London: Michael Joseph, 1974), p. 156.

13 Thorold Dickinson, 'The work of Sir Michael Balcon at Ealing Studios', in Roger Manvell (ed.), *The Year's Work in the Film 1950* (London: Longmans, Green, for British Council, 1951), p. 13.

14 Clarke, *This Is Where I Came In*, p. 29.

15 Charles Barr, *Ealing Studios* (London: Studio Vista, 2nd edn, 1993), p. 201.

16 George Perry, *Forever Ealing* (London: Pavilion Books, rev. edn, 1984), p. 125.

17 *Daily Mirror* (9 February 1952), p. 8.

18 A. Carr-Saunders, D. Caradog Jones and C. A. Moser, *A Survey of Social Conditions in England and Wales as Illustrated by Statistics* (London: Oxford University Press, Clarendon Press, 1958), Table 4.7, p. 44.

Examining class assumptions in films is akin to cleaning an old painting: aspects of the subject and its treatment are revealed which have hitherto been ignored or hidden. The model is not useful in all circumstances. War films fit uneasily within its parameters, while films such as *The Third Man* (d. Carol Reed, 1949) have little to say about working-class Britain, whatever their virtues. Teasing out every last class nuance is possible in these cases, but hardly worthwhile.

The dimensions of the model outlined in Chapter Two provide a way of ordering the conclusions.

Place in the authority structure

Although workers know their place, authority can be challenged (*Chance of a Lifetime*, d. Bernard Miles, 1950), infiltrated (*Vote for Huggett*, d. Ken Annakin, 1949), or guyed (any film involving Old Mother Riley or Frank Randle). Infiltration seems most successful, though at no time is the authority structure seriously threatened. Where workers do achieve a better class position, it is through individual effort as in *Blue Scar* (d. Jill Craigie, 1949) rather than through collective effort. Nor is the achievement without cost as existing relationships come under pressure.

Overt authority structures are evident in films about service life, though differences in rank receive surprisingly little emphasis once individuals are socialised into the institution by initial training. In spite of this, distinctions are implicit in the convention that those who give the orders are upper or middle class, as *They Were Not Divided* (d. Terence Young, 1950) illustrates, with NCOs occupying an ambiguous supervisory role. On the evidence of *The Blue Lamp* (d. Basil Dearden, 1950), the authority of rank was stressed more explicitly in the police force than in the armed services, as though the latter had been tested and transformed by war while the police force was mired in the 1930s.

Cohesion/fragmentation within the working class

There is scant evidence of a coherent working-class community in any of the films. Landladies often represent the respectable working class, whose world is disrupted by rougher elements such as Gwen in *Good Time Girl* (d. David Macdonald, 1948). Crime fragments the community in *The Blue Lamp*, with police, delinquents, 'real' criminals and the rough working-class pursuing separate agendas, yet the final scenes of the film tell another story. At least in films, a crime such as murder can override differences, encouraging cohesion. This process is also seen at work in *London Belongs to Me* (d. Sidney Gilliat, 1948), though here the murderer is supported rather than condemned by the community.

Particularly in Ealing films such as *The Blue Lamp* and *It Always Rains on Sunday* (d. Robert Hamer, 1947), the police control a working class which cannot discipline itself. This puts working people on a par with children such as the middle-class Johnny in *The Magnet* (d. Charles Frend, 1950), for whom the ubiquitous policeman functions as a conscience. Yet it is in an Ealing film, *Hue and Cry* (d. Charles Crichton, 1947), that children come together to fight crime where the police fail.

A Boy, a Girl and a Bike (d. Ralph Smart, 1949) comes nearest to presenting a coherent community – in a small town with a dominant industry which harks back to an earlier stage of industrial development. Even here there are aberrant figures whom the community cannot control and who have to be handed over to the police. In general, the family is more important than the community. An exception is *Chance of a Lifetime* (d. Bernard Miles, 1950), which seems as dated as *Sing as We Go* (d. Basil Dean, 1934).

Internalised values

Nationalisation makes little difference to the attitudes of management or workers in *Blue Scar*, but elsewhere attitudes are changing. This applies particularly to the younger generation, where there is a stress on education in *Waterfront* (d. Michael Anderson, 1950) and *Floodtide* (d. Frederick Wilson, 1949) as much as in *The Guinea*

Pig (d. Roy Boulting, 1948). It is also noticeable in the initiative of the children making Joe's election posters in *Vote for Huggett*. Between the wars, activities of this kind would have been the province of Arthur Ransome's upper-middle-class children rather than those from upper-working-class or lower-middle-class families. The Huggett films reveal other social changes. It is difficult to imagine Joe Huggett contemplating emigration without his wartime experience of life abroad. Even going to a holiday camp is an innovation. The contrast between Joe and the feckless father in *Waterfront* illustrates shifting perceptions of the working-class father. There is also the assumption in the Huggett films that girls should have a good education and a career – something which was less usual in working-class homes a generation earlier. Surviving from the earlier generation is that most conservative of figures: the working-class mother whose life is bounded by the home. She appears in *Waterloo Road* (d. Sidney Gilliat, 1945) and *Once a Jolly Swagman* (d. Jack Lee, 1948), as well as in the Huggett films. Yet her qualities should be acknowledged, notably her devotion to her family. Nor can she hold back the social changes which her children embrace, even if she tried.

Not unexpectedly after a war, liberty is more than an abstract ideal. Working-class characters such as Joe Huggett are breaking free of outdated social constraints – a process which the education system and other social reforms might have achieved, but which the war accelerated. The paradox is that in parallel with this new freedom comes the burden of an expanded bureaucracy. There are more rules for the unwary to transgress, as Joe Huggett discovers when he builds his garage without planning permission.

The built environment

The railway provides an abiding symbol of the working-class environment. The middle class travel by train; the working class live beside the tracks and watch them. The blast of an steam engine's whistle or the rhythmic clatter of wheels over rail joints provides an accompaniment to many of the films, except where a gasometer or a power station serves as a visual symbol of working-class status. The working-class world is smelly, dirty and noisy. Travellers can look down on the back yards and into living-room windows, making it a world without privacy.

The Huggetts' home, like that of Frank Randle in *Home Sweet Home* (d. John E. Blakeley, 1945), is a product of the speculative building boom which created between-the-wars suburbia. Jim and Tillie in *Waterloo Road* aspire to this housing class, even if they end the film sharing Jim's parental home. The postwar housing short-age means that Sam and Susie in *A Boy, a Girl and a Bike* are willing to take whatever is available.

Internally, working-class homes are notable for their outdated-ness and lack of space rather than obvious impoverishment. Limited resources are implicit: a larger home cannot be bought and furniture cannot be replaced. As a consequence, Victorian furnish-ings and decorations predominate. The living room is seen most often, reflecting the working-class pattern of one-room living. The mantelshelf is covered by a runner and adorned with ornaments; runners cover the shelves of the dresser which is used to display crockery. An ornate clock is prized, most obviously by the Jossers in *London Belongs to Me*. The coal-fired range is a standard fitment even where a cooker is installed, as in *Home Sweet Home*, though in reality the back boiler had ousted the range in working-class houses by the 1930s. When friends drop in, a line of washing might be left hanging over the range, as in *The Blue Lamp*. Where the family are on their own, a clotheshorse draped with washing is likely to stand in front of the range. Heat cannot be wasted. In older houses, the living room is the only heated room and is used for bathing, as in *It Always Rains on Sunday*. Even in the Huggetts' home, the front room is reserved for special occasions and receiving visitors.

Film-makers often had a problem in matching interior and exterior shots. Inside quite modern houses, or houses which once had higher status, the layout reverts to the traditional pattern of one-room living. This is noticeable in *Home Sweet Home* as well as Jackie's home in *Boys in Brown* (d. Montgomery Tully, 1949). Film-makers seemed intent on projecting a traditional view of working-class home life. Dramas set in prefabs are conspicuous by their absence.

Signifiers of class, notably speech, hairstyles and clothing

Working-class speech was a stumbling block for film-makers in the 1940s. It had to be bowdlerised for acceptability by the censors. It also had to be intelligible for audiences, which ruled out strong regional accents, genuine or otherwise. A cockney-born actor com-plained that even East End audiences could not understand what cinematic cockneys were saying, while Willie Gallacher declared to his fellow MPs that when a British film was shown in Scotland, scarcely any of the audience could understand a word that was said.[1] Though older male actors such as Jack Warner and William Hartnell achieved acceptable working-class personas with anglicised cockney accents, the conventions of drama school imposed received pronunciation on younger players, particularly on girls. The result can be an uneasy compromise which becomes apparent in family scenes. Outside of Mancunian films, authentic working-class voices from the regions are a rarity.

There is no clear distinction between formal and informal clothes, or between the clothes worn by younger and older men, as *Holiday Camp* (d. Ken Annakin, 1947) reveals. Generational differences are apparent in women's dress, with older women being more likely to wear hats. These conclusions apply across the classes, though the clothing of working-class men lags behind the times. The exception is the spiv, who is kept firmly in his working-class place by his desire for instant gratification and his speech. Though spivs existed before the war, the black market which arose as a response to rationing provided more opportunities to make money and greater public exposure.

For men this was the age of Brylcreem, as the immaculate hairstyles in *The Wooden Horse* (d. Jack Lee, 1950) testify. Although this was common to all ages and classes, the conscious use of hairstyles to indicate status was notable among upwardly mobile young men like Dirk Bogarde's Bill Fox in *Once a Jolly Swagman* and spivs such as Bill Owen's Dave Robinson in *Dancing with Crime* (d. John Paddy Carstairs, 1947). Distinctions based on dress and appearance become less sustainable when all social groups have access to cosmetics and good-quality clothing. In consequence, speech and deportment assume more importance as signifiers of class. This became more noticeable in films of the 1950s.

Common to many of the films is their reliance on stock characters, including the disapproving landlady, the dependable policeman, the drunken, violent father and the teenage tearaway. The limited roster of actors willing or able to take on working-class parts accentuated the problem of how to portray ordinary people and led to typecasting. Gladys Henson provides a convenient and enduring image of the respectable, caring, working-class mum, endlessly preparing meals for worldly-wise Jack Warner, while daughter Susan Shaw is forever looking for love – usually with an unsuitable man. A shortage of suitable actors does not provide a full explanation for these preconceived notions of working-class behaviour, since military officers were also stereotyped. The process is indicative of shared values, so that a nonverbal shorthand can be used, recalling Bernstein's restricted code. *The Gorbals Story* (d. David MacKane, 1950) and *Blue Scar* broke free from stereotypes by using actors who were not household names, but these films failed to attract audiences.[2] Their lack of success is attributable in part to the circuits' booking departments determining, rightly or wrongly, that both films had limited commercial potential – something which became a self-fulfilling prophesy. Despite the risk of stereotyping, the presence of familiar names in a film served a dual function. Firstly, a star such as Margaret Lockwood could attract fans to whatever she appeared in. Secondly, a name could signal to potential audiences the nature of what was on offer. The mention of Frank Randle on a poster left little doubt that they were going to see visual comedy in which the upper classes got their comeuppance. Transgressing stereotypes carried risks, an example being *Against the Wind* (d. Charles Crichton, 1948), in which Jack Warner played the agent who was shot for his treachery. The scriptwriter, T. E. B. Clarke, later admitted that this was gross miscasting.[3] In the mind of the public, Warner was the reliable working-class family man epitomised by Joe Huggett. He could be the villain in a comedy such as Crichton's *Hue and Cry* (1947). He could be shot doing his duty as George Dixon in *The Blue Lamp*, but shooting him as a traitor was too much. His foray into being a criminal on the run in *My Brother's Keeper* (d. Alfred Roome and Roy Rich, 1948) was no more successful: in spite of the lowest production costs of the thirty Rank films for which data is available, it still made a loss (Appendix, Table 1).

If the familiar attracts audiences, this encourages the industry to play safe. If the artifice of the stereotype is part of the attraction for audiences, this is inimical to realism. In later years, T. E. B. Clarke saw the comparative failure of *Against the Wind* as attributable to the decision to concentrate on realism, as opposed to the romanticism and predictable roles of wartime British films.[4] In looking back on Stewart Granger's performance in *Waterloo Road*, Sidney Gilliat considered that there was no school of realistic acting.[5] Against these latter-day views detecting a lack of realism in films made during the war, Norman Swallow, writing in 1947, complained that the wartime lessons in sociological drama had been forgotten: 'We are once more offered the old list of colourful escapism: *An Ideal Husband*, *Uncle Silas* and *Bonnie Prince Charlie*.'[6] Other critics endorsed his view. Harking back to wartime films which 'meant something', Milton Schulman lamented the absence on the screen of real people doing real things, while on the left, Joan Lestor also looked back fondly to wartime films portraying real people with real problems.[7] *It Always Rains on Sunday* and *Brighton Rock* (d. John Boulting, 1947) were castigated by D. A. Yerrill for their 'imposed realism'.[8] Directors and critics may have sought realism, yet the concept is nebulous enough for diverging, even contradictory definitions to become apparent. This is not a matter of opinions changing over time. The opposing views are crystallised in a study of Carol Reed's films by Basil Wright: a mine owner considered *The Stars Look Down* (1939) to be 'a film that lacks completely any feeling of reality,' while a Durham miner claimed that it was 'the most successful attempt to present to the public the life of mining folk'.[9] Realism is in the eye of the beholder. It signifies something beyond camera technique, affecting the representation of working-class people on film. Working-class audiences of the 1940s were in a better position to judge the results than the critics, however much the latter enjoyed their vicarious slumming. Somehow the term realism was never bandied about when upper-class characters were portrayed.

Realism should be seen as one of a competing range of perspectives available to film-makers in the 1940s. John Harlow and Michael Powell were among those who chose to explore other routes. Though Anthony Asquith used nonprofessional actors and improvised dialogue in *The Way to the Stars* (1945), he appreciated the skills of the actor, who offered something more real than the real thing (Chapter Three). This is an expression of Ien Ang's psychological reality noted in the context of Old Mother Riley films (Chapter Ten). Whatever the faults of *It Always Rains on Sunday*, Hamer sought psychological as well as physical veracity. The risk in abandoning any pretence of realism is the sentimentality which afflicts *The White Unicorn* (d. Bernard Knowles, 1947). A century earlier, Charles Dickens walked the same tightrope and it is no coincidence that characters like Hermione Baddeley's boarding-house keeper, Mrs Spry, in *It Always Rains on Sunday* might have sprung from the pages of a Dickens novel.

Victorian notions linger. In many of the films, notably those revisiting the war or dramatising the punishment of delinquents, working-class people lead simple lives. Like animals, the working class follow their instincts, leaving middle-class characters or narrators to draw morals or reveal psychological insights. The verbal complexity of Frank Randle and Old Mother Riley gives the lie to these misconceptions, but it is in the characters of Pinkie in *Brighton Rock* and Leo in *Appointment with Crime* (d. John Harlow, 1946) that psychological depths are to be found. The same might be said of Rose Sandigate in *It Always Rains on Sunday*. Because working-class women are normally relegated to subsidiary roles, her case is even more unusual.

Among the films considered, the commercial success of *The Way to the Stars* is beyond question. Audiences knew a good film when they saw it. Given the meagre number of screenings achieved in the sample Leeds cinemas by many of the films in which working-class characters are prominent, these is no evidence that audiences felt an empathy towards characters on the basis of their comparable class position. *Waterloo Road* was probably the most successful of these films. The likely attraction was Stewart Granger, who came second only to James Mason in popularity among male stars in the Bernstein Film Questionnaire (John Mills was sixth).[10] The only working-class film to rival *Waterloo Road* in popularity was *Holiday Camp*. This came close to portraying postwar life as many people knew it: the upheavals of the annual holiday, the teenage son being lured into gambling and the problems of the young widow struggling to bring up a child on her own. The screenwriters contrived to combine these elements in an amiable comedy with a dark undercurrent. One problem which did not appear was the complaining mother-in-law, though this deficiency was remedied in the subsequent Huggett series.

The name of Ted Willis keeps recurring in film credits. Though his leadership of Unity Theatre ended in acrimony and recrimination, his continuing sympathy with working people shines through the films which he scripted, even if cosiness crept into George Dixon's television reincarnation at Dock Green.[11] For Raymond Durgnat, 'Too many of Ted's nice people are just visiting from the middle-class.'[12] This undervalues Willis's achievement in bringing the working class to the screen. Though his vision can seem all-pervasive given the number of scripts in which he had a hand, the likely alternative was working-class people being marginalised in favour of more home counties dramas about middle-class couples.

The popularity of films can be gauged by using a combination of quantitative and qualitative sources – the first objective specified in Chapter One. Audience preferences provide a corrective against generalisations based on the few films such as *Brief Encounter* (d. David Lean, 1945) which have stood the test of time – and which were not always popular on their first release. More local studies are needed to give a better understanding of geographical and class-based differences in cinemagoing. Until then, any conclusions about what audiences liked must be treated with caution.

The second objective is to demonstrate how film might be used as source material by other disciplines. Comparing a novel with the filmed version or comparing films can illustrate changes over time in attitudes to childhood and the family, or in fashions of dress and interior design. The proviso is that as many films as possible should be viewed to ensure that genuine social trends are being revealed rather than the predilections of individual film-makers. Inevitably these glimpses of class perceptions in the past are filtered through the sensibilities of film-makers, but this is no worse than the distortions of memory which affect oral testimony or the bias inherent in written sources. Providing film is set alongside other sources and checked against them, it yields comparable insights.

An unresolved issue is which period serves as a model for traditional working-class culture. By ignoring the cinema, Richard Hoggart seems to hark back to Leeds in the early years of the century even though he was not born until 1918; Gareth Stedman Jones makes out a persuasive case for the late nineteenth century; Bernard Waites sees the notion of a friendly community developing in the 1930s, while Geoff Eley spoils his insistence on historical specificity by opting for the 1880s to the 1940s.[13] For Ross McKibbin, 'The traditional working class of the 1940s was traditional only in the sense that economic circumstances permitted it to behave for the first time in the way people – not least the working men and women – assumed that the "traditional" working class should behave.'[14] Why they should want to look back given the improvement in their economic circumstances is not clear and McKibbin does not offer any evidence for this tortuous interpretation.

Four sources of variation in definitions of 'traditional' can be distinguished: differences of time and locale, differences in determining what elements contribute to traditional working-class culture and differences in assessing the evidence once a definition is agreed. Most obviously in the case of Hoggart, reasoned argument is not the only factor involved. It may be possible to demonstrate with impeccable academic rigour why aspects of working-class culture in Edwardian days should be considered worthwhile, but Hoggart's attitude to subsequent developments stems as much from conviction as from logic.[15] It is tempting (and easy) to dismiss the cultural influences on academic writers as speculative, but this need not invalidate them, nor diminish their potency. Enoch Powell's verdict on the emotional factor in history is apposite: '... it is unquantifiable, it is rather shameful and it is difficult to handle, but without the emotional factor I do not think one can understand the turnaround which occurred in this country or some of the surprising things which this country did in the second half of the twentieth century.'[16] Writers who fail to declare their cultural influences are apt to lay false trails for those who follow.

Some elements of working-class life in the 1940s, notably the housing of large sectors of the population, were little changed from the late nineteenth century and can justifiably be termed traditional. In other spheres, life was very different. The reduction in family size discussed in Chapter Eleven implies changed attitudes towards contraception, while the emphasis on leisure evident from the enthusiasm for cinemas, dance halls, holiday camps and sport was a legacy from the interwar years, when it was charted in painstaking detail by Mass-Observation.[17] Social, economic and technological change are inextricably linked, finding expression in an ever-evolving culture.[18] Tradition offers a way of maintaining cultural continuity in the face of change, yet tradition itself adapts and evolves along with the culture. The seasonal television screening of *White Christmas* (d. Michael Curtiz, US, 1954) has established itself in the national psyche almost as much as that other recent tradition, the Christmas turkey.

As primary source material, film provides evidence on the social consequences of the Second World War – the third objective. Family life was changed. The Huggetts are a postwar family in their attitudes to children and local politics, while *Blue Scar* reveals a cynicism towards nationalisation which can be overlooked if reliance is placed on official documents. One inevitable legacy of war – the absence of a father – was seen as contributing to the upsurge in juvenile delinquency and this belief is evident in films. Changes in the role of women can be seen in the younger generation of the Huggett family, even if women of Ethel Huggett's age are wary of change. The Welfare State did little to inspire filmmakers, though the absence of unemployment as an issue is noteworthy compared with films from the 1930s. *Waterloo Road* and *A Boy, a Girl and a Bike* emphasise the importance of affordable housing for the working class – something which the war set back.

The final objective is to test Durgnat's dictum that a middle-class cinema only acknowledges the working class insofar as they are subservient to middle-class ideals, shade into the feckless or criminal, or are presented humorously.[19] The Huggetts are edging into the middle class, even if Ethel remains staunchly working class, but they are hardly subservient. The feckless and the criminal working class are there aplenty in films of the 1940s, though criminal masterminds belong to the higher echelons of society. Humorous working-class characters are also much in evidence. They abound in the comedies of Frank Randle and Old Mother Riley, which owe a debt to the music hall, though Durgnat may have had in mind those working-class characters who lurk in middle-class comedies such as *The Perfect Woman* (d. Bernard Knowles, 1949). Yet in *Once a Jolly Swagman*, *Chance of a Lifetime* and *A Boy, a Girl and a Bike*, the working class are treated seriously.

Nor are humorous characters exclusively working class, as the frequent pairing of Basil Radford and Naunton Wayne as a cricket-loving duo illustrates. Durgnat's generalisation is just that: a generalisation.

An issue which can only be touched on is how the lives of working-class audiences were influenced by the cinema. The problems of establishing a methodology and amassing evidence are formidable. There are also inconvenient facts to be explained. *The Way to the Stars* was popular in working-class Leeds, yet why should those forgotten audiences show a preference for films about the middle class? Durgnat offers a solution:

Since the working class and below account for between 55 per cent and 70 per cent ... of the population, it's surprising, on the face of it, that film-makers didn't from the beginning stake everything on intensively appealing to it by portraying its standards and customs.

On closer examination, reasons become apparent. Daydream and wish fulfilment are satisfied with more obvious ease by 'identification upwards'. Moreover, the middle and lower middle classes shade only gradually and confusingly into the upper-working classes. Thus it's natural and easy for many working-class people to take middle-class characteristics as their ego ideal.[20]

The success of Mancunian films and the Old Mother Riley series means that Durgnat's solution needs to be qualified. Their failure to achieve West End releases certainly suggests an absence of identification downwards: the middle class were little influenced by working-class values until the youth culture phenomenon of the 1960s. The working class could identify upwards, but given the opportunity, they could equally well identify with their own class. The trouble was that, at least in the cinema, they were rarely given the opportunity. Too often, films were about rather than of the working class. Working-class characters were safely contained within the trappings of a middle-class morality story, notably in *Good Time Girl*, with the existing order being accepted and the values of the working-class community being ignored. This failure of vision may be ascribed to the upper-middle-class outlook of censors and dominant figures in the industry including Michael Balcon and J. Arthur Rank.[21] It did not help that the proportion of film directors coming from public schools rivalled the proportion of cabinet ministers educated there. Whatever socialism meant, it was not control by the working class; whatever constituted an indigenous British cinema, it was not a cinema stemming from the concerns of the working class.

The cinema could provide the working class with desirable role models: in this paternal aspiration, the censors and J. Arthur Rank were in agreement. But the working class were enjoying relative affluence and as Durgnat points out, 'Affluence is double-edged. To some extent it exposes working-class warmth to middle-class "refainment" ... But at the same time it enables the working-classes to pay the piper, and call more of his tunes.' [22] In the longer term, Durgnat's economic logic seems inescapable – the spending power of the working class gave them the ability to make their demands heard – but the period 1945 to 1950 was not the long term and British film production was not attuned to its market. By the end of 1950, 28 per cent of British films released between 1945 and 1949 had not been shown in the sample Leeds cinemas (independents in southeast Essex failed to book 17 per cent) while Rank's film production arm was making losses (Appendix, Table 1).[23] If workers were calling for different tunes in the late 1940s, the piper was not always listening.

Escapism is a word often used by former cinema-goers, including my own interviewees.[24] The term can apply to the experience of being in the cinema as much as to the fantasy world conjured by specific films – memories of individual films are often hazy.[25] The notion of escapism is fostered in the films themselves (*The Holly and the Ivy*, d. George More O'Ferrall, 1952):

MARGARET: Mick, let's get out of here – let's go to the pictures.
MICHAEL: Okay. Suits me.
MARGARET: Come on then. Quick.
MICHAEL: We've missed the beginning. I don't suppose the film will be any good, anyway.
MARGARET: Never mind. Escape – the foundation of all entertainment.
MICHAEL: Get your Keating's – it's a flea-pit.

Yet escapism lacks academic respectability. As Paul Swann observes:

Films were regarded, in the words of Leavis and Thompson, as 'substitute living', a seductive form of shallow but unsatisfying escape which they felt had come to dominate industrial culture ... This kind of position was responsible in large part for the emergence of the documentary impulse in British film-making and literature in the 1930s and 1940s, which can be viewed as a concerted attempt to make the viewer 'face reality'.[26]

Shadows of an earlier prescriptive force, the Protestant work ethic, hang over the Leavisite approach. If the influence of Leavis has waned, escapism has not been rehabilitated. The very process of reading a film implies uncovering a deeper level of meaning which is denied to somebody who is merely carried along by the story.

Reading requires consideration of the film as embodiment of ideas as well as an entertainment to be taken at its face value – a duality into which the middle-class child is socialised.[27] Yet, like many of life's pleasures, escapism derives its power from being experienced rather than intellectualised. Star quality is one factor which distinguishes the cinema from other media and which contributes to its power to make the audience forget the everyday world. Yet analysing the mystique of the star carries the danger that its essence is lost, just as dissecting a butterfly does nothing to explain its beauty. The strain shows as Richard Dyer wrestles with this dilemma in his study of stardom.[28]

Feminist critics have had more success in squaring the circle of how to analyse something which cannot be put into words. Jackie Stacey finds wanting such stratagems as decoding, which attempt to shift the problem rather than resolving it. Her preferred solution involves getting people to offer experiences in their own words – a process which has since been developed by Joanne Lacey in her use of the film memories of working-class women in Liverpool.[29] Their approach has its antecedents. Hoggart trod a similar path in trying to discover how material was received, albeit with less emphasis on oral testimony:

Helped by Orwell and C. S. Lewis, I became more and more drawn to the question of what people might make of that material [from popular culture], by the thought that obviously poor writing might appeal to good instincts, that the mind of a reader is not a *tabula rasa* but has been nurtured within a social setting which provides its own forms and filters for judgments and resistances, that one had to know very much more about how people used much of the stuff which to us might seem merely dismissable trash, before one could speak confidently about the effects it might have.[30]

The work of Stacey, Lacey and others has gone some way to answering Hoggart's question, as well as addressing Annette Kuhn's concern, expressed in the 1980s, that a gulf was opening between textual analysis and contextual enquiry.[31] It has also helped to strip escapism of its pejorative connotations. The concept deserves to be taken seriously. As well as embodying what cinema-going meant for audiences of the 1940s, it can offer a means of analysing the experience. The possibility is opened up by Sally Mitchell in her study of popular reading in the nineteenth century: 'Escape reading gives us a clue about what is being escaped from; it may reflect a reverse image of the tone of the times.'[32] Escapist films such as the American musicals of the 1930s may be approached in this way. When a girl from a poor background is plucked from the chorus line and becomes a star, what does this say about a world in which opportunities are so conspicuously lacking for most of her class that even aspiring to the chorus line is something which only happens in dreams?

A similar perspective is adopted by the oral historian Luisa Passerini, whose ideal is to allow individual responses to prevail over collective responses. The interest for Passerini resides in the differences between individual responses: 'People could have gone in other directions, could have decided to cherish other myths or to alter them, could have interpreted a certain myth in an alternative or new way.' The result is the construction of single mythbiographies 'using a choice of resources, that include myths, combining the new and ancient in unique expressions'.[33] In Passerini's terms, cinema audiences combine images from a film with images from the memory store of other films, other media and life experiences to produce expressions which are unique to the individual. The film is reconstructed in the memory according to the individual's preoccupations and longings. This approach to how people use escapist entertainment may be juxtaposed with Michael Denning's study of dime novels. Denning distinguishes an allegoric mode of reading from the dominant novelistic mode. In an echo of Basil Bernstein's restricted code, the former is used by subordinate groups and relies on a master plot or some existing body of narrative such as Christian allegory, with individuals standing in for social groups.[34] Both the star and the genre – from costume drama to western – fit neatly into the allegoric mode, while critics root for the novelistic mode. Yet the contrast with Passerini's approach is more apparent than real. In Denning's terms, audiences can still use their own life experiences to fashion allegory into something which has personal meaning.

Like Passerini, but coming from a background of social psychology, Elihu Katz and David Foulkes also discern an area of variability in how the media are used, concluding that though a drive may be escapist, this need not apply to its fulfilment.[35] University of Birmingham studies made in the late 1940s provide a rich cache of material for examining sub-cultural attitudes derived from films towards such matters as dress and hair styles.[36] Echoing the terms of the pioneer social scientist, David Riesman, following the fashions derived from films encourages conformism within the group. At the same time, other groups such as teachers may interpret the same attitudes as oppositional.[37] Here the area of variability becomes an issue of discipline and generational difference.

What links all these researchers is the implication that audiences need not derive the intended values from a film, a notorious example being the furore over copycat violence associated with

A Clockwork Orange (d. Stanley Kubrick, 1971), which led to the film being withdrawn from circulation in Britain until the director's death. The working-class audience in Rochester who laughed at the preview of *Brief Encounter* were making a similar point: the nature of their response could not be taken for granted. Though the portrayal of the higher echelons of society in interwar films may have been intended to bolster the existing order, a large sector of working-class adolescents considered the characters to be hypocritical, lazy, boring, snobbish and deserving of pity.[38]

As if acknowledging this variability in reception, not all British films of the 1940s are prescriptive in their attitudes and values, notwithstanding the efforts of Balcon, Rank and the censors. *It Always Rains on Sunday* gives audiences a choice of role models, not all of whom would have met with Balcon's approval. *Holiday Camp* condones sex outside marriage (so long as the offending couple, Valerie and Michael, eventually get married) and cheating at cards (so long as Joe Huggett teaches the card sharps a lesson). Similar moral ambiguities can be found in *Good Time Girl* and *A Boy, a Girl and a Bike*. Seeing a simple choice between two options is tempting but misleading. Pat Kirkham discerns in *Dance Hall* (d. Charles Crichton, 1950) a choice between respectability and temptation, but the girls offer audiences a variety of options between these two poles as ways of reconciling their dreams with reality.[39] *The Blue Lamp* comes closest to offering a stark choice between good and evil embodied in the characters played by Hanley and Bogarde; the trouble is that at least for Andy Medhurst it is a one-sided contest in favour of Bogarde.[40]

The prevalence of stock characters and stereotypes in British films of the 1940s – a feature of Denning's allegoric mode – accords with the view of Paul Lazarsfeld, that founding father of media research: 'In general, ... people look not for new experience in the mass media but for a repetition and an elaboration of their old experiences into which they can more easily project themselves.'[41] By this view, people seek the comfortingly familiar as a backdrop against which they can see their own problems rehearsed. Mitchell sees such identification as a characteristic of open-ended light fiction as distinct from tightly-constructed major fiction in which every event is sequential, inevitable and related to the character's psychology within an artistically complete plot. The postwar melodramas from Gainsborough Studios certainly fall into the open-ended category. Yet defining quality in terms of a work's construction has its problems, leading Mitchell to classify *Jane Eyre* as light fiction.[42] Different forms can be accepted without having to be ranked in terms of quality. Because jazz is open-ended, it need not be inferior to a sonata with its clearly defined structure.

Lazarsfeld's approach implies that films have a conservative role, helping to reinforce values and maintain the existing order, though the elaboration of old experiences allows for evolutionary change. This is broadly the line taken by Raymond Williams in seeing a key to the popularity of *Coronation Street* (Granada TV, 1960– current) in the engagement by audiences with the sense of continuity of human lives.[43] The Huggett films and the Old Mother Riley series offered audiences a similar elaboration of experiences by familiar characters. One reason for the success of *The Way to the Stars* with its emphasis on children and the waiting woman must be its powerful sense of the continuity of human life as experienced even when coming to terms with death – an impulse which transcends class.

The cinema can elaborate experience as Lazarsfeld proposes, while still providing an escape. A bridge between the two approaches is provided by Karlheinz Stierle, for whom a distinctive feature of fiction is its ability to articulate a system of perspectives providing experiences which are radically different from those in ordinary life. Though this is akin to escapism, Stierle echoes Lazarsfeld in noting how this system prestructures for the reader potential paradigms of experience.[44] This viewpoint is equally applicable to the feature film. Frank Randle and Old Mother Riley offered the escapism of preposterous plots involving larger-than-life characters. They rehearsed attitudes to employers which many workers must have yearned to emulate. If audiences never tried, they could at least leave the cinema with a healthy cynicism towards middle-class pomposity.

'[The mass media] must roughly show us as we at present are. But their mirror image progressively distorts. Clever shifts of angle and deceptions of lighting can slowly bring about a change; we begin to believe what the mirror says and do not notice its subtle alterations.'[45] Hoggart's metaphor is seductive, particularly in its emphasis on the distorting power of the media, but the fact that the debate on the moral effects of the cinema has raged for a century suggests that the internalisation of values derived from films is less certain than Hoggart implies.

If reading a film is to be more than an exercise in aesthetics, it needs to be seen in the context of cinema-going as a social experience: which cinemas people prefer, how often they go and with whom, how they dress and which films they see. Determining what films meant to audiences of the past is more difficult, though clues can be gleaned from oral testimony and written sources ranging from fan magazines to the anthropological studies of Pearl Jephcott and others. Research has hardly begun, yet it is not without urgency. The passage of time may bring objectivity, but the patina of nostalgia for the war and its aftermath may prove harder to penetrate as the attitudes and mores of working-class communities of fifty years ago slip into history.

In the late 1940s, Lazarsfeld and his fellow sociologists at Columbia University conducted the largest investigation into mass communication and popular taste since the Payne Fund studies of 1933. Subsequent research has not substantially improved on their conclusion that although the mass media can affect social norms to an extent, they can also function as a social narcotic.[46] In Passerini's terms, this allows film to have a spectrum of functions and meanings. A seemingly cautious conclusion opens up a range of research options. The problem is giving them enough precision to make them testable, but fortunately a range of specific examples of the effect of film can be found. Jim Wolveridge, an East End costermonger born in 1920, records that rhyming slang was hardly used in the 1930s and would have died out if it had not been taken up by the professional cockney comedians of stage and radio. He also provides an interesting example of social change by an unexpected route, maintaining that the portrayal in films of the working class as dim-witted clowns was hated by the younger generation of East Enders, causing a lot of young people to try to improve their speech as a way of proving that they were not the oafs they were made out to be. 'Resentment did what education couldn't.' [47] Arthur La Bern noted the popularity of names like Shirley and Deanna in the East End of London, 'for in these days the all-pervading influence of the cinema plays its part in the choice of names for back-street offspring.' [48] Jerry White cites a 1934 newspaper reporting how young people in an Islington cafe adopted American styles of speech and clothing copied from movies.[49] Film may reinforce class attitudes; it also exposes audiences to wider cultural influences with unpredictable results.

Two caveats are in order. One is pinpointed by Andrew Davies:

Tracing the formation of social consciousness is one of the most difficult and sensitive of the tasks undertaken by the social historian, and care must be taken in discussing the ways in which the attitudes of young people were formed. However, undue emphasis upon the role of the cinema can easily obscure the importance of experiences at home, on the streets and at work, in forging young people's outlooks.[50]

The cinema had to compete with other leisure pursuits. The film *The Lambeth Walk* (d. Albert de Courville, 1939) doubtless reached more people than the stage show, yet Mass-Observation concluded that broadcasting the hit song was by far the most important means of popularising the dance, which became a craze.[51] Interdependence between media is difficult to demonstrate and is apt to be avoided for this reason. It is difficult to gain an idea of the relative influence of the cinema in the middle years of the twentieth century. The fact that it did influence adolescents is indisputable, though it was not necessarily the dominant cultural influence.

The other danger is put starkly by Walter Brandis and Dorothy Henderson:

In a work concerned with comparative socialisation within a society, there is always a danger that the differences such studies reveal will be transformed into statements of 'better' or 'worse' ... Once such judgements are made, implicitly or explicitly, that one form of socialisation is 'better' than another, it is but a short step to consider how we can transform the 'worse' into the 'better'. Can we transform the working-class into the middle-class? This question is based upon the dubious premise that socialisation within contemporary middle-class strata and the education we offer in schools represents the acme of three quarters of a million years of civilisation. It equally and inevitably leads on to a view of the child as a deficit system, his parents as inadequate and their culture deprived.[52]

Several researchers whose work is touched on in this chapter, including Mitchell and Medhurst, do not avoid the pitfall. Though some sectors of the working class suffered material deprivation, this should not be taken as evidence that working-class culture lacked richness. It was different. Books might have been less in evidence than in middle-class households and formal education may not always have been held in the same esteem, but was this such a loss if the family ties and social contacts vividly evoked by commentators such as Jephcott and Hoggart were so much more extensive? Lack of financial security meant that the working-class adolescent had no alternative but to face the world with realism, while acquiring the sophistication to walk between two cultures. As one of Jephcott's girls put it:

I used to love College films ... where they were always having fun and doing about two hours' work a day. You talk about a picture for days after at work, and go over special scenes. You envy the glamour and the big houses make you discontented. You try to copy their ways of dress, talk and walk, or in going for a job. By 18 you know that a lot of it was more or less lies.[53]

One of my interviewees took the opposite position: dissatisfaction with life made the cinema seem more real.[54] What both views have in common is that what was seen on the screen was compared with real life – and real life was the loser. The cinema might have been a distorting mirror, but at least it was a mirror. In reflecting the hopes and aspirations of audiences, it allowed people to make sense of their own lives in a communal setting – something which could not be achieved in any other way.

In his study of working-class youth in Manchester during the interwar years, Davies concludes that although the cinema might be seen as favouring consensus, audiences were too cynical for attitudes to be channelled by Hollywood.[55] It is easy to see the working class as passive recipients of what the media feed them. As a Manchester researcher pointed out in 1932, working-class youth made up a critical audience, quick to recognise poor films and with a strong idea of the types of films which they preferred – those with excitement, humour, or good music and singing – while they disliked 'impossible' (unrealistic), dull or boring films.[56] Roger Manvell, that high priest of the film as aesthetic experience, could hardly have quibbled. Nor is there any reason to suppose that war made working-class audiences any less critical; if anything, the opposite might be expected as new experiences and greater prosperity expanded their range of cultural references. In a study of how film propaganda was received in Britain, Nicholas Reeves detects the same healthy cynicism found by Davies.[57] Yet in spite of this, the working class were still at the bottom of the social hierarchy and still realistic about their life chances. The difference was that they had more opportunity of being heard.

Notes

1 Gerald Young, 'The voice of the people', *Film Quarterly*, 1:2 (1946–47), 46; *Parliamentary Debates (Commons)*, 5th series (1945), vol. 415, col. 2564.

2 Ironically, Edgar Anstey complained about the stereotyped acting and dialogue in *Blue Scar*. Edgar Anstey, 'The year's work in the documentary film', in Roger Manvell (ed.), *The Year's Work in the Film 1949* (London: Longmans, Green, for British Council, 1950), p. 34.

3 T. E. B. Clarke, *This Is Where I Came In* (London: Michael Joseph, 1974), p. 158.

4 *Ibid.*, p. 158.

5 Geoff Brown, *Launder and Gilliat* (London: BFI, 1977), p. 110.

6 Norman Swallow, 'Social realism in film and radio: a comparative analysis', *Sight & Sound*, 16:64 (1947–48), 170–1.

7 *Evening Standard* (4 June 1948), *Reynolds News* (25 April 1948). Both items contained in BFI, 'British films 1948' cuttings file.

8 D. A. Yerrill, 'The technique of realism', *Sight & Sound*, 17:65 (1948), 24.

9 Basil Wright, 'A study of Carol Reed', in Manvell (ed.), *The Year's Work in the Film 1949*, p. 16.

10   Sidney Bernstein, *The Bernstein Film Questionnaire 1946–7* (London: [Granada Theatres], 1947), p. 2.

11   For Willis's days at Unity Theatre, see Colin Chambers, *The Story of the Unity Theatre* (London: Lawrence and Wishart, 1989), pp. 231–89 *passim*.

12   Raymond Durgnat, *A Mirror for England: British Movies from Austerity to Affluence* (London: Faber & Faber, 1970), p. 61.

13   Richard Hoggart, *The Uses of Literacy: Aspects of Working-Class Life with Special Reference to Publications and Entertainments* (Harmondsworth: Penguin Books, 1958), pp. 26 and 31; Gareth Stedman Jones, 'Working-class culture and working-class politics in London 1870–1900: notes on the remaking of the working class', *Journal of Social History*, 7:4 (1974), 460–508; Bernard Waites, 'Popular culture in late nineteenth and early twentieth century Lancashire', in Open University, *Historical Development of Popular Culture in Britain 1* (Milton Keynes: Open University Press, 1981), p. 97; Geoff Eley, 'Distant Voices, Still Lives. The family is a dangerous place: memory, gender, and the image of the working class', in Robert A. Rosenstone (ed.), *Revisioning History: Film and the Construction of a New Past* (Princeton, NJ: Princeton University Press, 1995), p. 121.

14   Ross McKibbin, *Classes and Cultures: England 1918–1951* (Oxford: Oxford University Press, 1998), p. 161.

15   Hoggart is aware of the problem. Hoggart, *The Uses of Literacy*, p. 224.

16   J. Enoch Powell, 'Commentary one', in Brian Brivati and Harriet Jones (eds), *What Difference Did the War Make?* (London: Leicester University Press, 1995), p. 14.

17   Gary S. Cross (ed.), *Workers at Blackpool: Mass-Observation and Popular Leisure in the 1930s* (London: Routledge, 1990).

18   A persuasive study of the relationship of technology to economic and social change is Richard Wilkinson, *Poverty and Progress: An Ecological Model of Economic Development* (London: Methuen, 1973).

19   Durgnat, *A Mirror for England*, p. 48.

20   *Ibid.*, pp. 46–7.

21   For a censor's discouraging view of a film about a working-class football pool winner, *Easy Money* (d. Bernard Knowles, 1948), see BFI Library, British Board of Film Censors scenario notes, 14 August 1947. The comments are reproduced in Sue Harper, *Picturing the Past: The Rise and Fall of the British Costume Film* (London: BFI, 1994), p. 150.

22   Durgnat, *A Mirror for England*, p. 54.

23   For statistics on films in the two areas, see Philip J. Gillett, 'British feature films and working-class culture 1945–1950', Ph.D. thesis. University of North London, 2000, Table 6.13, p. a57.

24   *Ibid.*, pp. 406–7.

25   For a similar point, see Ashley Franklin, *A Cinema Near You: 100 Years of Going to the Pictures in Derbyshire* (Derby: Breedon Books, 1996), p. 88.

26   Paul Swann, *The Hollywood Feature Film in Postwar Britain* (New York: St Martins Press, 1987), p. 21.

27   Walter Brandis and Dorothy Henderson, *Social Class, Language and Communication* (London: Routledge & Kegan Paul, 1970), p. 47.

28   Richard Dyer, *Stars* (London: BFI, 1979).

29 Jackie Stacey, *Star Gazing: Hollywood Cinema and Female Spectatorship* (London: Routledge, 1994); Joanne Lacey, 'Seeing through happiness. Class, gender and popular film: Liverpool women remake the 50's film musical', Ph.D. thesis, University of London, 1997.

30 Richard Hoggart, *Life and Times*, vol. 2: *A Sort of Clowning 1940–59* (London: Chatto & Windus, 1990), p. 135.

31 Annette Kuhn, 'Women's genres', *Screen*, 25:1 (1984), 19–20.

32 Sally Mitchell, *The Fallen Angel: Chastity, Class and Women's Reading 1835–1880* (Bowling Green, OH: Bowling Green University Popular Press, 1981), p. 92.

33 Luisa Passerini, 'Mythology in oral history', in Raphael Samuel and Paul Thompson (eds), *The Myths We Live By* (London: Routledge, 1990), p. 59. See also Stuart Voytilla, *Myth and the Movies: Discovering the Mythic Structure of 50 Unforgettable Films* (Studio City, CA: Michael Wiese Productions, 1999).

34 Michael Denning, *Mechanic Accents: Dime Novels and Working-Class Culture in America* (London: Verso, 1987), pp. 72–4.

35 Elihu Katz and David Foulkes, 'On the use of the mass media as escape: clarification of a concept', *Public Opinion Quarterly*, 26:3 (1962), 381.

36 W. D. Wall, 'The adolescent and the cinema', *Educational Review*, 1:1 (1948), 34–46; W. D. Wall and W. A. Simpson, 'The effects of cinema attendance on the behaviour of adolescents as seen by their contemporaries', *British Journal of Educational Psychology*, 19:1 (1949), 53–61; Barbara Kesterton, 'The social and emotional effects of the recreational film on adolescents of 13 and 14 years of age in the West Bromwich area', Ph.D. thesis, University of Birmingham, 1948.

37 David Riesman, with Nathan Glazer and Reuel Denney, *The Lonely Crowd: A Study of the Changing American Character* (New York: Doubleday Anchor Books, [1960?]), p. 184.

38 A. Fielder, 'Adolescents and the cinema: report of an enquiry', Dip. Social Studies thesis, University of Manchester, 1932, p. 28, cited in Andrew Davies, *Leisure, Gender and Poverty: Working-Class Culture in Salford and Manchester 1900–1939* (Buckingham: Open University Press, 1992), p. 95.

39 Pat Kirkham, 'Dress, dance, dreams and fantasy: fashion and fantasy in *Dance Hall*', *Journal of Design History*, 8:3 (1995), 195–207.

40 Andy Medhurst, 'Dirk Bogarde', in Charles Barr (ed.), *All Our Yesterdays: 90 Years of British Cinema* (London: BFI, 1986), p. 347.

41 Paul F. Lazarsfeld, 'Audience research', in Bernard Berelson and Morris Janowitz (eds), *Reader in Public Opinion and Communication* (New York: Free Press of Glencoe, 1953), p. 343.

42 Mitchell, *The Fallen Angel*, pp. 165–7.

43 Stephen Heath and Gillian Skirrow, 'An interview with Raymond Williams', in Tania Modleski (ed.), *Studies in Entertainment: Critical Approaches to Mass Culture* (Bloomington and Indianapolis, IN: Indiana University Press, 1986), p. 6.

44 Karlheinz Stierle, 'The reading of fictional texts', trans. Inge Crosman and Thelka Zachrau, in Susan R. Suleiman and Inge Crosman (eds), *The Reader in the Text: Essays on Audience and Interpretation* (Princeton, NJ: Princeton University Press, 1980), p. 100.

45 Richard Hoggart, *Speaking to Each Other*, vol. 1: *About Society* (London: Chatto & Windus, 1970), p. 33.

46 Wilber Schramm, *Men, Messages and Media: A Look at Human Communication* (New York and London: Harper & Row, 1973), p. 238.

47 Jim Wolveridge, 'Ain't it grand', in Venetia Murray, *Echoes of the East End* (London: Viking: 1989), pp. 134 and 137.

48 Arthur La Bern, *It Always Rains on Sunday* (Leeds and London: Morley-Baker, 1969), p. 7.

49 *Islington and Highbury Post* (7 April 1934), cited in Jerry White, *The Worst Street in North London: Campbell Bunk, Islington, between the Wars* (London: Routledge & Kegan Paul, 1986), p. 166. The possibility that the reporter took a jaundiced view of Islington's young people cannot be overlooked.

50 Davies, *Leisure, Gender and Poverty*, pp. 96–7.

51 Mass-Observation, *Britain* (Harmondsworth: Penguin Books, 1939), pp. 142–74.

52 Brandis and Henderson, *Social Class, Language and Communication*, pp. 121–2.

53 Pearl Jephcott, *Rising Twenty: Notes on Some Ordinary Girls* (London: Faber & Faber, 1948) p. 156.

54 Interview with June McDowell, Southend-on-Sea (2 March 1997).

55 Davies, *Leisure, Gender and Poverty*, p. 96.

56 Fielder, 'Adolescents and the cinema' cited in *ibid.*, p. 95.

57 Nicholas Reeves, *The Power of Film Propaganda: Myth or Reality* (London: Cassell, 1999), pp. 240–1.

Appendix

For the late 1940s, the Board of Trade returns summarised in Tables 1–4 provide the only precise sources of box-office revenues nationwide. The basis for the calculations by each company is not clear, so comparisons between tables are unreliable. Later releases will have had less time to accrue revenue; all other things being equal, their rankings should be correspondingly lower. With these provisos, the figures do provide a guide to the relative popularity of films released by each company, together with production costs. All box-office revenues quoted are likely to be net of entertainments tax.

Table 1 UK revenues, production costs and profits of Rank films to 24 December 1949 (£)

	Net revenue to date	Expected total net revenue	Cost	Profit or loss [a]
Oliver Twist (1948)	328,900	370,000	371,540	8,900
Great Expectations (1947)	303,700	303,700	391,569	21,200
The Upturned Glass (1947)	211,300	211,300	195,958	45,800
Blanche Fury (1948)	200,500	201,800	382,175	(135,400)
The Blue Lagoon (1949)	189,500	250,000	311,094	40,300
Holiday Camp (1947)	184,300	184,300	150,376	16,000
Miranda (1948)	181,300	182,200	170,372	5,600
Hungry Hill (1947)	180,700	180,700	375,591	(201,600)
Green for Danger (1947)	159,300	159,300	202,388	(26,600)
The Woman in the Hall (1947)	133,900	134,000	201,244	(83,400)
The Man Within (1947)	128,100	128,200	161,845	(6,500)
Easy Money (1948)	125,300	127,700	116,821	2,200
London Belongs to Me (1948)	122,500	130,000	271,275	(158,200)
Broken Journey (1948)	118,200	119,500	196,962	(63,900)
The Weaker Sex (1948)	115,800	122,000	175,171	(69,400)
The Brothers (1947)	111,000	111,100	162,868	(55,700)
Take My Life (1947)	105,500	107,100	211,849	(84,900)
Portrait from Life (1949)	100,200	120,000	132,827	4,100
My Brother's Keeper (1948)	96,300	105,000	113,595	(9,400)
The Root of All Evil (1947)	96,100	96,600	155,032	(64,300)
Uncle Silas (1947)	96,000	96,400	366,254	(283,600)
The End of the River (1947)	95,500	96,300	217,336	(78,000)
The Mark of Cain (1948)	92,000	94,000	253,449	(177,600)
Passionate Friends (1949)	90,400	115,000	346,827	(127,400)
Mr Perrin and Mr Traill (1948)	83,200	90,000	190,731	(104,600)
One Night with You (1948)	74,600	76,100	236,195	(173,000)
The History of Mr Polly (1949)	69,600	95,000	253,535	(172,100)
Esther Waters (1948)	47,700	50,000	338,551	(305,700)
The Bad Lord Byron (1949)	22,400	45,000	223,872	(179,200)
Marry Me (1949)	21,100	50,000	117,941	(67,600)

Source Calculated from PRO BT 64/4490, Schedules 2, 4 and 6.
Note [a] Figures include unidentified adjustments, possibly including overseas earnings. Losses are shown in brackets.

Table 2 Revenues and production costs of Ealing features to 1950 (£)

	Revenue [a]	Cost
It Always Rains on Sunday (1947)	229,706	180,936
Frieda (1947)	227,017	168,435
Scott of the Antarctic (1948)	214,223	371,588
Nicholas Nickleby (1947)	139,313	191,246
Hue and Cry (1947)	115,781	104,222
Passport to Pimlico (1949)	104,443	276,787
Against the Wind (1948)	94,995	202,330
Saraband for Dead Lovers (1948)	87,335	371,205
The Loves of Joanna Godden (1947)	82,908	167,073
Eureka Stockade (1948)	55,855	not given
Another Shore (1948)	35,370	180,794

Source Calculated from PRO BT 64/4491.
Note [a] Whether foreign earnings are included is not specified.

Table 3 **Revenues and production costs of ABPC films to March 1950 (£)**

	Net revenue [a]	Cost	Loss
My Brother Jonathan (1948)	527,970	193,851	46,878
The Guinea Pig (1948)	415,692	252,418	125,648
Brighton Rock (1947)	366,496	192,436	95,066
Noose (1948)	311,749	136,500	58,015
Temptation Harbour (1947)	276,771	133,174	39,152
Bond Street (1948)	275,045	163,629	100,341
Silent Dust (1949)	272,786	149,854	78,323
While the Sun Shines (1949)	253,603	110,840	40,397
For Them that Trespass (1949)	195,891	150,232	109,761
Man on the Run (1949)	175,716	110,090	72,566
The Silver Darlings (1947)	152,943	not given	not given
The Queen of Spades (1949)	141,309	232,500	213,108
Private Angelo (1949)	110,720	218,713	198,454

Source Calculated from PRO BT 64/4492.
Note [a] Whether foreign earnings are included is not specified.

Table 4 **UK revenues and production costs of British Lion films to April 1950 (£)**

	Revenue	Cost
Spring in Park Lane (1948)	366,985	238,000
The Courtneys of Curzon Street (1947)	328,568	315,810
An Ideal Husband (1948)	216,166	506,000
The Winslow Boy (1948)	215,110	425,915
The Fallen Idol (1948)	202,020	397,568
A Man about the House (1947)	164,331	304,521
Bonnie Prince Charlie (1948)	154,611	760,000
Mine Own Executioner (1947)	143,632	295,000
Anna Karenina (1948)	135,341	553,000
Elizabeth of Ladymead (1949)	129,074	298,654
The Shop at Sly Corner (1947)	124,197	76,715
Night Beat (1948)	118,578	175,118
The Small Back Room (1949)	103,547	232,972
White Cradle Inn (1947)	99,666	135,000
The Small Voice (1948)	79,364	121,000
Forbidden (1949)	67,758	100,000
Call of the Blood (1948)	45,713	66,295

Source Calculated from PRO BT 64/4493.

Table 5 **Top ten programmes at the Gaumont, Sheffield, from January 1947 to December 1950, with comparative attendance figures and rankings for films discussed** [a]

Main feature [b]	Second feature [b]	Attendances	Rank (n = 197)
Great Expectations	none	77,427 [c]	1
The White Unicorn	The Royal Wedding	73,448 [c]	2
Oliver Twist	COI short	71,628 [c]	3
Birth of a Baby (US)	Cigarette Girl (US)	69,685 [c]	4
Spring in Park Lane	none	69,223 [c]	5
The Best Years of Our Lives (US)	none	67,426 [c]	6
Forever Amber (US)	none	65,927 [c]	7
Monsieur Verdoux (US)	none	63,414 [c]	8
The Long Night (US)	They Got Me Covered (US)	53,315 [c]	9
The Jolson Story (US)	Fear (US) [d]	46,661 [c]	10
It Always Rains on Sunday	A Haunting We Will Go (US)	30,283	23
Here Come the Huggetts	Thirteen Lead Soldiers (US)	28,709	31
Good Time Girl	Bush Pilot (Canada)	28,207	38
Holiday Camp	Avalanche (US)	28,033	41
The Huggetts Abroad	Illegal Entry (US)	23,771	92
Once a Jolly Swagman	The Connors Case (Canada)	22,702	115
Dance Hall	The Overlanders	22,093	125
Waterfront	The Man in Grey	21,746	129
Against the Wind	The Moon and Sixpence (US, 1943)	20,674	152
Boys in Brown	Miss Pilgrim's Progress	20,630	153
Ticket to Tomahawk (US)	Old Mother Riley, Headmistress	19,012	172
Hue and Cry	God's Country (US)	18,615	178
A Boy, a Girl and a Bike	He Walked by Night (US)	16,627	189
Floodtide	Canon City (US)	11,252	197

Sources CTA, weekly returns for Gaumont, Sheffield, October 1948–December 1950; Allen Eyles (personal communication).

Notes

[a] Sunday attendance figures are included in the totals. As different programmes were screened on Sundays, the true attendances for the weekday programmes will be lower. Rankings may be slightly inaccurate if Sunday attendances showed marked variation.

[b] British registered unless indicated.

[c] Running for two weeks.

[d] Second feature replaced by documentary – *Olympic Preview* – for second week of run.

Table 6 **Film popularity in working-class Leeds, 1945–50: the nine films screened on the greatest number of days in ten independent cinemas compared with days of screening of the films discussed**

Film [a]	Days of screening
Up in Arms (US, 1944)	42
The Jolson Story (US, 1946)	36
The Princess and the Pirate (US, 1944)	36
The Royal Wedding (1947)	36
State Fair (US, 1945) [b]	36
The Way to the Stars (1945)	33
Nob Hill (US, 1945)	30
The Seventh Veil (1945)	30
The Bandit of Sherwood Forest (US, 1946)	28
Waterloo Road (1945)	23
Holiday Camp (1947)	18
Home Sweet Home (1945)	17
The White Unicorn (1947)	15
The Hasty Heart (1949)	15
They Made Me a Fugitive (1947)	14
Appointment with Crime (1947)	12
Dancing with Crime (1947)	12
Brighton Rock (1947)	12
The Guinea Pig (1948)	12
Old Mother Riley's New Venture (1949)	12
Waterfront (1950)	10
It Always Rains on Sunday (1947)	9
The Captive Heart (1946)	6
Hue and Cry (1947)	6
Good Time Girl (1948)	6
London Belongs to Me (1948)	6
Chance of a Lifetime (1950)	6
Over the Garden Wall (1950)	6
Fame is the Spur (1947)	3
Here Come the Huggetts (1948)	3
Once a Jolly Swagman (1948)	3
Blue Scar (1949)	3
Boys in Brown (1949)	3
Vote for Huggett (1949)	3
The Blue Lamp (1950)	3
The Gorbals Story (1950)	3
Night and the City (1950)	3
Old Mother Riley, Headmistress (1950)	3

Source Calculated from *Yorkshire Evening Post*, 1945–50.
Notes
[a] British registered unless marked.
[b] All screenings assumed to be the 1945 remake rather than the 1933 version.

Table 7 **Film popularity in southeast Essex, 1945–50: the eleven films screened on the greatest number of days in all cinemas compared with days of screening of the films discussed**

Film [a]	Days of screening
The Royal Wedding (1947)	88
The Jolson Story (US, 1946)	79
The Seventh Veil (1945)	63
The Rake's Progress (1945)	59
The Third Man (1949)	55
The Bandit of Sherwood Forest (US, 1946)	54
Great Expectations (1946)	54
The Red Shoes (1948)	54
Spring in Park Lane (1948)	54
The Way to the Stars (1945)	53
The Wicked Lady (1945)	53
Dancing with Crime (1947)	51
Holiday Camp (1947)	49
The Captive Heart (1946)	44
Home Sweet Home (1945)	41
It Always Rains on Sunday (1947)	41
London Belongs to Me (1948)	37
Waterloo Road (1945)	37
The White Unicorn (1947)	35
The Blue Lamp (1950)	35
Hue and Cry (1947)	34
The Guinea Pig (1948)	31
The Hasty Heart (1949)	31
Brighton Rock (1947)	28
Here Come the Huggetts (1948)	28
Old Mother Riley's New Venture (1949)	28
Vote for Huggett (1949)	28
Good Time Girl (1948)	25
Once a Jolly Swagman (1948)	25
They Were Not Divided (1950)	25
Fame is the Spur (1947)	23
The Huggetts Abroad (1949)	22
Dance Hall (1950)	22
Appointment with Crime (1946)	20
They Made Me a Fugitive (1947)	19
Night and the City (1950)	19
The Wooden Horse (1950)	19
Blue Scar (1949)	16
Boys in Brown (1949)	16
Chance of a Lifetime (1950)	13
Over the Garden Wall (1950)	13
Floodtide (1949)	10
Waterfront (1950)	10
The Gorbals Story (1950)	9
A Boy, a Girl and a Bike (1950)	7
The Magnet (1950)	7
Old Mother Riley, Headmistress (1950)	7

Source Calculated from *Southend Standard*, 1945–50.
Note [a] British registered unless marked.

Table 8 **Children aged eight to sixteen found guilty of indictable offences in England and Wales, 1938–60 – all courts**

	Number of male offenders		Number per 100,000 of the population of boys in the age group		Number of female offenders		Number per 100,000 of the population of girls in the age group	
	8–13 yrs	14–16 yrs	8–13 yrs	14–16 yrs	8–13 yrs	14–16 yrs	8–13 yrs	14–16 yrs
1938	14,724	11,645	798	1,131	835	912	46	90
1939	16,724	12,281	930	1,248	941	889	53	91
1940	23,167	16,071	1,304	1,674	1,449	1,500	83	158
1941	23,083	17,000	1,324	1,824	1,530	1,981	89	214
1942	20,382	14,691	1,184	1,613	1,563	1,913	93	212
1943	21,058	14,212	1,234	1,591	1,666	1,827	100	206
1944	22,525	14,625	1,330	1,654	1,558	1,846	94	211
1945	22,922	17,349	1,361	1,967	1,500	1,732	92	199
1946	19,912	14,347	1,175	1,638	1,433	1,396	87	162
1947	19,567	13,027	1,140	1,515	1,591	1,509	96	178
1948	24,684	15,980	1,433	1,902	2,043	1,727	123	212
1949	23,164	14,126	1,351	1,708	1,717	1,423	104	177
1950	20,412 [a]	14,624						
1955	16,185 [a]	13,517	924 [a]	1,603			73 [a]	172
1960	24,425 [a]	24,749						

Sources
1938–49: Home Office and Ministry of Education joint circular, *Juvenile Delinquency*, HO 99/1953, Min. of Ed. 265/1953, 20 July 1953, p. 6.
1950–60: F. H. McClintock, N. Howard Avison and G. N. G. Rose, *Crime in England and Wales* (London: Heinemann, 1968), Table 6.9, p. 165 and Table 6.20, p. 179.
Note [a] 10–13 years.

Table 9 **Standardised fertility rate of married women by social class, 1931 and 1951**

	Social class					
	I	II	III	IV	V	All
1931	79	84	94	108	124	100
1951	90	93	96	110	123	100

Source Peter R. Cox, *Demography* (Cambridge: Cambridge University Press, 4th edn, 1970), p. 358, reproduced in Constance Rollett and Julia Parker, 'Population and family', in A.H. Halsey (ed.) *Trends in British Society since 1900: A Guide to the Changing Social Structure of Britain* (Basingstoke and London: Macmillan, 1972), Table 2.38, p. 57.

Select filmography

Appointment with Crime, 1946
Production company: British National
Distributor on first release: Anglo-American
Director and screenplay: John Harlow
Producer: Louis H. Jackson
Source: Michael Leighton, Vernon Sewell
Leading actors: William Hartnell, Robert Beatty, Joyce Howard, Raymond Lovell, Herbert Lom

The Blue Lamp, 1950
Production company: Ealing
Distributor on first release: General Film Distributors
Director: Basil Dearden
Producer: Michael Balcon
Screenplay: T. E. B. Clarke, Alexander Mackendrick
Source: Jan Read, Ted Willis
Leading actors: Jack Warner, Jimmy Hanley, Dirk Bogarde, Robert Flemyng, Peggy Evans

Blue Scar, 1949
Production company: Outlook
Distributor on first release: British Lion
Director and screenplay: Jill Craigie
Producer: William MacQuitty
Leading actors: Emrys Jones, Gwyneth Vaughan

A Boy, a Girl and a Bike, 1949
Production company: Gainsborough
Distributor on first release: General Film Distributors
Director: Ralph Smart
Producer: Ralph Keene
Screenplay: Ted Willis
Leading actors: John McCallum, Honor Blackman, Diana Dors, Leslie Dwyer, Patrick Holt

Boys in Brown, 1949
Production company: Gainsborough
Distributor on first release: General Film Distributors
Director and screenplay: Montgomery Tully
Producer: Anthony Darnborough
Source: (play) Reginald Beckwith
Leading actors: Jack Warner, Richard Attenborough, Jimmy Hanley, Dirk
  Bogarde

Brighton Rock, 1947
Production company: ABPC
Distributor on first release: Pathe
Director: John Boulting
Producer: Roy Boulting
Screenplay: Graham Greene, Terence Rattigan
Source: (novel) Graham Greene
Leading actors: Richard Attenborough, Hermione Baddeley, Carol Marsh,
  William Hartnell

The Captive Heart, 1946
Production company: Ealing
Distributor on first release: General Film Distributors
Director: Basil Dearden
Producer: Michael Balcon
Screenplay: Angus Macphail, Guy Morgan
Source: Patrick Kirwan
Leading actors: Michael Redgrave, Mervyn Johns, Jack Warner, Basil Rad-
  ford, Jimmy Hanley

Chance of a Lifetime, 1950
Production company: Pilgrim Pictures
Distributor on first release: British Lion
Director: Bernard Miles
Producers: Bernard Miles, John Palmer
Screenplay: Bernard Miles, Walter Greenwood
Leading actors: Basil Radford, Bernard Miles, Julien Mitchell, Geoffrey Keen

Dance Hall, 1950
Production company: Ealing
Distributor on first release: General Film Distributors
Director: Charles Crichton
Producer: Michael Balcon
Screenplay: E. V. H. Emmett, Diane Morgan, Alexander Mackendrick
Leading actors: Petula Clark, Natasha Parry, Diana Dors

Dancing with Crime, 1947
Production company: Coronet-Alliance
Distributor on first release: Paramount
Director: John Paddy Carstairs
Producer: James A. Carter
Screenplay: Brock Williams
Source: Peter Fraser
Leading actors: Richard Attenborough, Sheila Sim, Barry K. Barnes, Barry
  Jones

Fame is the Spur, 1947
Production company: Two Cities
Distributor on first release: General Film Distributors
Director: Roy Boulting
Producer: John Boulting
Screenplay: Nigel Balchin
Source: (novel) Howard Spring
Leading actors: Michael Redgrave, Rosamund John

Floodtide, 1949
Production company: Aquila
Distributor on first release: General Film Distributors
Director: Frederick Wilson
Producer: Donald B. Wilson
Screenplay: George Blake, Donald B. Wilson
Source: George Blake
Leading actors: Gordon Jackson, Rona Anderson, Jack Lambert

Good Time Girl, 1948
Production company: Triton
Distributor on first release: General Film Distibutors
Director: David Macdonald
Producers: Sydney Box, Samuel Goldwyn jr
Screenplay: Muriel and Sydney Box, Ted Willis
Source: (novel) Arthur La Bern
Leading actors: Jean Kent, Flora Robson, Dennis Price, Herbert Lom

The Gorbals Story, 1950
Production company: New World
Distributor on first release: Eros
Director: David MacKane
Producer: Ernest Gartside
Screenplay: David MacKane
Source: (play) Robert McLeish
Leading actors: Howard Connell, Betty Henderson, Russell Hunter, Roddy
    McMillan

The Guinea Pig, 1948
Production company: Pilgrim
Distributor on first release: Pathe
Director: Roy Boulting
Producer: John Boulting
Screenplay: Warren Chetham Strode, Bernard Miles, Roy Boulting
Source: (play) Warren Chetham Strode
Leading actors: Richard Attenborough, Cecil Trouncer, Robert Flemyng

The Hasty Heart, 1949
Production company: ABPC
Distributor on first release: Associated British Pictures
Director and producer: Vincent Sherman
Screenplay: Ronald MacDougall
Source: (play) John Patrick
Leading actors: Richard Todd, Ronald Reagan, Patricia Neal

Here Come the Huggetts, 1948
Production company: Gainsborough
Distributor on first release: General Film Distributors
Director: Ken Annakin
Producer: Betty Box
Screenplay: Mabel and Denis Constanduros, Peter Rogers, Muriel and
Sydney Box
Leading actors: Jack Warner, Kathleen Harrison, Jane Hylton, Susan Shaw,
Petula Clark

Holiday Camp, 1947
Production company: Gainsborough
Distributor on first release: General Film Distributors
Director: Ken Annakin
Producer: Sydney Box
Screenplay: Muriel and Sydney Box, Peter Rogers, Mabel and Denis Con-
standuros, Ted Willis
Source: Godfrey Winn
Leading actors: Jack Warner, Kathleen Harrison, Hazel Court, Flora Robson,
Esma Cannon

Home Sweet Home, 1945
Production company: Mancunian
Distributor on first release: Butchers
Director and producer: John E. Blakeley
Screenplay: Roney Parsons, Anthony Toner
Leading actors: Frank Randle, Tony Pendrell, H. F. Maltby

Hue and Cry, 1947
Production company: Ealing
Distributor on first release: General Film Distributors
Director: Charles Crichton
Producer: Michael Balcon
Screenplay: T. E. B. Clarke
Leading actors: Harry Fowler, Joan Dowling, Alastair Sim, Jack Warner

The Huggetts Abroad, 1949
Production company: Gainsborough
Distributor on first release: General Film Distributors
Director: Ken Annakin
Producer: Betty Box
Screenplay: Mabel and Denis Constanduros, Ted Willis, Gerard Bryant
Leading actors: Jack Warner, Kathleen Harrison. Susan Shaw, Petula Clark,
Dinah Sheridan

It Always Rains on Sunday, 1947
Production company: Ealing
Distributor on first release: General Film Distributors
Director: Robert Hamer
Producer: Michael Balcon
Screenplay: Robert Hamer, Henry Cornelius
Source: (novel) Arthur La Bern
Leading actors: Googie Withers, John McCallum, Jack Warner

London Belongs to Me, 1948
Production company: Independent Producers-Individual
Distributor on first release: General Film Distributors
Director: Sidney Gilliat
Producers: Frank Launder and Sidney Gilliat
Screenplay: Sidney Gilliat and J. B. Williams
Source: (novel) Norman Collins
Leading actors: Richard Attenborough, Alastair Sim, Susan Shaw, Joyce Carey

The Magnet, 1950
Production company: Ealing
Distributor on first release: General Film Distributors
Director: Charles Frend
Producer: Michael Balcon
Screenplay: T. E. B. Clarke
Leading actors: William (James) Fox, Stephen Murray, Kay Walsh

Night and the City, 1950
Production company and distributor on first release: 20th Century Productions
Director: Jules Dassin
Producer: Samuel G. Engel
Screenplay: Jo Eisinger
Source: (novel) Gerald Kersh
Leading actors: Richard Widmark, Gene Tierney, Googie Withers, Francis L. Sullivan

Old Mother Riley's New Venture, 1949
Production company: Harry Reynolds
Distributor on first release: Renown
Director: John Harlow
Producers: Harry Reynolds, John Gilling
Screenplay: Con West, Jack Marks, John Gilling
Source: Con West, Jack Marks
Leading actors: Arthur Lucan, Kitty McShane, Chilli Bouchier

Old Mother Riley, Headmistress, 1950
Production company: Harry Reynolds
Distributor on first release: Renown
Director: John Harlow
Screenplay: John Harlow, Ted Kavanagh
Source: Con West, Jack Marks
Leading actors: Arthur Lucan, Kitty McShane

Once a Jolly Swagman, 1948
Production company: Pinewood-Wessex
Distributor on first release: General Film Distributors
Director: Jack Lee
Producer: Ian Dalrymple
Screenplay: Jack Lee, William Rose, Cliff Gordon
Source: (novel) Montagu Slater
Leading actors: Dirk Bogarde, Renee Asherson, Bill Owen, Bonar Colleano

Over the Garden Wall, 1950
Production company: Film Studios Manchester
Distributor on first release: Mancunian
Director and producer: John E. Blakeley
Screenplay: Harry Jackson
Source: Anthony Toner
Leading actors: Norman Evans, Jimmy James

They Made Me a Fugitive, 1947
Production company: Gloria-Alliance
Distributor on first release: Warner Brothers
Director: Cavalcanti
Producers: Nat Bronsten, James Carter
Screenplay: Noel Langley
Source: (novel) Jackson Budd
Leading actors: Trevor Howard, Sally Gray, Griffith Jones

They Were Not Divided, 1950
Production company: Two Cities
Distributor on first release: General Film Distributors
Director and screenplay: Terence Young
Producer: Herbert Smith
Leading actors: Edward Underdown, Ralph Clanton

Vote for Huggett, 1949
Production company: Gainsborough
Distributor on first release: General Film Distributors
Director: Ken Annakin
Producer: Betty Box
Screenplay: Mabel and Denis Constanduros, Allan Mackinnon
Leading actors: Jack Warner, Kathleen Harrison, Susan Shaw, Petula Clark

Waterfront, 1950
Production company: Conqueror
Distributor on first release: General Film Distributors
Director: Michael Anderson
Producer: Paul Soskin
Screenplay: John Brophy, Paul Soskin
Source: (novel) John Brophy
Leading actors: Robert Newton, Kathleen Harrison, Susan Shaw, Richard
    Burton, Avis Scott.

Waterloo Road, 1945
Production company: Gainsborough
Distributor on first release: General Film Distributors
Director and screenplay: Sidney Gilliat
Producer: Edward Black
Source: Val Valentine
Leading actors: John Mills, Stewart Granger, Alastair Sim, Joy Shelton

The Way to the Stars, 1945
Production company: Two Cities
Distributor on first release: United Artists
Director: Anthony Asquith
Producer: Anatole de Grunwald

Screenplay: Terence Rattigan, Anatole de Grunwald
Source: Terence Rattigan, Richard Sharman
Leading actors: Michael Redgrave, John Mills, Rosamund John, Douglass Montgomery

The White Unicorn, 1947
Production company: John Corfield
Distributor on first release: General Film Distributors
Director: Bernard Knowles
Producer: Harold Huth
Screenplay: Robert Westerby, A. R. Rawlinson
Source: (novel) Flora Sandstrom
Leading actors: Margaret Lockwood, Joan Greenwood, Dennis Price

The Wooden Horse, 1950
Production company: British Lion-Wessex
Distributor on first release: British Lion
Director: Jack Lee
Producer: Ian Dalrymple
Screenplay and source: Eric Williams
Leading actors: Leo Genn, David Tomlinson, Anthony Steel

The Yellow Balloon, 1953
Production company: Marble Arch
Distributor on first release: Associated British Pictures
Director: J. Lee Thompson
Producer: Victor Skutezky
Screenplay: Anne Burnaby and Jack Lee Thompson
Source: Anne Burnaby
Leading actors: Andrew Ray, Kenneth More, William Sylvester

Select bibliography

Social history

Addison, Paul. *Now the War Is Over: A Social History of Britain 1945–1951* (London: Pimlico, 1995).

Annan, Noel. *Our Age: The Age That Made Post-War Britain* (London: Fontana, 1996).

Brivati, Brian, and Harriet Jones (eds). *What Difference Did the War Make?* (London: Leicester University Press, 1995).

Calder, Angus. *The Myth of the Blitz* (London: Pimlico, 1992).

Calder, Angus. *The People's War: Britain 1939–1945* (London: Pimlico, 1992).

Hennessy, Peter. *Never Again: Britain 1945–51* (London: Jonathan Cape, 1992).

Hopkins, Harry. *The New Look: A Social History of the Forties and Fifties in Britain* (London: Readers Union and Secker & Warburg, 1963).

Jenkins, Alan. *The Forties* (London: William Heinemann, 1977).

Morgan, Kenneth O. *The People's Peace: British History 1945–1989* (Oxford: Oxford University Press, 1990).

Riley, Denise. '"The free mothers": pronatalism and working women in industry at the end of the last war in Britain'. *History Workshop Journal*, no. 11 (1981), 59–118.

Sissons, Michael, and Philip French (eds). *The Age of Austerity* (Harmondsworth: Penguin Books, 1964).

Smith, Harold L. (ed.). *War and Social Change: British Society in the Second World War* (Manchester: Manchester University Press, 1986).

Wilson, Elizabeth. *Only Halfway to Paradise: Women in Postwar Britain 1945–1968* (London: Tavistock Publications, 1980).

Class and social structure

Blackwell, Trevor, and Jeremy Seabrook. *A World Still to Win: The Reconstruction of the Post-War Working Class* (London: Faber & Faber, 1985).

Brandis, Walter, and Dorothy Henderson. *Social Class, Language and Communication* (London: Routledge & Kegan Paul, 1970).

Bulmer, Martin (ed.). *Working-Class Images of Society* (London: Routledge & Kegan Paul, 1975).

Clarke, John, Chas Critcher, and Richard Johnson (eds). *Working-Class Culture: Studies in History and Theory* (London: Hutchinson, 1979).

Davies, Andrew. *Leisure, Gender and Poverty: Working-Class Culture in Salford and Manchester 1900–1939* (Buckingham: Open University Press, 1992).

Halsey, A. H. (ed.). *Trends in British Society since 1900: A Guide to the Changing Social Structure of Britain* (Basingstoke and London: Macmillan, 1972).

Hopkins, Eric. *The Rise and Fall of the English Working Classes 1918–1990* (London: Weidenfeld & Nicholson, 1991).

Humphries, Stephen. *Hooligans or Rebels? An Oral History of Working-Class Childhood and Youth 1889–1939* (Oxford: Basil Blackwell, 1995).

Jackson, Brian. *Working-Class Community: Some General Notions Raised by a Series of Studies in Northern England* (London: Routledge & Kegan Paul, 1968).

Laing, Stuart. *Representations of Working-Class Life 1957–1964* (Basingstoke and London: Macmillan, 1986).

Lancaster Regionalism Group. *Localities, Class and Gender* (London: Pion, 1985).

Lee, David J. and Bryan S. Turner. *Conflicts about Class: Debating Inequality in Late Industrialism* (Harlow: Longman, 1996).

Lockwood, David. *The Blackcoated Worker: A Study in Class Consciousness* (Oxford: Oxford University Press, Clarendon Press, 1989).

McKibbin, Ross. *The Ideologies of Class: Social Relations in Britain 1880–1950* (Oxford: Oxford University Press, Clarendon Press, 1994).

McKibbin, Ross. *Classes and Cultures in England 1918–1951* (Oxford: Oxford University Press, 1998).

Marsh, David C. *The Changing Social Structure of England and Wales 1871–1961* (London: Routledge & Kegan Paul, rev. edn, 1965).

Marwick, Arthur. *Class: Image and Reality in Britain, France and the USA since 1890* (London: Collins, 1980).

Mungham, Geoff, and Geoff Pearson (eds). *Working Class Youth Culture* (London: Routledge & Kegan Paul, 1976).

Obelkevich, James, and Peter Catterall (eds). *Understanding Post-War British Society* (London: Routledge, 1994).

Payne, Geoff. *Mobility and Change in Modern Society* (Basingstoke and London: Macmillan, 1987).

Roberts, Elizabeth. *Women's Place: An Oral History of Working-Class Women 1890–1940* (Oxford: Basil Blackwell, 1984).

Tebbutt, Melanie. *Women's Talk? A Social History of 'Gossip' in Working-Class Neighbourhoods 1880–1960* (Aldershot: Scolar Press, 1995).

Williams, Raymond. 'The working class and leisure: class expression and/or social control'. *Society for the Study of Labour History Bulletin*, no. 32 (1976), 5–18.

Cultural studies

Ang, Ien. *Watching Dallas: Soap Opera and the Melodramatic Imagination*, trans. Della Couling (London: Routledge, 1989).

Bromley, Roger. *Lost Narratives: Popular Fictions, Politics and Recent History* (London: Routledge, 1988).

Carey, James. *Communication as Culture* (London: Routledge, 1992).

Geertz, Clifford. *The Interpretation of Cultures: Selected Essays* (London: Fontana Press, 1993).

Gray, Nigel. *The Silent Majority: A Study of the Working Class in Post-War British Fiction* (London: Vision Press, 1973).

Hewison, Robert. *Culture and Consensus: England, Art and Politics since 1940* (London: Methuen, 1995).

Hoggart, Richard. *The Uses of Literacy: Aspects of Working-Class Life with Special Reference to Publications and Entertainments* (Harmondsworth: Penguin Books, 1958).

Hoggart, Richard. *Speaking to Each Other* (London: Chatto & Windus, 2 vols, 1970).

Keddie, Nell (ed.). *Tinker, Tailor ... The Myth of Cultural Deprivation* (Harmondsworth: Penguin Books, 1973).

Kirkham, Pat, and David Thoms (eds). *War Culture: Social Change and Changing Experience in World War Two* (London: Lawrence & Wishart, 1995).

MacCabe, Colin (ed.). *High Theory/Low Culture* (Manchester: Manchester University Press, 1986).

Marquand, David, and Anthony Seldon (eds). *The Ideas that Shaped Post-War Britain.* (London: Fontana Press, 1996).

Martin, Bernice. *A Sociology of Contemporary Cultural Change* (Oxford: Basil Blackwell, 1981).

Marwick, Arthur. *Culture in Britain since 1945* (Oxford: Basil Blackwell, 1991).

Miles, Peter, and Malcolm Smith. *Cinema, Literature and Society* (London: Croom Helm, 1987).

Modleski, Tania (ed.). *Studies in Entertainment: Critical Approaches to Mass Culture* (Bloomington and Indianapolis, IN: Indiana University Press, 1986).

Parker, Stanley. *The Sociology of Leisure* (London: George Allen & Unwin, 1976).

Samuel, Raphael, and Paul Thompson (eds). *The Myths We Live By* (London: Routledge, 1990).

Sinfield, Alan. *Literature, Politics and Culture in Postwar Britain* (Oxford: Basil Blackwell, 1989).

Stam, Robert. *Reflexivity in Film and Literature: From Don Quixote to Jean-Luc Godard* (Ann Arbor, MI: UMI Research Press, 1985).

Suleiman, Susan R. and Inge Crosman (eds). *The Reader in the Text: Essays on Audience and Interpretation* (Princeton, NJ: Princeton University Press, 1980).

Swingewood, Alan. *The Myth of Mass Culture* (Basingstoke and London, Macmillan: 1977).

Williams, Raymond. 'A lecture on realism'. *Screen*, 18:1 (1977), 61–74.

Williams, Raymond. *Culture and Society 1780–1950* (London: Hogarth Press, 1987).

Film

Aldgate, Anthony and Jeffrey Richards. *Britain Can Take It: The British Cinema in the Second World War* (Edinburgh: Edinburgh University Press, 2nd edn, 1994).

Austin, Bruce A. *The Film Audience: An International Bibliography of Research with Annotations and an Essay* (Metuchen, NJ: Scarecrow Press, 1983).

Barr, Charles. *Ealing Studios* (London: Studio Vista, 2nd edn, 1993).

Barr, Charles (ed.). *All Our Yesterdays: 90 Years of British Cinema* (London: BFI, 1986).

Broadley, John. 'A life in Leeds cinemas'. *Picture House*, no. 11 (1987–88), 7–13.

Broadley, John. 'The film trade in Leeds'. *Picture House*, no. 12 (1988), 25–9.

Broadley, John. 'Facing the fifties: a life in Leeds cinemas 3'. *Picture House*, nos 14–15 (1990), 31–8.

Burton, Alan, Tim O'Sullivan and Paul Wells (eds). *Liberal Directions: Basil Dearden and Postwar British Film Culture* (Trowbridge: Flicks Books, 1997).

Chibnall, Steve, and Robert Murphy (eds). *British Crime Cinema* (London: Routledge, 1999).

Cook, Pam (ed.). *Gainsborough Pictures* (London: Cassell, 1997).

Curran, James and Vincent Porter (eds). *British Cinema History* (London: Weidenfeld & Nicholson, 1983).

Drazin, Charles. *The Finest Years: British Cinema of the 1940s* (London: Andre Deutsch, 1998).

Durgnat, Raymond. *A Mirror for England: British Movies from Austerity to Affluence* (London: Faber & Faber, 1970).

Ellis, John. 'Art, culture and quality – terms for a cinema in the forties and seventies'. *Screen*, 19:3 (1978), 9–49.

Geraghty, Christine. *British Cinema in the Fifties: Gender, Genre and the 'New Look'* (London: Routledge, 2000).

Gledhill, Christine, and Gillian Swanson (eds). *Nationalising Femininity: Culture, Sexuality and the British Cinema in the Second World War* (Manchester: Manchester University Press, 1996).

Harper, Sue. *Picturing the Past: The Rise and Fall of the British Costume Film* (London: BFI, 1994).

Harper, Sue, and Vincent Porter. 'Moved to tears: weeping in the cinema of postwar Britain'. *Screen*, 37:2 (1996), 152–73.

Harper, Sue, and Vincent Porter. 'Cinema audience tastes in 1950s Britain'. *Journal of Popular British Cinema*, no. 2 (1999), 66–82.

Hill, John. *Sex, Class and Realism: British Cinema 1956–1963* (London: BFI, 1986).

Landy, Marcia. *British Genres: Cinema and Society 1930–1960* (Princeton, NJ: Princeton University Press, 1991).

Lant, Antonia. *Blackout: Reinventing Women for Wartime British Cinema* (Princeton, NJ: Princeton University Press, 1991).

McCabe, Colin, and Duncan Petrie (eds). *New Scholarship from BFI Research* (London: BFI, 1996).

McFarlane, Brian. *An Autobiography of British Cinema as Told by the Filmmakers and Actors Who Made It* (London: Methuen, 1997).

Murphy, Robert. *Realism and Tinsel: Cinema and Society in Britain 1939–49* (London: Routledge, 1992).

Murphy, Robert. *British Cinema and the Second World War* (London: Continuum, 2000).

Murphy, Robert (ed.). *The British Cinema Book* (London: BFI, 1997).

Richards, Jeffrey. *The Age of the Dream Palace: Cinema and Society in Britain 1930–39* (London: Routledge, 1989).

Richards, Jeffrey. *Stars in Our Eyes: Lancashire Stars of Stage, Screen and Radio* (Preston: Lancashire County Books, 1994).

Richards, Jeffrey. *Film and British National Identity from Dickens to 'Dad's Army'* (Manchester: Manchester University Press, 1997).

Richards, Jeffrey (ed.). *The Unknown 1930s: An Alternative History of the British Cinema* (London: I. B. Tauris, 1998).

Robertson, James C. *The British Board of Film Censors: Film Censorship in Britain 1896–1950* (London: Croom Helm, 1985).

Rosenstone, Robert A. (ed.). *Revisioning History: Film and the Construction of a New Past* (Princeton, NJ: Princeton University Press, 1995).

Sedgwick, John. *Popular Filmgoing in 1930s Britain: A Choice of Pleasures* (Exeter: Exeter University Press, 2000).

Shafer, Stephen C. *British Popular Films 1929–1939: The Cinema of Reassurance* (London: Routledge, 1997).

Shindler, Colin. *Hollywood Goes to War: Film and American Society 1939–1952* (London: Routledge & Kegan Paul, 1979).

Short, K. R. M. (ed.). *Feature Films as History* (London: Croom Helm, 1981).

Stacey, Jackie. *Star Gazing: Hollywood Cinema and Female Spectatorship* (London: Routledge, 1994).

Stead, Peter. *Film and the Working Class: The Feature Film in British and American History* (London: Routledge, 1991).

Sutton, David. *A Chorus of Raspberries* (Exeter: Exeter University Press, 2000).

Swann, Paul. *The Hollywood Feature Film in Postwar Britain* (New York: St Martin's Press, 1987).

Taylor, Philip M. (ed.). *Britain and the Cinema in the Second World War* (Basingstoke and London: Macmillan, 1988).

Thumim, Janet. *Celluloid Sisters: Women and Popular Cinema* (Basingstoke and London: Macmillan, 1992).

Trevelyan, John. 'Film Censorship in Great Britain'. *Screen*, 11:3 (1970), 19–30.

Index

Note: 'n.' after a page reference indicates the number of a note on that page.

The British working class in postwar film